WHAT CAPITALISM NEEDS

From unemployment to Brexit to climate change, capitalism is in trouble and ill-prepared to cope with the challenges of the coming decades. How did we get here? While contemporary economists and policymakers tend to ignore the political and social dimensions of capitalism, some of the great economists of the past – Adam Smith, Friedrich List, John Maynard Keynes, Joseph Schumpeter, Karl Polanyi, and Albert Hirschman – did not make the same mistake. Leveraging their insights, sociologists John L. Campbell and John A. Hall trace the historical development of capitalism as a social, political, and economic system throughout the twentieth and early twenty-first centuries. They draw comparisons across eras and around the globe to show that there is no inevitable logic of capitalism; rather, capitalism's performance depends on the strength of nation-states, the social cohesion of capitalist societies, and the stability of the international system – three things that are in short supply today.

JOHN L. CAMPBELL is Class of 1925 Professor and Professor of Sociology at Dartmouth College. He is the author of *American Discontent* and other books.

JOHN A. HALL is James McGill Professor of Comparative Historical Sociology at McGill University. He is the author of *The Importance of Being Civil* and other books.

WHAT CAPITALISM NEEDS

Forgotten Lessons of Great Economists

JOHN L. CAMPBELL

JOHN A. HALL

CAMBRIDGE
UNIVERSITY PRESS

CAMBRIDGE
UNIVERSITY PRESS

University Printing House, Cambridge CB2 8BS, United Kingdom

One Liberty Plaza, 20th Floor, New York, NY 10006, USA

477 Williamstown Road, Port Melbourne, VIC 3207, Australia

314–321, 3rd Floor, Plot 3, Splendor Forum, Jasola District Centre,
New Delhi – 110025, India

103 Penang Road, #05-06/07, Visioncrest Commercial, Singapore 238467

Cambridge University Press is part of the University of Cambridge.

It furthers the University's mission by disseminating knowledge in the pursuit of
education, learning, and research at the highest international levels of excellence.

www.cambridge.org
Information on this title: www.cambridge.org/9781108487825
DOI: 10.1017/9781108768054

© Cambridge University Press 2021

First published 2021

Printed in the United Kingdom by TJ Books Limited, Padstow Cornwall

A catalogue record for this publication is available from the British Library.

ISBN 978-1-108-48782-5 Hardback

CONTENTS

v

TABLES

This book is about the social conditions necessary for capitalism to prosper – and about the weakening of those conditions in recent years. It could not come at a better time because the world is reeling economically from the coronavirus pandemic. Things may not return to normal for a very long time – if ever. If we want capitalism to perform well in ways to be specified, it is imperative that we understand the conditions of its existence.

Capitalism has vastly enhanced human productive powers, initially in northwestern Europe and now in China. Yet it has been subject to periodic crises. At the end of the last century, neoliberal economists dreamed of a utopian world of perfect markets with minimal state interference in which individuals would calculate their best interests in some seamless web of perfection. It is a dream that has not been fulfilled. Indeed, it is a dream that was badly shaken by the 2008 financial crisis that brought the advanced capitalist world to its knees. For the next ten years, capitalism faced growing instabilities. Europe remained mired in high unemployment and sluggish economic growth, and it was manifestly weakened both by Britain's decision to leave the European Union (commonly known as Brexit) and its inability to deal with structural problems with the euro. The structure of the world political economy was also changing: East Asia emerged as a hub of capitalist innovation and production, with China its ascendant economic powerhouse, poised to be the world's next superpower. World capital flows became dangerously imbalanced as the advanced capitalist countries borrowed more from the leading emerging market economies. Inequality continued to rise in many capitalist countries. Nationalism of a particularly nasty sort burst out all over, and immigrants were scapegoated for all sorts of problems. Finally, capitalism suffered from expensive trade wars and geopolitical disruption sparked by the erratic and malicious behaviors of Donald Trump, including the arbitrary imposition of tariffs and withdrawal from various multilateral agreements, all aiming to force countries around the world to bow to his wishes. The Golden Age of capitalism that had followed the Second World War was at an end.

And then the coronavirus pandemic hit. First identified in December 2019 in Wuhan, China, the COVID-19 virus spread rapidly around the world. By November 2020, more than 40 million cases had been reported in 185 countries and territories, and more than 1 million people had died worldwide, nearly a quarter of them in the United States, with the numbers looking set to climb yet further. Many countries locked down their economies: governments mandated that all but essential businesses close their doors, and many employers furloughed their workers; others tried to find ways of supporting their employees to work from home – but huge numbers of workers were simply fired. More than 100 countries restricted travel. Schools closed. Social distancing became the "new normal." Hospitals filled up with infected patients, and health workers struggled to find masks, gowns, ventilators, and other necessary equipment.

Capitalism faced its worst crisis since the Great Depression. Some economists worried that the pandemic's impact would be even worse. During the first three months of the outbreak, the Dow, Nikkei, and FTSE stock indexes lost about 30 percent of their value. Unemployment skyrocketed in many countries. Nearly 1 million people in the United Kingdom applied for unemployment benefits in just two weeks; some 26.5 million Americans filed for benefits in a little over a month. Major industrial supply chains broke down. And the International Monetary Fund forecast that most of the world's major economies, including Canada, France, Germany, Italy, Japan, the United Kingdom, and the United States, were headed for deep recessions by the end of 2020. China alone looked like it might avoid that fate even though its industrial production had plunged roughly 10 percent during the first quarter of the year.[1] In short, the pandemic led to economic disaster.

We had nearly finished writing a draft of this book when COVID-19 first emerged. When we began, our purpose in writing it was to identify the sociological conditions under which capitalism had performed better or worse during the twentieth and early twenty-first centuries. But when the pandemic overwhelmed the world, we worried that our argument was suddenly out of date. The world seemed to have changed in fundamental ways. However, it soon became clear that the opposite was true: our argument was more relevant than ever – and it is likely to remain so, unfortunately, even now that the particular scourge of the presidency of Donald Trump has come to an end. Like an X-ray of the capitalist system, the crisis has revealed with tremendous clarity that the key variables we originally thought were necessary for capitalism to work well are especially important when it comes to managing the potentially devastating economic consequences of a horrendous health crisis.

We had hoped to vet a draft of the manuscript with colleagues at a workshop at Dartmouth College in early spring 2020, sponsored by the Rockefeller Center for Social Science, for which we are appreciative, and then at the Copenhagen Business School. But the conditions of the pandemic made that impossible. Nevertheless, we still benefited from the comments of several people who either discussed the project with us or read earlier versions or pieces of the manuscript at various stages of the project. They include William Cats-Baril, Mike Cummins, Marc Dixon, Francesco Duina, Lev Grinberg, Brooke Harrington, Doug Irwin, Peter Katzenstein, Lane Kenworthy, Sunmin Kim, Krzysztof Pelc, and Kathy Sherrieb. Sara Doskow, our editor at Cambridge University Press, also provided sage advice and very helpful comments, as did an anonymous reviewer for the Press. Vanessa Plaister did a wonderful job copyediting the manuscript. We are grateful to them all.

1

Sociology from Economics

As sociologists, we view capitalism and its optimal needs differently from conventional economists. Ironically, however, our own perspective draws on the work of well-known early economists – sociologically astute, but often misunderstood or neglected in economics today. Those earlier economists provide us with most of the important building blocks for our argument. They also remind us that the foundations of economics are fundamentally different from the widespread contemporary belief that markets work best when political and social forces do not interfere with them. The historical perspective suggests that this contemporary view is wrong and that putting it into practice has caused serious economic damage. *We will show that capitalism performs best when states possess the intellectual and institutional capacities to manage their economies effectively and when societies are blessed with basic social cohesion, so that the interests of the many in widespread prosperity are not outweighed by those of the privileged few.* Our concern, however, is that state capacity and social cohesion are in short supply these days because their conditions of existence have been badly damaged; hence our plea to reverse this situation is quixotic. We do not suffer from the illusion that a better way will necessarily be found that will realize our desires. But we do believe that, without a better understanding of what makes capitalism work well, the situation will not improve.

Sociologists see capitalism as a much more complex system of social relations than do most economists. Economic activity is based not only on people pursuing their economic interests but also on trust, historical tradition, and personal identity. Sociologists also recognize that capitalism is embedded in a wide variety of institutions – political and cultural, as well as economic. And sociologists understand that the way in which capitalism operates varies significantly across countries and over time. But what is perhaps most noticeable about sociology is its fundamental criticism of capitalism. The greatest sociologists on the subject spoke of the alienation, anomie, and disenchantment associated with capitalism. There is nothing inherently wrong with this view, given the exploitation of workers in many capitalist societies both past and present, and we really speak warmly in this book only about the Golden Age of capitalism – that is, the first few decades following the Second World War – when, by contemporary standards, the interests of the many carried greater weight relative to those of the few. To be sure, those economists whose thought we admire had their own reservations about capitalism. But they differ from the sociologists in two ways: First, they were aware of and appreciated the dynamism and prosperity that capitalism can produce; second, they provided useful sociological insights about the mechanisms of capitalism and the institutions needed to make it work – and whose absence brings chaos. It is for this reason that we rely on the work of six historically eminent economists: Adam Smith, Albert Hirschman, Friedrich List, John Maynard Keynes, Joseph Schumpeter, and Karl Polanyi. Many of their insights have been forgotten; we resurrect and expand them here.

It might seem strange to focus on this group of economists. After all, they lived during very different eras of capitalism and, as a result, had very different views of capitalism. Smith was a leading member of the eighteenth-century Scottish Enlightenment, writing during the early years of capitalism when the factory system was just emerging, with the logistics of transportation and communication still essentially primitive. List lived in the early nineteenth century, when tariff barriers inside Germany were being torn down so as to increase specialization and trade. Keynes lived through the Great Depression and two world wars. He died just after the Second World War and lived in Britain as its power in the world was diminishing. Schumpeter, an Austrian, lived during the same period, but he spent the last two decades of his life in the United States at a time when its hegemonic power was blossoming. This latter pair witnessed the rise of multinational corporations, steam ships, automobiles, air travel, and telephones. Polanyi was another mid-twentieth-century economist, but he was one who lived in Austria, Britain, the United States, and Canada, and who lived long enough to see the emergence of the Cold War, the European Economic Community (forerunner to the European Union), and the full weight of the United States as an international superpower. Finally, Hirschman, the youngest member of our group, was born during the First World War in Berlin, where he witnessed Hitler's rise to power, before fleeing to France. Hirschman fought on behalf of the Spanish Republic in the Spanish Civil War, helped Jews and others to escape Nazi-occupied France, and eventually emigrated to the United States, where he died in 2012 having seen the moon landing, the globalization of capitalism, the collapse of the Soviet Union, the birth of the Internet, and the emergence of China as a leading economic player on the world stage. Yet, despite their different experiences, these economists shared two things in common: Each developed views of economics that were unorthodox for their time, and each appreciated in varying degree how important social cohesion and state capacities are if capitalist societies are to prosper.

Contemporary economists tend to forget the lessons learned by their predecessors. This is unfortunate because taking that intellectual heritage seriously can inform a more complete understanding of how capitalism works – one that incorporates the important roles that states and social relations play in capitalism both domestically and internationally. In this regard, it is worth remembering that some of the economists we discuss did not describe their work as the study of economics at all but rather as the study of political economy – a much more encompassing approach to the analysis of capitalism than is typical of most economists today.[1] There are some exceptions to this generalization – notably, institutional economists and those concerned recently with economic inequality.[2] But modern economics evolved from a discipline based on institutional, historical, and comparative analysis to one based on formal mathematical modeling and parsimonious explanation – and then, as one economist told us, to narrow-minded empiricism focusing on small questions, thanks to the rise of computers and large data sets.[3]

Mainstream economists, as well as the policymakers and media pundits who heed their advice, take a very different view from ours. They believe that markets work best if politicians do not "interfere" with market processes. Perhaps most famously, former University of Chicago economist Milton Friedman argued, in his bestselling *Capitalism and Freedom*, that maximizing shareholder wealth through markets is the best way of delivering prosperity, and that most attempts by government to improve markets are doomed to failure and may even make things worse. He believed that the government should refrain from imposing tariffs, setting minimum wage rates, regulating industries, and requiring people to contribute to social security programs. Nor should the government license particular enterprises, occupations or professions, operate national parks or toll roads, redistribute income or provide social services to alleviate poverty.[4] Friedman won the Nobel Prize in Economics for his work. Other influential schools of economic thought held similar views. Rational expectations theory suggested that people anticipate the government's economic policies and then behave proactively in ways that nullify the intended effects of those policies; the efficient market hypothesis maintained that unfettered markets are the best way of establishing value and setting prices. Friedman's view and that of his likeminded compatriots is mistaken. Yet it is their perspective that helped to pave the way for the neoliberal (sometimes called free-market or laissez-faire) economic reforms that led to the 2008 financial crisis, perpetuated much of the economic misery that followed, and which may yet exacerbate the disastrous economic fallout of the coronavirus pandemic.

Some economists disagree with this orthodox view of what makes capitalism work well. Some even point occasionally to the importance of our two key variables, state capacities and social cohesion. Joseph Stiglitz complains that, in the mainstream view, "there is little need for community and no need for trust. Government is a hindrance; it is the problem, not the solution."[5] Paul Krugman scolds his fellow economists for neglecting that "economics inevitably takes place in a political context."[6] Stiglitz and Krugman, also both Nobel Prize winners, have concluded that the economics profession went astray when it followed orthodoxy, ignoring mountains of evidence indicating that it was the wrong path to follow, and that, as a result, it succumbed to a flawed ideology rather than subscribed to reasoned argument.[7] We agree, but we will have much more to say about how state capacities and social cohesion affect capitalism.

Before going any further, we must point to complexities in the character of capitalism. Every economist would agree that a minimal definition begins with the presence of private property, production for the market, and the principle of profit maximization by rational means. But, as noted, there is more to it than that, as becomes obvious once we ask ourselves about the nature of the society in which we live. Countries are marked not only by capitalism but also by national sentiment and by the character of their political regime. You cannot understand capitalism without understanding what unites or divides a society. Nor can you understand capitalism without understanding how the economy and state engage each other. Then, there is the fact that what happens inside a country often depends on events in the external world. The larger world is, of course, capitalist too, and nation-states must navigate within it. As a result, domestic political and social arrangements are subject to economic

6

pressure from that larger world. But the larger world involves geopolitics that also affect capitalism inside countries.

Two implications follow from this last point. First, capitalism changes because of geopolitics, just as geopolitics change because of developments within capitalism. When the Chinese invented gunpowder, they banned its use for military production, limiting it instead to fireworks, because they had no geopolitical rivals. In Europe, where states were often at each other's throats, that move was not possible: it would have led to the destruction of any state that tried, because its rivals would not have done the same thing. Equally, the geopolitical agreement among members of the Organization of the Petroleum Exporting Countries (OPEC) to increase oil prices in the 1970s sent shock waves through the world's capitalist economies. In turn, this escalated geopolitical tensions between these capitalist countries and the OPEC cartel. Second, changes within international capitalism have been managed differently by states over time. World capitalism is far from politically neutral. Notably, its postwar institutions were largely created by the United States, thanks to both its military and economic strength in 1945, and the role of this hegemonic power remains exceptionally important today, even though its character has changed. These considerations make for complexities that we cannot ignore. Nonetheless, our focus is on capitalism, whose geographic range and intensity of interaction have increased significantly since the Second World War – and all the more so in the decades that followed the collapse of the Soviet bloc.

We live life forward and understand it backward. We now possess enough hindsight to see that there was an exceptional postwar period in which the advanced core of the capitalist world benefited from peace and prosperity thanks largely to the United States setting the rules by which capitalism operated. That relatively benign era of stability has come to an end; history is on the move again, with destabilizing effects – in part, because the United States now chooses to use some of its power to renegotiate those rules, such as those it helped to establish for the General Agreement on Tariffs and Trade (GATT), now the World Trade Organization (WTO), and also because the international architecture of capitalism is changing, driven primarily by the rise of China.

We now turn to our general argument by describing our two variables, social cohesion and state capacity. We do this with help from the great economists mentioned earlier. Chapter 2 begins by examining the disasters of the mid-twentieth century in which capitalism was thoroughly disrupted by geopolitical forces. It then turns to the amazing postwar recovery – the Golden Age – that was made possible by geopolitical settlement. Chapter 3 chronicles the slow decline of the Golden Age; then, in the next two chapters, we consider capitalism's contemporary difficulties. Chapter 4 looks at the deterioration of social cohesion. Growing economic inequality and stifled economic mobility, on the one hand, and rising nationalist discontent, on the other, are undermining social cohesion and therefore destabilizing politics and state capacity throughout the advanced capitalist world. Chapter 5 analyzes in detail this deterioration of state capacity. No description is neutral, so we will conclude in Chapter 6 by discussing prospects for the future, particularly in light of the unprecedented challenges to capitalism posed by the coronavirus pandemic, the digital information age, and climate crisis.

Building Blocks

It makes sense to begin with Adam Smith, often seen as the founding father of economics. He favored competitive markets – an idea best captured in his notion of the "invisible hand," a process that stems from individuals pursuing their economic interests by rationally calculating costs and benefits, then striking the best deals they can in the marketplace. In the aggregate, the accumulation of these many individual deals constitutes the forces of supply and demand, which express the general economic interests of society and increase national prosperity and wealth.[8] This idea has become the foundation of today's mainstream economics. However, mainstream economists forget that Smith had much more to say about all this. He also recognized the importance of social cohesion and state capacity for the development and success of capitalism.

Consider social cohesion first. As is well known, Smith argued in *The Wealth of Nations* that prosperity in capitalism stemmed from the division of labor – or, more precisely, the specialization, dexterity, and innovative powers of workers. His famous example was a pin factory: when the task of manufacturing pins was broken down into its component steps and each step was assigned to a different worker, pin manufacturing became much more efficient and productive. Smith shows here his continual sympathy for labor, his insistence being that high levels of human capital resulting from basic social cohesion underlie prosperity, which in turn increased social solidarity.

But there was another source of social cohesion of greater importance. While Smith praised the rational pursuit

9

of self-interest in *The Wealth of Nations*, his earlier book *The Theory of Moral Sentiments* maintained that something else is the principal motivation of human behavior.[9] The single most important human motivation was not the pursuit of material well-being but the longing to be loved, to which he added at the end of his life the desire to find oneself lovable. As he put it, "the chief part of human happiness arises from the consciousness of being beloved."[10] In other words, people are fundamentally social creatures driven by what other people think of them. Those around us serve as a looking-glass through which we can gauge and adjust our own behavior.[11]

From this, Smith derived a crucial point: we tend to admire success and often flaunt it. As a result, we are jealous of and want to catch up with those above us in the economic pecking order. For Smith, this is the most essential source of social cohesion – less a belief in capitalism in and of itself than an appreciation of the role that money-making has within the comparisons to others that marks social life.[12] What this suggests metaphorically is an ascending escalator – one without end – on which people are aware of each other, constantly trying to catch up with those above them, running and running until their death. As long as you believe that you might catch up, cohesion is assured, even if the odds are against you, because everyone above and ahead of you is running too. If people cease to hold the belief that they can catch up, illusory though it may be, then trust in the system will decline, social cohesion will break down, and capitalism will run into trouble. For Smith, the illusion of the societal escalator keeps the wheels of capitalism turning even though it is neither morally admirable nor indeed sensible.

The point is that the founding father of economics recognized that social cohesion was a necessary condition for capitalist prosperity. For this reason, he insisted in *The Wealth of Nations* that "basic measures of equality" were important too. Smith believed that the rate of profit was "naturally low in rich [countries], and high in poor countries" and was always highest in countries that were "going fastest to ruin."[13] Countries in which capitalists hoarded too many of the profits for themselves and limited workers' wages would fail to fulfill the promise of capitalism for greater national wealth and prosperity – the standard by which he felt a social order should be judged. He recognized that the interests of capitalists and those of the rest of society were frequently at odds with each other – particularly when it came to regulating monopoly and competition.[14] Furthermore, *The Wealth of Nations* makes it clear that he admired a contractual world in which those at the bottom of society have the power to resist oppression from those above – a world that abolishes uncompensated apprenticeships, domestic servitude, and clerical domination – altogether destroying a world of hierarchy based on debt, favor, and gift.[15] In short, Smith favored a certain measure of both economic and political equality.

But what about our second variable, state capacity? Smith described *The Wealth of Nations* as a handbook for the legislator – a guide for practical political action. He believed that such action was necessary because capitalists disliked competition, as noted, and were keen wherever possible to gain advantages, such as special licenses, subsidies, and tariff protection, that would help them to avoid the risks of competing in the marketplace.[16] In other words, capitalists cannot be trusted with capitalism, so the market must be regulated and never captured by capitalists.

In Smith's view, two sets of tasks confront the state elite. Book V of *The Wealth of Nations* is devoted to the positive functions of the state. The first set is domestic. The tasks include the protection of private property and the provision of public works and infrastructure. The state should not let inequality get out of hand, as noted, so Smith favored progressive tax regimes that recognize the limited incomes of the poor and avoid taxes on necessities such as food and clothing. The state should also guard against monopolies. Crucially, the state should provide basic education because both economy and society benefit from a well-trained population. There is absolutely no truth to the notion that Smith saw no positive role for the state, as Milton Friedman once maintained in a celebrated public lecture.[17]

The second set of tasks confronting the state is external. Smith was well aware of the importance of national defense, but he went well beyond this basic point. The traditional European attitude of the early modern period – mercantilism – had been to see economic affairs in zero-sum terms, with the gain for one state coming at the expense of a rival. This was a reason for war – something that should and could be avoided. Smith suggested that it was madness for each country to act independently like this; it was far better for countries to specialize and then to trade. Why produce terrible wine in England and poor-quality woolens in Portugal, when it was possible to obtain good Portuguese wine in return for high-quality English woolens? In this matter, Smith was arguing a normative, as well as a descriptive, case. The state should ensure free and open trade with its neighbors. Doing otherwise, Smith believed, leads to a world of high profits and low wages that he feared would diminish the benefits that capitalism can bring. It is not much of a stretch to infer from Smith that trade was a form of international social cohesion through which all capitalist nations could prosper.

Social Cohesion

Albert Hirschman adds something to the sources of cohesion that Smith identified. Hirschman explained that when people have voice in an organization or system, they are likely to be loyal to it; they will have a sense of belonging to it.[18] Even when they perceive it as being poorly managed, unfair or oppressive, they will neither rebel nor leave as long as they believe that they can improve things through voice, by expressing their hopes and concerns to those in charge. In contrast, the denial of voice makes for anger and hence the desire to exit. Hirschman's most famous book *Exit, Voice, and Loyalty* shows that these concepts are useful for understanding how capitalism works.[19]

We will show that the provision of voice is a way of facilitating a sense of social inclusion and, by extension, the social cohesion that is so important for capitalist prosperity. This was abundantly clear in Denmark and Switzerland, as we will see, where institutionalized voice helped policymakers to manage the 2008 financial crisis effectively. Voice increases the possibility for dialogue, negotiation, and cooperation among people in all quarters of the capitalist system. Workers, for instance, are more likely to cooperate with employers to solve problems, resolve their differences, and seek mutually acceptable responses to crises if they are organized and enjoy corporatist means of being heard in front offices and corporate board rooms. Similarly, employers can benefit from the knowledge and insights of their employees in improving the production process and quality of the products they produce. West Germany, Japan, and the Scandinavian countries took this lesson to heart with great success during the Golden Age of capitalism. When voice fails to work, people rebel against the system. This is clear from the history of many class, populist, and nationalist movements; they often began as vocal expressions of dissatisfaction that eventually morphed into exit.[20]

Hirschman would probably not have disagreed with Smith's account of social cohesion – that is, the insistence that if inequality is minimized and people believe in the societal escalator, the cohesion will be maintained. But Hirschman went a step further, recognizing that political feelings mattered too. He suggested that political inclusion might work even in the absence of basic equality: "In societies which inhibit passage from one social stratum to another, resort to the voice option is automatically strengthened: everyone has a strong motivation to defend the quality of life at his own station."[21]

State Capacity

An important part of our argument is that capitalism benefits from states with the capacities to promote development and manage the ups and downs that any capitalist economy is going to experience. Nineteenth-century economist Friedrich List offered a critique of Smith's antimercantilist argument to make this point. In *The National System of Political Economy*, List insisted that, in addition to taking a role in training labor and creating social cohesion, the state needed to protect newly developing industries from international competition. List had spent several years in North America when he was young and was deeply impressed by Alexander Hamilton's 1791 *Report on Manufactures*. The United States would always be subservient to Britain, Hamilton maintained, if it failed to develop its own industries. This was the consequence of Britain's advanced economic status and its consequent ability to flood the American market with cheap goods. The only way for the United States to move forward was through protectionism – that is, import barriers that would give domestic producers time to improve their production processes and the quality of their products, and therefore to slowly create national comparative advantage. For a while, of course, consumers within such a regime would have to buy inferior domestic goods compared to those they might purchase from abroad. But, in List's view, this short-term sacrifice would yield long-term benefits. Once domestic producers had improved the quality of their goods sufficiently to compete in the international market, protectionism could and should be abandoned. What we have here is nationalism from above: state leaders wanting to develop their societies not only to increase domestic wealth but also to ensure survival within the international economic and geopolitical system. We will have more to say about nationalism soon because that protean force can take different forms.

What List failed to realize, however, is that there can be a downside to protectionism. Protectionism diminishes trust among nations, which can cause conflict in a variety of ways. One is by enabling a country to become so powerful economically that it tips the balance of power internationally. That is the story of Germany in the nineteenth century. But another way in which protectionism may be disruptive is when a great power losing its predominance tries to maintain it through protectionist means – that is, protectionism to cling to power rather than to create it. This was the troubling case of the United States during Donald Trump's presidency.

List recognized the virtues of state intervention for helping fledgling capitalist societies with their initial development. In contrast, John Maynard Keynes, the great twentieth-century British economist, saw the need for states to manage capitalist economies once they were mature. In this regard, Keynes disagreed with the economic orthodoxy of his day, which held that, if left to their own devices, markets would self-correct during booms and busts without government assistance. Keynes provided an analysis of capitalism's tendency toward chronic market failure, reflected in unemployment. Although markets occasionally crash with disastrous consequences, he believed that even their normal condition was one of unnecessary unemployment.[22]

Keynes argued that unemployment was the result not of workers being lazy or poorly motivated but rather of insufficient aggregate demand for the things they produced. Crucially, demand tends to be insufficient because people tend to save more and consume and invest less than is needed to sustain full employment – especially with high levels of inequality when spending power is concentrated at the top.[23] Wealthier people tend to save more than poorer people because the wealthy have more discretionary income. If the distributions of income and wealth are skewed too much in favor of the privileged few, aggregate spending and therefore aggregate demand in the economy will suffer, and chronic unemployment will result. To be blunt, excessive inequality will cripple capitalism.[24]

For Keynes, then, inequality was not so much a problem of social cohesion, as it was for Smith, but a problem of macro-economic performance. He explained all this in his masterpiece *The General Theory of Employment, Interest, and Money*, published at the height of the Great Depression.[25] The implication of this for orthodox economics was devastating: laissez-faire policies did not work.[26] Accordingly, as one economist put it, the "essence of Keynes's economics ... was to save capitalism from the stupidity of its managers."[27] In this regard, the need for intellectually well-informed and institutionally well-resourced political elites was clear.

Keynes encouraged political leaders to use fiscal and monetary policy to regulate consumption, investment, and demand to achieve full employment.[28] Policymakers could, for instance, cut taxes, reduce interest rates, and invest in the economy through public works projects or social welfare programs if they needed to stimulate demand and create jobs in a recession. They should do this, he maintained, even if it meant borrowing money and running up budget deficits in the short term. Once the economy recovered and unemployment declined, tax revenues would rise, and the government would be able to reduce those deficits and pay down its debt. Keynes saw wise political elites wielding the state's policy tools, including deficit financing, as the fire brigade saving capitalism from itself.[29] Living at a time when large portions of Europe were in the grips of Hitler and Stalin, Keynes hoped to make capitalism work better to avoid the two great alternative power systems of the day, fascism and communism. In his view, "It is better that a man should tyrannize over his bank balance than over his fellow-citizens."[30]

The Instability of Capitalism

Conventional economics assumes that markets tend toward equilibrium – that is, that problems such as slack demand, unemployment, or even financial crises such as that of 2008 will eventually resolve themselves. We do not share that assumption, which is why we believe that state capacities and social cohesion are necessary for capitalism's well-being. Nor was that assumption shared by two of the great economists, Joseph Schumpeter and Karl Polanyi.

Schumpeter disagreed with most economists of his day because he saw capitalism as a process of continuous disruption, not equilibrium. He insisted in *Capitalism, Socialism and Democracy* that the hallmark of capitalism is inevitable change as entrepreneurs develop new products, technologies, and production methods that replace the old ones. He called this the process of "creative destruction" and viewed it as the routine essence of capitalism.[31] He also believed that, as capitalism evolved, the process of creative

destruction would shift from the hands of individual entrepreneurs to those of large, centralized corporations.[32] So, for
instance, Alexander Graham Bell invented the telephone,
which begat the very innovative Bell Telephone Company
(now AT&T) and Bell Labs, its phenomenally creative technology incubator.

As Schumpeter saw it, there were two problems here.
First, with the development of larger, more bureaucratized
firms, economic decision making would become routinized
and rationalized, slowly extinguishing the creativity required
for entrepreneurial breakthroughs. But the second and far
more serious problem was that the growing dominance of
ever larger corporations would eliminate small and medium-
sized businesses, and eventually the innovative bourgeoisie, as
a class. Their demise would pave the way for intellectuals
advocating socialism.[33] So creative destruction had revolutionary, as well as routine, implications for capitalism. His predic-
tion that centralization would lead to socialism has proved to
be essentially inaccurate. But the point that capitalism involves
continual disruption has gained in salience since his death.

The thinker who most fully realized what the societal
consequences of continual economic disturbance would
mean was Karl Polanyi, who had also experienced the disruption of the First World War and the chaos of the interwar
period. In *The Great Transformation*, published at the end of
the Second World War, Polanyi argued that the development
of capitalism involved a "double movement," whereby the
problems created by liberal capitalism, particularly for the
working class, would create counter-movements to alleviate
them. One such counter-movement was Soviet-style

socialism, rooted in an antidemocratic Marxist-Leninist ideology.[34] An alternative and wholly repulsive counter-movement on which the book concentrated most was fascism, as seen in Italy, Germany, and Japan.[35] This involved the state cracking down on labor unions, intervening in the economy in harsh ways, and excluding religious and ethnic groups from politics and society. Fascism was thus firmly linked to nationalism of the worst kind, infused with deep distrust of other nations and international institutions. For Polanyi, "[f]ascism, like socialism, was rooted in a market society that refused to function."[36] He sought for a different type of counter-movement – one akin to what we would call social democracy. His hope was that a more benevolent type of capitalism would prevail, with democratic politics holding sway over the economy and mitigating its worst effects. In such a society, all social groups would be included in the political system, their voices heard and respected by elites. The state would respond to problems caused by the market by providing legal protections for workers and social welfare programs for the poor. President Franklin Roosevelt's New Deal was one inspiration for his vision, but so was the democratic socialist movement he had seen in the 1920s in Vienna.

Polanyi argued that two things were required to mitigate the instabilities of market society: One was a state with the capacity to disarm capitalism's self-destructive potential; the other was the sort of social cohesion afforded nations by institutions that provided voice for its many stakeholders and by the possibility for social mobility and economic prosperity. In this regard, Polanyi had a clearer reading of Smith than conventional economists – a reading that appreciated Smith's recognition that the success of capitalism depended on more than the invisible hand of the market.[37] Polanyi's Jewish background certainly sensitized him to questions of inclusion and exclusion. In short, he recognized that the state was necessary for saving capitalism from itself and for facilitating social cohesion. Through institutionalized voice, the forces of social cohesion could help to ensure that the state did what was necessary to sustain capitalism and distribute its benefits widely throughout the population. This was the essence of what we would call his social democratic vision.

We must note that no book on the instabilities of capitalism could be complete without mentioning Karl Marx. No thinker exposed the cruelties of exploitation more graphically, while his emphasis on class structure remains at the core of any sociology of capitalism. But we do not base our argument on his work for several reasons. First, he refused to accept that state power can affect capitalist dynamics. He believed that capitalism always dominated the state, never the other way around. In this regard, he was simply wrong. Second, the experience of two world wars has made it obvious that peace among nation-states is a necessary condition for capitalist prosperity.[38] Marx was silent on this issue. Third, Marx's belief that capitalism was doomed and prone to revolution has also been proven to be wrong. The system can be and has been subject to reforms that have allowed it to survive for well over two centuries, albeit in different forms. In particular, the crucial problem of overproduction and underconsumption that Marx worried about can be counteracted in various ways, not least by the creation of new "needs" – that is, the creation of goods designed to achieve the status

21

distinctions of the societal escalator, whose workings we have already discussed. Finally, Marx's analysis of class conflict is flawed, as we will see shortly.

The International Architecture of Capitalism

The final lesson we take from the great economists comes once again from Keynes – although the spirit of his work at this point builds on the ideas of Smith. Bitter experience as a participant taught Keynes about the character of international capitalism, thereby giving his ideas range and power. He had attended the meetings at Versailles that followed the First World War, writing as a result his bestselling *The Economic Consequences of the Peace*. That book is a scathing condemnation of what he thought was the utter stupidity of French, British, and American political leaders in crafting the treaty – a treaty whose treatment of Germany (notably, its demand for exorbitant reparations) was so harsh that he predicted correctly that it would sow the seeds for another war. Furthermore, the protectionism that followed the Great Depression amplified the importance of international state leadership in Keynes's thinking.

Keynes became an important political actor. As the British delegation's leader at the meetings at Bretton Woods in July 1944, he played a major role in creating a new world economic order. His plan sought to provide rules by which the leading states could cooperate. In particular, he insisted that countries in fiscal trouble should be helped, while those with huge surpluses should be penalized, on the grounds that currency imbalances could cause serious difficulties for international capitalism. Imbalances like these became very important later, as we shall see – particularly those between China and the United States, as well as those between Germany and the other members of the eurozone. To solve this problem, Keynes proposed an international clearing union that would regulate international trade, credit, and exchange rates. Underscoring his concern about leaving economic policymaking to foolish politicians, the union would be run by impartial economic technocrats not swayed by narrow national interests. Keynes believed that this system would avoid conflict, mitigate crisis, and produce balanced economic trade across nations, as well as stable employment within them.[39]

But Keynes's plan for the architecture of world capitalism was defeated at the hands of the U.S. representative Harry Dexter White, loath to accept any constraints on the United States. The institutions created at that time demonstrate that capitalism after 1945 has been American in character. Capitalism has lived under the hegemony of the United States, which was at first relatively benign but has recently become more predatory.[40] Although Keynes may not have envisioned or applauded this outcome, he certainly appreciated that some sort of international state leadership – either by a single hegemon or a small group of states – was necessary to forge not only sound economic policy for the capitalist world but also a modicum of social cohesion and cooperation among the nation-states involved. In sum, he realized that state capacities and social cohesion mattered for capitalism at the international, as well as domestic, levels.

Our Argument Elaborated

We can now flesh out our argument about the sociology of capitalism using the conceptual building blocks given to us by these great economists. It is summarized schematically in Figure 1.1. Note immediately the presence of background

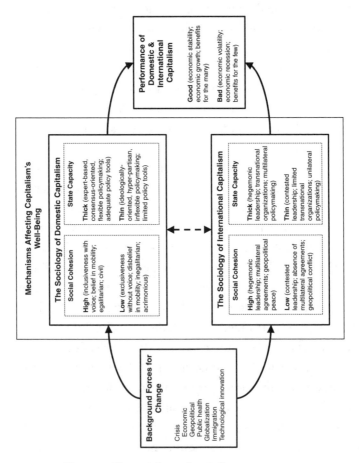

Figure 1.1 The sociology of capitalism

forces that either strengthen or undermine social cohesion and state capacity. Our claim, of course, is that when these forces strengthen social cohesion and state capacity, capitalism works well; when they do not, things go badly. Smith was one of the first economists to recognize this. But it is also an acknowledgement of the arguments of Schumpeter and Polanyi that capitalism is an unstable system, prone to constant change and occasional crisis.

Social cohesion ensures the success of capitalism in three ways. First, social cohesion brings the political stability on which capitalism depends. The presence of voice creates loyalty because actors feel they are stakeholders in their society. The presence of voice rests on a shared national sense of solidarity and collective interest. This is most readily available when a population is ethnically, religiously, and linguistically homogeneous, but it can also be created by institutions that ensure that a more heterogeneous population feels included.

Second, a socially inclusive society provides all with access to educational and training opportunities. The high levels of human capital that result create prosperity. So, capitalism for the few is not only morally disturbing but also structurally dangerous for the entire system. This is why Smith favored a modicum of equality and why he argued that the ability of capitalists to gain special privileges would undermine competition, lower wages, and raise prices so as to increase profits in a way certain to lead a country quickly to economic ruin. Contemporary French economist Thomas Philippon makes this point about the American economy in recent decades.[41] He explains that competition has declined, profits have risen, and the share of those profits going to labor has declined. Inequality has grown as a result. He calculates that "the lack of competition has deprived American workers of $1.5 trillion of income. More than the entire cumulative growth of real compensation between 2012 and 2018."[42] However normatively reprehensible this may be, the trouble does not end there. Philippon, like Smith, stresses that innovation – the root of capitalist growth – often comes from below, from talented people – that is, people with substantial human capital – and easy entry into the market. He argues that if competition is further reduced and labor's share of the economic pie continues to shrink, then innovation will stall, market access for newcomers will be blocked, political instability will rise, and capitalism will suffer.

This brings us to the final point. Those at the bottom of capitalist society do not necessarily believe in the system; what usually matters more is their acceptance of what the system promises to bring – notably, upward economic mobility – combined with an absence of perceived alternatives.[43] Social cohesion is, in a sense, blind, driven by conspicuous consumption and the desire to catch up with those ahead on the societal escalator. For this mechanism to work, there must be some general sense that one has a foot on the escalator, even if it is at the bottom of the conveyance in motion.

The intellectual and institutional capacities for flexible policymaking determine the resilience and effectiveness of the state. These capacities can be thick and abundant or thin and in short supply. Thick intellectual capacity includes well-trained elites blessed with an esprit de corps, a willingness to listen to qualified and experienced experts, and a reliance on well-established facts and data rather than ideology. Policymakers working in such an environment tend to be consensus-oriented and have an ability to think outside the box in innovative ways when necessary.[44] We are not suggesting that this is simply a matter of smart versus stupid politicians or good versus bad political leadership; it is much more a matter of the conditions that bring people into political power who are more or less ideologically partisan and intellectually myopic. Thick institutional capacity includes a wide array of fiscal, monetary, and regulatory policy tools and the authority to use them when necessary – authority that is enhanced when it is derived from consensus-oriented political institutions. Where state capacities are thin, policymakers have fewer policy tools at their disposal, and policymaking tends to be partisan. It is also less data-driven, less attentive to expertise, and less innovative and flexible.

Polanyi saw that social cohesion and state capacities are very often linked in reciprocal fashion. When societies are not socially cohesive, state capacities tend to be thin, because policymaking is partisan and divisive. And when partisan leaders make policy that exacerbates inequality, not to mention racial and ethnic tensions, social cohesion suffers still more. This has happened recently in the United States, where society has become divided along economic, political, ideological and racial lines. As a result, voters have elected strikingly divisive and ill-informed politicians who have weakened the state's fiscal and regulatory capacities, thereby further undermining social cohesion. This is happening in other countries where the deterioration of social cohesion, marked by rising economic inequality, ideological polarization, and distrust of government, has undermined the intellectual and institutional capacities of states to manage capitalism effectively, especially in times of crisis.[45] As those capacities diminish, they further undermine social cohesion in a vicious feedback loop.

Social cohesion and state capacities are important not only at the domestic level but also for the external world, as Keynes realized. Geopolitical peace is fundamental. Beyond that, the more states cooperate with each other as a cohesive group through multilateral agreements, the better capitalism will perform. The thicker the capacity of states to manage international capitalism, either because they rely on skilled technocrats and advisers in international institutions such as the European Union or the WTO, or because they have their own expertise in international affairs, the more willing they are to set aside their national interests when necessary for the sake of the international capitalist system. This too helps capitalism to perform better. The degree to which the international community is cohesive and possesses transnational state capacities, in the form of organizations such as the WTO or World Bank, depends on a variety of historical factors, but the presence or absence of American hegemony since the Second World War has been particularly important.

Figure 1.1 is not a perfect model of reality; it is merely a tool to encourage thought. Two necessary clarifications make this clear. First, we need to go beyond the contrast between two simple self-reinforcing cycles – between, on the one hand, cohesive societies that allow intelligent political elites to serve them, not least by adding to social cohesion, and, on the other hand, acrimonious societies that breed opportunistic elites that play on and deepen the social divisions that already exist. There can be complexities involving opposing forces. A powerful leader can remind a potentially divided society of what holds it together, as has been true of the leadership of Jacinda Ardern in New Zealand, or do a great deal to create division in an otherwise relatively cohesive society, as has been true of Viktor Orbán in Hungary. But the reverse is also true: a socially cohesive society, especially if it rests on powerful national sentiment, can restrain a wayward leader, thereby preventing too much damage. Second, we recognize that the dynamics of capitalism can affect both the factors that concern us. Over time, the performance outcomes on the right side of Figure 1.1 may feed back, influencing the background factors on the left side of the figure. For example, unfettered capitalism tends to generate economic crises. How well states manage these crises affects social cohesion. If states are effective and social cohesion is maintained, then capitalism performs well, and the possibility of future crises diminishes; otherwise, crises are more likely in the future.

The problem for capitalism now is that, in many countries, social cohesion is being destroyed and state capacity undermined – contributing to the decline of the rate of economic growth in the Organisation for Economic Co-operation and Development (OECD) since the 1970s, as Figure 1.2 illustrates. Things were better during the postwar Golden Age. Mass participation in war had done much to equalize social conditions, although racial and gender inequality persisted in many countries. States were so aware

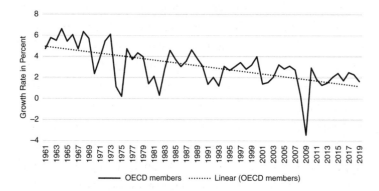

Figure 1.2 OECD average annual growth in gross domestic product (GDP), 1961–2019
Source: World Bank (2020b).

of the disasters of two world wars and the Great Depression that they sought greater political inclusion and class compromise. But times have changed. Many capitalist societies have increased inequality and fostered exclusion, leading to politics that are less civil and more divisive. Moreover, these problems are reverberating internationally. For instance, rising inequality in the United Kingdom has undermined social cohesion, allowing the political and economic entrepreneurs who fostered it to come to power on the basis of wholly absurd fantasies and promises that fueled the desire for Brexit. This example adds nuance to our earlier point about the two-dimensional nature of state capacity. Certainly, the institutional capacities of policymakers are important: they need the right policy tools for the job at hand. But the state's intellectual capacity matters too. Political entrepreneurs can have fantasies and ideas all of their own for which the people never voted; these can have a tremendous impact, not necessarily for the good. This is certainly true in the case of Brexit – for example in the neo-imperial illusions still very present in the English upper classes. Brexit is sure to damage the economy of the United Kingdom and is creating constitutional problems that threaten the unity of the country.

This example allows us to make another key point – the only one in this book not derived from great economists. In principle, all regimes can be overthrown from below, but this is especially likely in modern times when the masses enter politics. Accordingly, we have asked whether mechanisms of political inclusion are necessary for the stability of capitalism. This is most obviously a question for liberal democracy, which gives the vote to economic classes at the bottom of society. But the question also needs to be directed to groups with varying national identities within liberal democracies – particularly racial, ethnic, religious, and linguistic identities – because nationalism is the second equally vital form of popular politics. Does the stability and prosperity of capitalism also require the political inclusion of these distinct national groups? We believe it does. The long-term health of capitalism requires the political inclusion of all social classes and all significant national groups, presumably through democratic means. In this matter, we follow a central idea of Ernest Gellner, the great theorist of nationalism. Economic class conflict is real, and it matters – but it is the combination of class grievance with nationalist difference that produces real social dynamite.[46] We see this throughout the capitalist world today, especially in the hostility shown to immigrants and minorities for general economic troubles. Recall that, for

List, nationalism was about advancing and protecting the nation's economic interests; as Gellner recognized, nationalism can also be about the nation's political and cultural interests.

With that in mind, we need to make a few further clarifications about nationalism. First, at times, nationalist movements are instigated by an elite at the top, as we have seen; on other occasions, they may be a movement of the masses from below. Second, we must distinguish between those forms of nationalism that help to bolster capitalism and those that destabilize it. It is a major error to see nationalism always in negative terms, as a destructive force. It most certainly has that capacity, both domestically and internationally, but it can be positive as well, as a source of cohesion and vitality. A final point needs to be made here. Authoritarian capitalism, including capitalism managed by putatively socialist regimes, is not free from such pressures, despite its greater capacity for control. That said, capitalism combined with liberal democracy is our preferred system for two reasons. It is morally better than the alternatives because it is most likely to entail a measure of political inclusiveness, equality, and fairness that other forms of capitalism lack. And, as a result, it may be better equipped to contain social tensions and manage crises to the extent that the establishment of inclusiveness, equality, and fairness can enhance the possibility for individual self-sacrifice on behalf of the nation when trouble occurs.

One caveat is important. Economists recognize that many things affect the performance of capitalism, including natural disasters and technological change. We accept that without question. Our claim is that social cohesion and state capacities at both the domestic and international levels do so as well, and we insist firmly that mainstream economists largely ignore these factors.[47] Neglecting these two things is a grave mistake if we want to understand the mechanisms of capitalism. The great forefathers of contemporary economics did not make this mistake.

Conclusion

The central plank of our argument has been that the societal escalator provides essential stability for capitalism. For this mechanism to work, the state must control the immediate interests of capitalists to protect the market mechanism from their depredations.

All of this varies by place and time. A quick look back at the fortunes of the working class makes this clear. Before 1914, a range of working-class activism could be detected across countries, from the United States and Britain at one end of the scale, marked by the relative passivity of trade unionism, to Imperial Germany and the Romanov Empire at the other end, marked by full revolutionary working-class consciousness. The reason for this variation is simple: social movements take on the character of the political regimes with which they interact. White American working-class men gained the vote as early as the 1830s and thereafter felt that the state was their own. As a result, their grievances and struggles were directed at employers not politicians; at industry not the state, and decentralized thanks to the state's federalist structure that never produced a significant labor party. In Great Britain, a short-lived exclusion of trade union rights and a more centralized state helped to create a Labour Party, but the allegiance to socialist ideas remained very limited, as it did in America, because the state was essentially liberal.[48] In contrast, at the other end of the spectrum, antisocialist laws at the end of the nineteenth century in Germany radicalized the working class, creating struggles not only at the industrial level but also politically – as was necessary given the way in which the state tried to stifle working-class voice.[49] And in Imperial Russia the autocracy created a working class that became fully revolutionary, able to seize power in Saint Petersburg and Moscow in 1917.[50]

This analysis builds on Hirschman's insights about voice. It amounts to saying that liberalism diffuses conflict throughout society, while authoritarianism tends to concentrate it. Some forms of state are more amenable to stabilizing capitalism than others.

Let us conclude this discussion of social cohesion by returning to the claim that class inequality alone is a much less powerful force than class inequality tied to ethnic difference. Over the last decades, economic inequality has certainly increased within countries, as has the debilitating speed of change of occupational structure. Those suffering from these developments have come to see themselves as a distinctly disadvantaged group. Their frustrations are twofold. First, they are opposed to the elite – that is, to the cosmopolitans of the upper level of society who can move easily beyond the nation-state in a globalized world. Yet, perhaps ironically, those who are stuck – that is, caged – within the nation-state are far more patriotic than the elite. Their desire to protect their nation involves wanting to rein in, to recage, or to renationalize the elite who have left it behind.[51] Second, such antielitism is very often linked to worries about immigrants based on mistaken beliefs that these take away job opportunities that would otherwise have been the birthright of the "authentic" members of the nation. It is noticeable that elites favor such immigration because of the economic talent it brings, just as they tend to support affirmative action programs that often irritate those below who are excluded from such programs – people who feel that their place on the societal escalator has been taken by others who are culturally different from themselves, thereby limiting their prospects for the future.

Both frustrations constitute the origins of a new form of politics that pervades the contemporary capitalist world. This is best seen as a new form of nationalism, sometimes referred to as populism, nativist in character, replete with anxiety and rooted in people's desire to "take back control" of their country from both the elite and those they perceive to be foreigners unlike themselves. The crucial point is that social cohesion is breaking down because this group feels excluded both economically and culturally. The sense of being part of a single national entity has gone; the desire to protect their society becomes visceral as a result. The radical political style that results is a major concern of this book.

2

Phoenix from the Ashes

Adam Smith died in 1790, just before the French Revolutionary
and Napoleonic wars. The long peace of the nineteenth century
that followed rested on an implicit geopolitical deal. For decades after the Congress of Vienna of 1815 had established
a framework for peace, no one wanted to challenge Britain, in
part because they were exhausted from war but also because
doing so might upset the balance of power in Europe and
strengthen one's rivals. Furthermore, the world's leading economies subscribed to the gold standard – fixing their currencies
to the price of gold – thereby ensuring a stable international
payments system that steadied capitalism.[1] The hope was that
trade would now replace military conquest, and that peace and
prosperity would be assured. The first half of the twentieth
century crushed that hope. It was a time of war and economic
catastrophe.

Our first task in this chapter is to understand what
went wrong. Our explanation focuses on three factors: the
breakdown of social cohesion within countries as a result of
rising nationalist and class divisions; limited state capacities,
both domestically and internationally; and the absence of
international hegemonic leadership. We need to explain the
forces that determined capitalism's fate during the first half of
the twentieth century because it will help us to understand,
by sheer contrast, the unprecedented stability and economic
prosperity that came after 1945.

Our second task is to understand this sharp about-face. Like the phoenix of Greek mythology rising from the ashes, the era immediately after the Second World War turned out to be the Golden Age of capitalism – a time of remarkable peace and economic prosperity. Nationalist and class divisions were curtailed, and social cohesion was restored domestically by states more conscious of social needs and enjoying the capacities to achieve them, with both factors playing out within a stable international order led by the United States, capitalism's new hegemonic power. But behind all this is a paradox: War can destroy economies, but its consequences can quite unintentionally create the conditions for future prosperity.

The Darkest Days

By the end of the nineteenth century, thanks to trade policies of the sort advocated by List, every major European country had a similar portfolio of the industries needed for geopolitical autonomy. Wilhelmine Germany had become the largest European economy, its profits overwhelmingly coming from its large internal market and from trade with other developed areas. Nevertheless, what matters are often perceptions rather than facts. During the late nineteenth and first half of the twentieth centuries, many political leaders believed that imperialism was necessary if capitalism were to thrive, insisting that economic strength would ensure survival and prosperity within a world of geopolitical competition. They believed that huge territorial possessions were essential to state power because size enabled states to secure access to their own sources of raw materials and to their own markets, and hence to be geopolitically independent.[2] But with increased size came problems of nationalism, an immediate cause of war in 1914.

Several elements were involved. First, large territorial size meant the presence of different national groups – ethnic, religious, and linguistic – within the same empire. National diversity began to create demands from below. These might have been managed with the sort of inclusive cultural policies recommended by Hirschman, but that route was largely ruled out by the intense geopolitical rivalries of the era – a time, by the way, when Europe lacked a hegemonic leader able to hold these rivalries in check. What mattered most was a dreadful game of mirrors. The great powers sought to create nations within each other's territories. The Tsars encouraged Kurdish nationalism, knowing that it would irritate and weaken the Ottomans. The Habsburgs did the same for Ukrainian nationalists, thereby making it very difficult for the Tsars to force the Ukrainians in their territory to fully assimilate as "little Russians." In other words, geopolitical rivals tried to undermine social cohesion in each other's territories.

Second, the thought that diverse nationalities might be disloyal to the empire increased the pressure to assimilate them into a new shared identity. Empires sought to nationalize their peoples. The trouble here was that forcible assimilation added to the politicization of national groups, which exacerbated tensions and undermined cohesion inside the empires, not to mention irritated one's rivals outside, thereby further threatening international cohesion and stability.

There is a final factor concerning nationalism and social cohesion. The likelihood of German participation in geopolitical conflict was boosted by radical, right-wing, middle-class pressure for a much more aggressive nationalist policy than the political elite wanted. This is nationalism within a state, not nationalism wishing to secede. It reflected an inability to modernize politics – to integrate both the middle and working classes, so as to create loyalty to the regime.[3] The lack of voice undermined social cohesion.

Let us turn to the issue of state capacity. Political elites badly miscalculated in the years leading up to 1914. Bismarck, of course, had been an exception, able to abandon imperial demands at a key point, well aware that few economic profits lay in that direction. If only later German elites – and those of other countries – had calculated like capitalists, war might have been avoided. But they did not.

The German case is especially important, because the war involved the Anglo-German rivalry as much as the tensions in the Balkans and Central Europe. Imperial Germany lacked a cabinet government; it was a court society whose character was deeply affected by the personal character and whims of Kaiser Wilhelm II. This institutional thinness undermined the state's intellectual capacity for making well-reasoned policy, which was torn instead in different directions. One faction supported by heavy industrialists and the Social Democrats wanted to gain imperial possessions overseas; another faction, favored by the army, wished to continue the traditional policy of expansion to the east. The lack of unitary cabinet government meant that both sides influenced policymaking, thereby inspiring enemies on all sides – and so creating the encirclement by Russia and France from which Germany sought to break free in 1914. This was a self-inflicted wound, stemming from thin state capacities and setting the stage for war and economic disaster.

But limited state capacities ensured that elites in other countries made mistakes as well. Consider Conrad von Hotzendorf, chief of the Austrian General Staff. Desperately in love with a married woman, he advocated war, believing that military success would lead to a successful petition for divorce. More importantly, Conrad and his military peers wanted to prevent political reforms that threatened their elite privilege and power. They believed that, by taking Austria-Hungary to war, they could silence the voice of reformers at home.[4] This was a desperate move by a politically threatened faction of the state elite, who put their interests above those of their society as a whole.

Nationalist pressures combined with state elites prone to miscalculating created a fragile and febrile situation in July 1914. The assassination of Archduke Ferdinand, heir to the Habsburg throne, was the occasion for a war that changed the world. The hideous bloodletting that resulted hurt capitalism badly. Over the course of the war, gross domestic product (GDP) per capita declined, on average, by 12 percent in Europe. The population declined by about 3 percent.[5] Of the 65 million men who fought in the war, 10 million were killed in battle or died of disease, and 21 million were wounded. Some 7 million civilians were killed as well. The direct financial cost of the war for the participating countries was roughly $186 billion.[6]

The war damaged social cohesion. At the domestic level, the rise in labor militancy was marked.[7] Keynes observed that the prewar system had depended on what he called a double bluff: The working classes had accepted only a small piece of the economic cake that they helped to make, while the capitalists took the rest but with the understanding that they would consume only very little of it in practice.[8] This had been a source of social cohesion and stability. But working-class acquiescence now deteriorated because it had suffered the most during the war: food shortages, disease, and often the death of the family's primary earner pushed many families into poverty. Governments had promised military recruits a higher standard of living, but it never materialized. Internationally, the Ottoman, German, Habsburg, and Tsarist empires collapsed, allowing for the emergence of small new nation-states in Central Europe and the Balkans. None were culturally homogenous, and most had reasons to fight with their neighbors – which meant that international conflict was likely. Of course, the Russian empire was reconstituted under different management, but its communist principles threatened both capitalism and the geopolitical order – and later provided a model for Chinese communism. Equally importantly, the war destroyed the monetary foundations and economic stability of capitalism going forward. Crucially, France and Britain were deeply indebted to both American banks and the American state, and accordingly they unwisely demanded large reparations from the losers that led to endless political struggles undermining social cohesion in defeated Germany.

Problems of thin state capacities were equally apparent after the war. For instance, many states returned to the gold standard, beginning with Britain in 1925. This was a resurrection of economic orthodoxy that protected investors' interests by defending the value of the national currency. By pegging their currencies to their gold reserves – a scarce resource that states could not easily increase – states limited their institutional capacities for expanding the money supply to stimulate their economies when necessary, most obviously when the working class demanded help.[9] Furthermore, the reparations imposed on Germany and her allies were harsh, and they paid no attention to Germany's ability to pay – failing as well to realize that an impoverished Germany would not be able to buy British goods. Keynes bluntly chalked this up to the stupidity of political leaders in establishing the conditions for peace. He also argued that because France and Britain had suffered so much in the war, they lacked the institutional capacities to enforce the peace established at Versailles should Germany again turn to aggression. But the most obvious problem was the failure of statecraft on the part of the United States.[10] President Wilson wanted to establish a leading role for the United States in matters of European security, but his naivety at Versailles and in congressional politics at home undermined the League of Nations, his mechanism for bringing peace and stability to the world.[11] As a result, the interwar period lacked the sort of hegemonic leader that would prove to be so important for fostering international social cohesion and stabilizing capitalism in the second half of the century.

In sum, just as thin state capacities, deteriorating social cohesion, and the absence of hegemonic leadership had precipitated the Great War with such devastating consequences for capitalism, they also made it impossible to place capitalism on a sound footing during the interwar years.

Nonetheless, some things improved during the 1920s – at least for a while. The reparations question was addressed, and efforts were made to bring Germany back into the fold. Tariffs were reduced. Even the threat of militant communism diminished. But, driven in part by the return to the gold standard, mass consumption was weakening by the late 1920s, and many countries were slipping into recession. This, of course, was Keynes's great fear: that economic demand would diminish to a point at which growth stalled and unemployment rose. Farmers were hit particularly hard, but workers in manufacturing suffered too. Economic inequality increased, further threatening social cohesion.

The problems of austerity in Germany was compounded by the fact that it had taken loans from the United States to pay its postwar reparations. Because the United States maintained high tariffs on imports, averaging 33 percent, it was difficult for Germany to export enough to the United States to pay for those loans.[12] European countries scaled back tariffs because their industries and agriculture needed to recover; the United States kept tariffs high so as to protect already well-established producers from competition because their share of European markets was shrinking. This was a predatory move by a state on the verge of becoming a hegemonic power.

When the American stock market crashed in 1929, the situation went from bad to worse. Vast sums were suddenly lost, and banks began calling in loans, thereby setting off a vicious chain reaction. With less money available, people and businesses spent less, demand for goods and services declined, production was cut back, unemployment rose, and prices fell in a vicious deflationary spiral whereby falling prices created incentives for people to hoard money and delay their purchases. All this also made it harder for people and businesses to keep up with loan payments, so banks began to fail. Yet the U.S. Federal Reserve, refusing to abandon economic orthodoxy, did little to stop the financial hemorrhaging. Reflecting on the Depression over half a century later, economist Ben Bernanke, former head of the Federal Reserve Board and an expert on the events of the 1930s, remarked that one of the great lessons of the Depression was that "policymakers confronted with extraordinary circumstances must be prepared to think outside the box, defying orthodoxy if necessary."[13]

This, of course, is a matter of state intellectual capacity, unfortunately lacking in this case, because economic policy was dominated by the upper classes at the expense of the lower classes. Gold-standard austerity would please finance capital and investors; easing fiscal and monetary policy would please the populace.[14] But thin state institutional capacities were also to blame – specifically, lax financial regulation, which was corrected later, for example, by the separation of commercial and investment banking under the 1933 Glass-Steagall Act.

Meanwhile, as the crisis metastasized internationally, it unleashed new nationalist forces. German and Hungarian nationalists had already demanded not only an end to reparations but also the return of lands they had lost at Versailles. Furthermore, to boost export-oriented recovery, countries turned again to economic nationalism, further undermining international stability. Twenty countries abandoned the gold standard and devalued their currencies. Yet, because so many did the same, nobody gained a competitive advantage for very long. Several countries abrogated trade treaties and imposed higher tariffs that undermined international trade.[15] Between 1926 and 1931, tariff rates in France, Germany, Japan, Sweden, Great Britain, and the United States jumped anywhere from 1.5 to 3.5 times their initial levels.[16] This was virtually inevitable, because there were no international institutions to manage the crisis or coordinate national responses. Bankers and governments saw the need for more international economic cooperation, but they could not muster the domestic political support to make it happen. Had a hegemonic power pushed for coordinated policies across countries, things might not have spiraled out of control.

The Depression also undermined social cohesion domestically. Part of the problem was that capitalist economies were already transitioning from heavy manufacturing industries, such as textiles, mining, steel, and iron, to mass consumption industries, such as automobiles, consumer appliances, tobacco, and processed foods. This was the sort of creative destruction that Joseph Schumpeter described – but with an unfortunate twist. The productivity gains involved had not yet been matched with employment gains in these new industries. As a result, income inequality grew, and there was not enough consumer demand to absorb what was being produced. Yet, for a while, economic orthodoxy remained the preferred solution: Stick to austerity, balance government budgets, and – if possible – reduce wages, abolish unions, and get rid of fixed-wage contracts. But the workers rebelled, and social cohesion broke down further as rent strikes, food riots, and labor walkouts erupted in many countries.[17] As a result, the Labour Party came to power in Britain. But its tenure was brief. In contrast, the Social Democrats who won office in Scandinavian countries were able to begin building welfare states. In the United States, Franklin Roosevelt won the presidency, Democrats controlled Congress, and the New Deal was born. These new regimes finally began moving in Keynesian directions, building up – that is, thickening – institutional and intellectual state capacities to stimulate their economies and restore some semblance of social cohesion.

In Germany, however, the breakdown of social cohesion took a very different turn. Germany had suffered more than any country after the Great War and during the Depression. Germans felt humiliated by the steep reparations demanded of them – and even the eventual fact that they did not pay failed to soothe their resentment. The combination of extreme right-wing paramilitaries, anti-Semitism, vicious hyperinflation, rigid upper-class naivety, and nationalism led to the rise of the Nazi Party. Hitler's drive for empire represented a return to the belief that territorial size was essential to self-sufficiency and geopolitical independence. This was scarcely surprising: Germany was close to starvation by the time war ended in 1918. But Hitler's empire was to be different from that of Imperial Germany: This was not to be an empire ruling over different nations; this was to be an ethnically homogenous, sanitized nation-state – the most horrible and divisive form of nationalism imaginable.

In East Asia, similar forces were in motion. Imperial Japan had established colonies throughout the region to ensure access to raw materials, but it sought further expansion into Dutch and British territories to obtain access to oil and rubber. The military was largely in charge of the government – especially the state bureaucracy, whose power far exceeded that of the parliament and political parties. The emperor, deemed to rule by divine right, had little political impact other than inspiring devout patriotism and nationalism, which leaders used to build an ultra-nationalistic culture among the Japanese. But Japanese nationalism was fueled too by Western racism toward Japan at the League of Nations in the 1920s and 1930s – another example of social cohesion undermined at the international level. So, the need for natural resources and the growth of Japanese nationalism, compounded by fears of outside aggression from the Western powers as well as Russia and China, eventually led Japan to align with Germany and enter the Second World War.[18]

This war was even more destructive than the first in terms of lives lost, monies spent, and sheer economic destruction.[19] Some 75 million people died in the war as a consequence of combat, genocide, disease, bombings, massacres, and famine. The twelve leading West European countries saw their GDP decline by 23 percent between 1939 and 1946. It was especially severe in Germany, where GDP had grown slowly during the war but suddenly plummeted 67 percent between 1944 and 1946. The story in Japan was similar: GDP dropped by 50 percent between 1944 and 1945.[20] It is scarcely surprising that, at the height of the Second World War, both Polanyi and Schumpeter argued that capitalism was doomed.

They were wrong.

The Golden Age

The darkest days came before a new dawn. The capitalist world's rebound from the devastation of the Depression and Second World War was rapid and impressive, and it was a rebound that benefited the many rather than the few. Average annual economic growth per capita in Europe and Japan, which hovered around 1 percent from 1913 to 1950, jumped to about 4 percent and 8 percent, respectively, between 1950 and 1973. It also rose in the United States, although more modestly.[21] Exports, which had sagged especially during the Depression, bounced back sharply following the war and continued to climb throughout the rest of the century.[22] Unemployment rates dropped to about 2.5 percent in Europe and were even lower in Japan. They averaged about 4 percent in the United States.[23] Finally, inflation fell well within manageable bounds throughout the capitalist world.[24]

This Golden Age rested on new international and domestic foundations, with a good deal of institutional variation added in different areas of the world. Let us consider these elements in turn.

The Second World War ended very differently from the First – without a treaty, but with the ability to create stable political and economic rules of the game that went a long way toward restoring peace and prosperity to the capitalist world. Three crucial background factors were responsible for this. One was that social cohesion increased as nationalist conflicts diminished sharply. Ethnic cleansing and mass murder had been so extensive that European societies had become much more homogeneous, making such liberal openings as there were far easier to achieve. A second factor was that the United States and the Soviet Union, the two world powers that had done the most to win the war, restrained competition both between and within their two spheres of influence. It did not matter if Korea and Germany were divided if order were maintained. The leaders of the capitalist and socialist worlds imposed, as Stalin put it, their own social system on the areas under their control. Finally, a crucial change had immense global significance: Nuclear weapons were so powerful that they were not to be used; enemies had to cooperate so as not to annihilate each other.

The threat of communism, as well as the enormous financial and military power of the United States, helped to facilitate social consensus internationally within the capitalist world. States always face a security dilemma. With great skill and luck, peace can be achieved through balance-of-power politics. The tragedy of Europe lay in its inability to do this in the first half of the twentieth century. After 1945, the United States helped to provide the stability that Europeans had not been able to find themselves. The security dilemma of both Japan and Europe was solved by the power of the United States – guaranteeing military protection for the former and taking a leading role in the North Atlantic Treaty Organization (NATO) in the latter. This went a long way toward ensuring that international cooperation and consensus replaced conflict. But other things did too. France and Germany, the two great continental powers, signed the Treaty of Paris in 1951, which created the European Coal and Steel Community (ECSC). This was an agreement designed to pool French and German steel and coal production, thereby effectively removing complete geopolitical independence from each country and establishing interdependence instead. France was the driving force: having been invaded three times by Germany in a single lifetime, the French figured that if they could not beat their neighbor, then they should join them. This agreement was the opening gambit of what would eventually become the European Union (EU) – a set of institutions further integrating Europe, opening markets, and harmonizing economic activity. The United States played a role here: Jean Monnet, the French diplomat who spearheaded the ECSC, was able to push the project because of the help he received in Washington, D.C.

But why was the United States prepared at the end of the Second World War to embrace the leadership role it had rejected after the First? To begin with, American policymakers were susceptible to the demands of domestic capitalists to open world markets for them. Second, the political elite enjoyed the power and institutional capacities it had developed during the war, including a host of fiscal policy tools – notably, the massive expansion of the income tax. Of course, there was a considerable overlap between these two sets of actors, even though some state leaders were more worried about national security than the needs of the American economy, which is why, for instance, the Truman administration accepted continental involvement in NATO. In short, the political elite had arrived at an accommodation: It realized that political naivety and isolationism – the result of thin state capacities – had had dreadful consequences after the First World War; it was determined to do better. But it is important to note that European states reinforced this consensus, clamoring for American leadership. As Britain's Lord Ismay, NATO's first Secretary General, is said to have put it, the idea was "to keep the Russians out, the Americans in, and the Germans down."

The institutional foundations of postwar capitalist society were established in July 1944 when representatives from the forty-four allied countries met at the Mount Washington Hotel in Bretton Woods, New Hampshire. Recognizing that the allies would win the war, they assembled to design an ambitious system of multilateral institutions to regulate trade, facilitate national fiscal prudence, stabilize currencies, control inflation, encourage full employment, cope with national economic crises, and inspire economic development. The idea was to build international institutional capacities that would help the world to avoid another Great Depression after the war – something that allied leaders feared. There were two intellectual rationales for all this: First, the Depression had made it clear that markets required firm political foundations to function properly; second, there was a general realization that one country's domestic economic policies could affect those of others, and that policymakers should take this into account. The protectionism and economic nationalism of the interwar period had to be avoided.[25] President Franklin Roosevelt emphasized the point in his opening remarks at Bretton Woods: "The economic health of every country is a proper matter of concern to all its neighbors, near and far."[26] This was a call for institutional thickening – the establishment and continued maintenance of international institutions that could regulate things such as trade, exchange rates, and capital flows that affect capitalist prosperity worldwide.

The two principal negotiators were Harry Dexter White and Keynes, representing, respectively, the United States and Great Britain. White wanted to peg exchange rates to the dollar and open world markets to American exports and capital. Keynes strove to protect the sovereign right of nations to change their exchange rates. He also tried to preserve preferential trade relations within the British Empire. Already in declining health, Keynes was bested by White, particularly in the crucial area of exchange rate controls. This was the end of the British Empire and the rise of a new era in the international political economy – an era led by the first genuinely hegemonic power of capitalist society, the United States. One representative from the Bank of England called Bretton Woods "the greatest blow to Britain next to the war."[27] Among other things, it meant that the center of world finance would move from London to Wall Street.

The Bretton Woods agreements involved five major components. The first was a fixed, yet flexible, exchange-rate system. Currencies were pegged to the dollar, whose value was set to gold at $35 an ounce – a move designed to stabilize currencies and mitigate inflation. This cemented the dollar's international supremacy, because most of the world's trade-related transactions across borders would now be settled in dollars.[28] Second, the International Monetary Fund (IMF) was established and charged with policing the system, monitoring countries' economic performance, and providing financial assistance to those suffering serious balance-of-payments problems. The IMF could also give permission to countries that wanted to devalue their currency to resolve balance-of-payments problems and promote full employment. Third, the International Bank for Reconstruction and Development (IBRD) was established, which eventually became part of the World Bank. Its job was to provide loans and underwrite securities to facilitate the rebuilding of those economies that had been devastated by war and those otherwise in need of development assistance. Fourth, national governments were permitted to impose controls on capital flows across their borders. Finally, the Bretton Woods agreement laid the foundation for the General Agreement on Tariffs and Trade (GATT), signed in 1947, which decades later became the World Trade Organization (WTO). Its purpose was to reduce tariffs and import quotas, and to ensure global free trade. If a country were to want to protect a domestic industry such as automobiles or steel with tariffs, GATT officials would determine whether and how much it could do so without imposing excessive costs on foreign exporters of those products.[29]

This, then, was the new international architecture of capitalism. It provided the background and encouraged developments within states, to which we now turn.

What mattered most immediately was the decline of political extremism. In Europe, the extreme right had been defeated in war and replaced by Christian Democracy, perhaps the most important pillar of postwar social stability. The extreme left had been defeated too. Rarely did communist or socialist parties enter, let alone form, governments in capitalist countries. More moderate labor and social democratic parties took this role. These developments were aided by the United States, supporting the former and making life very difficult for the latter, given the context of the Cold War. But the result was clear: Between the two world wars, the average share of votes cast for far-right parties in twenty democracies was just shy of 7 percent; that figure dropped below 2 percent between 1950 and 1973, before rising again to about 6 percent between 1976 and 2014.[30]

Not only did this move to the center reflect diminished nationalist tensions in many countries, but also it involved historic class compromises that engendered national reconstruction and economic growth.[31] The voice of the working class in economic affairs, which Hirschman recognized as being so important, was institutionalized in ways that reduced class conflict. Furthermore, the capitalist class sought, as noted, to moderate national politics. Business elites strove to establish relatively peaceful relations with the labor unions and, as a result, were supportive of social spending and the taxes necessary to pay for it.[32] Finally, the threat of communism helped to foster moderation politically and economically within all the advanced capitalist countries, both the left and right recognizing communism as their common foe.[33]

At the very basis of everything was what French economist Thomas Piketty has called the "Great Compression" – a massive reduction in economic inequality in advanced capitalist countries. Equalizing social conditions has been extremely difficult historically, resulting characteristically from disaster, from war and revolution, and from plague and total societal collapse. It is war that matters most here. Two world wars, not to mention the Great Depression, had led to the widespread destruction of capital and property, thereby lessening the power of the rich. At the same time, mass conscription, together with a good deal of suffering on the home fronts, meant greater political pressure from the masses below for a voice in political affairs. As a result, vast amounts of wealth were wiped out, government spending soared, and progressive taxes, landing most heavily on the upper classes, hit record heights to pay for varied equalization policies. So, after the Second World War, economic inequality was comparatively low, and it remained so in most of the countries involved. It was only in the late 1970s and early 1980s that it began to rise again. For instance, the share of national income going to the richest 10 percent of Americans dropped from about 45 percent to 35 percent during the Second World War, and it remained stable for the next three decades.[34] Similar trends were present in other countries.[35]

Sound political judgement was called for here. The First World War provided the chance to establish greater equality, but political elites took only limited steps in that direction, chiefly through early efforts at building a welfare state in the 1930s. They had learned their lesson by the end of the Second World War, accepting and then amplifying a variety of state capacities – notably, in various forms of welfare, which helped to bolster political stability. In other words, improvements in the states' intellectual capacities – that is, learning from past mistakes – helped to thicken some of their institutional capacities in ways that improved social cohesion. For instance, the U.S. Congress passed the Servicemen's Readjustment Act of 1944, commonly known as the GI Bill, which established hospitals, vocational training programs, and unemployment benefits for veterans. It also provided veterans with low-cost mortgages and stipends for college tuition. A few years later, President Truman signed the Housing Act of 1948, providing liberal mortgage insurance for low-cost housing. The Eisenhower administration launched a massive national highway construction program that provided thousands of jobs. Millions of veterans benefited, the American economy boomed, unemployment remained low, wages rose, and much of the United States prospered.[36] The Europeans put more effort into building generous welfare states, had stronger unions that could cut better deals on wages and benefits, and had stronger center-left political parties protecting working- and middle-class interests. Nevertheless, on both sides of the Atlantic, this was the democratic expression of Polanyi's double movement.

This new world was Keynesian – one in which states developed thicker capacities for managing aggregate demand through the prudent use of fiscal and monetary policy tools to keep capitalism on an even keel, maintain relatively low levels of unemployment and inflation, and avoid severe recessions and depressions. Some countries had flirted with Keynesian-like policies in the 1930s. In the United States, a few Keynesian economists had gained jobs at the Federal Reserve Board in the early part of the decade, and the Roosevelt administration had started experimenting with Keynesianism in 1937.[37] Proto-Keynesians also began to find their way into government positions in France, Sweden, and a few other European countries. Having to cope with the Depression and increasing their military capabilities during a time of escalating geopolitical tensions caused some governments to engage in deficit financing during the 1930s.[38] Still, it was the enormous military spending during the Second World War that pulled the

United States out of the depths of the Depression, creating in the process an economy large enough to allow for the workings of Keynesianism. In the postwar period, more and more policymakers recognized the virtues of Keynesianism, thereby improving the intellectual and institutional capacities of their states – although experience with hyperinflation in the 1930s limited its appeal in Germany, where the fear that inflation might stem from excessive deficit spending was very much on policymakers' minds.[39] Nevertheless, in many countries, the acceptance of Keynesianism led to larger government budgets, heavier tax burdens, and more aggressive central bank policies, which afforded states greater capacities for managing their economies.[40]

In short, lessons learned from the disasters of the first half of the century, coupled with the rise of American hegemony and Keynesianism, bolstered social cohesion and thickened state capacities throughout the capitalist world. Yet we need to be careful not to paint with too broad a brush, for there were important differences between the United States and the rest of the capitalist world that we must now highlight. For example, spending in the United States was tilted toward the military.[41] The great power lacked corporatist arrangements, but business and labor unions nonetheless still came to certain accommodations – notably, agreements to link productivity increases to wages and benefits, the so-called capital-labor accord. This was established initially in the automobile industry in the 1940s, but it spread to other heavy manufacturing industries such as steel, rubber, and chemicals. Later, unions representing federal, state, and municipal employees, and then farm workers, also signed collective bargaining agreements. These helped to reduce labor strife and to usher in an era of relative calm in labor–management relations. In contrast, most European countries put more effort into building generous welfare states than did the United States. Corporatism in Germany, the Benelux countries, and Scandinavia facilitated all sorts of industrial policies involving the institutional coordination of state, business, and labor activities around issues such as infrastructural development, human capital formation, and financing for selected industries. The British did something similar for a while, although on a far less centralized scale. The French experimented with indicative planning, another form of state-business coordination. Small states seemed to be particularly good at these things, because they tended to be more homogeneous culturally and, as a result, enjoyed more social cohesion and trust, which facilitated cooperation in the national interest.[42] But, on both sides of the Atlantic, significant steps were taken to facilitate class compromise and full employment, thereby giving the working and middle classes a sense that their voices were being heard and that they were an important part of society, as Hirschman might have hoped. Again, social cohesion and state capacities developed in lockstep.

There were, however, striking regional developments that caused increasing divergence between the United States and its allies. The Treaty of Paris was the first step, as noted, toward European integration after the war. Members of the new European Union had to accept massive amounts of legislation designed to facilitate the smooth functioning of markets and trade within the region – and to protect those at the bottom of the social scale, including minorities.[43] Nevertheless, surveys have shown that, within the Union, most people's identities remain largely national rather than transnational – albeit with some variation. A stronger sense of European identity is more apparent among the more cosmopolitan upper reaches of European society. Furthermore, the countries that suffered most in the Second World War have tended to be the most Europhile.[44] The key point to be made is that European institutions are best seen as providing fora in which heads of state and government officials can meet, settle disagreements, and make deals. They were mechanisms for promoting cooperation among national political elites, in part by collecting and providing vast amounts of data to decision makers and their representatives. This is a sign of thick, developed transnational intellectual state capacity and informed voice for its members.

East Asian countries followed their own paths to prosperity. The Japanese pursued a package of developmental policies, mixing tariff protection, as List might have advised, with combinations of state subsidies and financing, often orchestrated by the Ministry of International Trade and Industry in cooperation with the Ministry of Finance and Bank of Japan. Indeed, the state had a formidable array of institutional capacities at its disposal, and policymakers used them wisely. Automobiles, consumer electronics, and other strategic industries that the state picked were protected and promoted in this way until the quality of their products was good enough to compete in international markets. Japan's postwar rise as an economic powerhouse was fundamentally the result of intellectual competence among the state's administrative elites – recruited from the top universities on the basis of merit, carefully screened through civil-service examinations, often possessing wide-ranging general knowledge of the bureaucracy, socialized in the ways of consensual decision making, and among the most powerful of their kind in the advanced industrial democracies.[45] In particular, a group of well-trained Japanese economists played key roles in economic policymaking both as advisers to government and as high-level state bureaucrats before, during, and after the war. They were averse to liberal capitalism, as well as communism, and after the war devised their developmental strategy to strengthen the nation's economic power by engaging in international competition.

A central concern of Japanese strategy was that of cultivating social cohesion. This was done in two ways. The first involved stabilizing labor relations by guaranteeing life-long job security and annual wage increases, and encouraging dialogue between managers and workers inside firms. The second involved cultivating cohesive networks among policymakers and business leaders in a system based on bargaining and reciprocal consent. In fact, such networks had long existed in Japan between state bureaucrats and large, family-owned business groups – the so-called *zaibatsu* that morphed into a more modern *keiretsu* after the war. As a result, the state, business, and labor all adopted a long-term, nationalist, productivity mentality to economic decision making rather than a short-term, individualistic, profit-oriented approach. It was this combination of social cohesion and state capacity that did so much to help Japan to transition quickly from a military-based economy to a trade-based one by the end of the 1960s, thereby becoming one of the world's largest and most successful economies by the 1980s.[46] Of course, American hegemony helped too, by providing military security to Japan, leaving the Japanese state free to devote more resources to economic development. The Japanese strategy worked like a charm. South Korea followed suit later with similar state-led approaches.[47]

Not all East Asian countries followed the same developmental path, but they did all rely heavily on states with thick intellectual and institutional capacities. Singapore, for instance, did not use protectionism, but in the 1960s it took its first bold steps to attract foreign direct investment from around the world. This was a story of intense strategic state intervention, aiming to create an institutional ecosystem conducive to economic development. The government did this by investing heavily in education, training, technology, and infrastructure. It also encouraged social cohesion, but, in contrast to Japan, it did so by using autocratic sticks as well as more benevolent carrots. The sticks included repressing opposition to the ruling party, cracking down on student political activities, emasculating the unions, preventing strikes, and handing out harsh penalties for minor infractions of the law. But the carrots entailed facilitating business networking, joint ventures, and public–private partnerships, ensuring religious freedom, and reminding citizens in this ethnically diverse country of ever-present external threats. The state also provided public housing to all ethnic groups and established English as the overarching state language, while allowing people to speak their first language at home.[48]

Other developing East Asian countries, such as Taiwan and Hong Kong, shared important developmental characteristics. One was bureaucratic coordination structures in which insulated, well-trained state bureaucrats, largely immune from intense private-sector lobbying, gathered information on the industries in question and formulated developmental policies accordingly. Another common trait was the formal and informal linkages and communication channels that existed between the state and industry. This facilitated information sharing helped to alleviate conflict between policymakers and business and bolstered social cohesion.[49] It was this paradoxical combination of state insulation with public–private connectedness that was the key to success in these, as well as other, developing countries – something sociologist Peter Evans calls the state's "embedded autonomy."[50] That many of these countries were culturally homogeneous surely enhanced social cohesion and the ability of policymaking and industrial elites to work together for the national economic good.[51]

There is an important point to be made here about the relationship between Hirschman's voice, social cohesion, and capitalism. Authoritarianism, as well as democratic voice, can ensure the social cohesion that capitalism needs. Our preference is for the latter but not only for normative reasons. Authoritarianism is a less politically stable mechanism for achieving social cohesion than is the provision of democratic voice. It is not surprising that South Korea eventually abandoned autocracy for democracy as its capitalist economy prospered. Prodemocracy demonstrations, the emergence of progressive political elites, and pressure from the United

States helped to usher in the change. Nor is it surprising that China has witnessed uprisings in Tiananmen Square and, more recently, Hong Kong as Chinese capitalism has flourished. Our point is that while social cohesion is a necessary condition for capitalist prosperity, voice is not a necessary condition for social cohesion – although it may provide more stability in the long run.

Overall, then, during its Golden Age capitalism was extraordinarily successful: an international economic order combining free trade and capital mobility, on one side, with domestic Keynesian-style stabilization policy, on the other, all nestled within the Bretton Woods architecture.[52] It was rooted in high levels of social cohesion and state capacities at both the domestic and international levels. The United States played a crucial role in facilitating all this as the world's hegemonic leader.

This does not mean that relations between different classes and ethnic, religious, or other groups were perfectly harmonious. Despite major breakthroughs in labor–management relations in the United States, there were still significant conflicts between the two sides – notably, over right-to-work laws and prohibitions on union activity at the state level.[53] Race relations have remained extremely fraught as well, although the U.S. Congress responded to the civil rights movement and international pressure by passing civil rights legislation affording Black and marginalized ethnic communities more political voice and economic opportunity than they had enjoyed previously. In some European countries, tensions revolved around ethnic groups, especially in Spain and Northern Ireland, with further tensions set to arise only later in response to immigration.

Conclusion

The story told in this chapter is utterly remarkable. Sheer hell was followed by decency and prosperity. Some have argued that this postwar period was merely one of catching up, or returning to normal, following the devastation many countries suffered in the Second World War. There may be some truth to that. However, catching up after war is neither automatic nor inevitable; it requires the right state capacities and a modicum of social cohesion. After all, Germany and Japan bounced back much better than did Italy. And there was much less catching up in the capitalist world following the First World War than there was following the Second. So, while there may be some credibility to the catching-up argument, one still needs to understand how state capacities and social cohesion were at work.

The remainder of this book explains how things eventually came unglued after the Golden Age and what the implications of this are going forward. For now, we can preview at least three critical reasons why this happened that are central to the arguments in the rest of this book. First, the key advance of the period was conjunctural – not fully anchored in permanent social structural change. The fundamental class compromise rested on the greater equality and societal escalator that resulted, in part, from mass participation in warfare. The sense of shared sacrifice that lay behind greater equalization was not to last. Upper classes everywhere almost always find ways of increasing their share of the cake and gaining more for themselves than for the many. The basis of social cohesion was always likely to be challenged. Second, in their push for self-enrichment, the upper classes eventually turned away from Keynesianism and, in doing so, launched an attack on state capacities that weakened the institutional and intellectual foundations of the postwar order. Third, the behavior of the United States changed. The proponents of "hegemonic stability theory" claim that the stability of capitalist society always depends on a leader capable of providing both a top currency and defense for its allies.[54] The military power and economic leadership of the United States did help capitalism to flourish after 1945. But it is important, as noted, to recognize a crucial contrast between two relatively distinct periods of American hegemony, the benign and the predatory. It was most often in the United States' interest to act generously in the years immediately after 1945, and that relatively benign role was made possible by the untrammeled power that it then possessed. As the hegemon's power has diminished, a predatory alternative has become increasingly attractive.

The institutional and social conditions of the Golden Age were never going to last.

3

Storm Clouds

Storm clouds began to threaten the postwar political economy rather quickly. By the late 1960s, war-torn countries had made great strides in revitalizing their economies, while competition was heating up in world markets, challenging the United States' economic primacy. Then, the price of oil skyrocketed in the 1970s, driving production costs higher. These years came to be dominated by stagflation – a toxic mix of inflation, sluggish economic growth, and high unemployment. On top of that, thanks to dramatic improvements in telecommunications and transportation, consumer demands began to change rapidly, and manufacturers raced to keep up. In 1909, Henry Ford had promised his customers that they could buy a Model T in any color so long as it was black; by 1973, the Ford Mustang came in three body styles, with five engine options, a choice of three transmissions, and more than a dozen colors. To compete effectively in this new environment of Schumpeterian creative destruction, manufacturers began to downsize their operations, establish international supply chains, seek wage and benefit concessions from workers, and move some of their operations to countries with lower wages and more lenient business regulations. Other countries began entering the game too – notably, Brazil, Russia, India, China, and South Africa, known as the BRICS countries – increasing international competition even further. Finally, many states began taking a new, more laissez-faire, approach to managing their economies – neoliberal in character and a fundamental alternative to Keynesianism. Capitalism was expanding through the whole world, but it was becoming less stable and more prone to crisis in the process.

This chapter explains how these forces began to unsettle capitalism during the last third of the twentieth century. Of course, these were not entirely bad times: International travel was increasing, many citizens of the capitalist world enjoyed more disposable income, and health and education outcomes were improving. Nevertheless, change was afoot, and trouble was looming. The story begins with the United States, whose hegemonic position started to change at the margins. Next, we examine the factors that led to the rise and widespread acceptance of neoliberalism – sometimes called market fundamentalism – an ideology that called for less government control over the economy. This was supposed to be a prescription for improving economic performance by unleashing market forces. But the move toward neoliberalism was, in effect, an attack on state capacities at both the national and international levels. It also involved an assault on the class compromise that had marked the socially cohesive postwar era. Much of this was driven by an increase in the power of capitalists. This helped to pave the way for mounting economic instability and economic crises, first in the capitalist periphery and then at the core.

Hegemony in Flux

The Bretton Woods system had established a "fixed but adjustable" exchange-rate system. This arrangement soon came under stress. Given the dollar's unique position, it afforded the U.S. government the privilege of seigniorage. Unlike other countries, the United States could expand its money supply at will. One way of doing so was simply to print more dollar bills on government printing presses; another involved buying securities. Just as you might have a checking account at your local bank, so too did many banks have accounts at the Federal Reserve (known as the Fed). The Fed can simply credit the banks' accounts with new deposits, thereby "printing money" out of thin air. It does this by using these credits to buy U.S. Treasury bonds and other securities from the banks. The banks then pump this newly created money into the economy as loans and other investments. It is worth noting that Treasury bonds are often in demand worldwide because they are backed by the "full faith and credit" of the U.S. government, the world's hegemonic power, and are therefore deemed to be an extremely safe investment. Investors can be assured that they will get their money back when the bonds reach maturity, because the government can always "print" more money if it has to. This, of course, also makes it easy for the government to borrow at very favorable interest rates by selling these securities.[1] This is an extraordinarily useful element of state capacity, if wielded carefully. The problem was that if the United States were to do this to excess, it would eventually be unable to redeem dollars for gold at the price agreed upon at Bretton Woods – that is, at $35 an ounce. It would also generate increasingly large budget deficits. Confidence in the dollar would erode, and the whole exchange-rate system would begin to teeter like a house of cards.[2]

European governments worried about the stability of the dollar. The combination of the Vietnam War and the War on Poverty, President Johnson's effort to reduce inequality in the United States during the 1960s, led to borrowing, "printing" money, budget deficits, and inflationary pressure. The dollar became overvalued, and American policymakers began to fear that foreign governments holding dollars might sense trouble and want to exchange them for gold, thus draining American gold reserves. In August 1971, President Richard Nixon unilaterally closed the gold window, cancelling the convertibility of dollars to gold. The so-called Nixon shock sent the exchange-rate system reeling.[3] One of the most stabilizing institutional elements of the capitalist system was suddenly in danger.

The Europeans were furious for several reasons. For years, the United States' Cold War allies had been forced to hold overvalued dollars, concerned that the currency's collapse would force the United States to pull its military forces out of Europe and East Asia.[4] Now, not only could they no longer exchange their dollars for gold, but the United States had devalued the currency. Anything on world markets priced in dollars – such as oil – suddenly became more expensive. Many countries began to experience inflation, which in Europe led to several years of massive strikes. Moreover, thanks to devaluation, exchange rates floated. Eventually, other countries devalued their own currencies, which led to a surge in the cost of imports to many countries: on average, 70 percent for nonfuel commodities and 100 percent for food by 1973.[5] The dollar remained the world's reserve currency, but the United States had destroyed one of the most important stabilizing pillars of the postwar international architecture of capitalism. The Bretton Woods exchange-rate system was dead. While Europeans tried to cope by devising their own exchange-rate mechanisms, none worked well. Adding fuel to the fire, the United States slapped a 10 percent surcharge on all imports into the country, aiming to lower its trade and current account deficits.[6] In short, the Europeans felt that the United States had abused its hegemonic power and stabbed them in the back. Hegemonic power had started to shift from a relatively benign form to a more predatory one based less on the well-being of the international community and more on American interests alone.

There were other problems too. We have seen that war had upset capitalism twice in the first half of the twentieth century; in the second half, it happened again. Egyptian and Syrian forces attacked Israel in October 1973, seeking to reclaim land lost to Israel in the 1967 Arab–Israeli war. Later that month, the Organization of the Petroleum Exporting Countries (OPEC) imposed an oil embargo on countries supporting Israel in the war, including the United States, Canada, Japan, and the United Kingdom. By the time the embargo was lifted a year later, the price of oil had quadrupled from $3 to $12 a barrel globally. In the United States, gasoline was suddenly in short supply and rationed. Those with even-numbered license plates could buy it only on even-numbered days of the month; those with odd-numbered plates, on odd-numbered days. People waited in long lines to fill their tanks at gas stations. A second oil crisis hit in the aftermath of the Iranian Revolution in 1979 and the Iran–Iraq War a year later. The price of crude oil on world markets, which had been rising anyway, shot up again, more than doubling within the year to $40 a barrel.

All of this contributed to the onset of stagflation. Figure 3.1 illustrates the trends in the advanced capitalist countries. Beginning with the 1973 oil crisis, economic growth dropped dramatically, while inflation spiked. Rising unemployment often accompanied these trends – on average, doubling during the second half of the 1970s from figures during the previous decade-and-a-half and continuing to worsen right through the mid-1990s.[7] Even in the United States, despite its hegemonic position, unemployment reached more than 8 percent following the first oil crisis and peaked at nearly 11 percent after the second. This sort of instability was unprecedented in postwar capitalism, and it left economists and policymakers perplexed, as we shall see momentarily.[8]

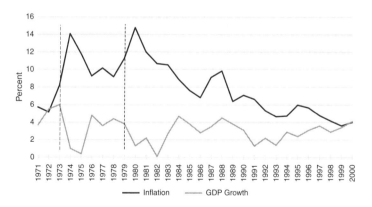

Figure 3.1 Stagflation in the OECD, 1971–2000
Source: OECD (2019a).

The hegemonic power of the United States was a factor in these events. The country had been the most powerful defender of Israel in the Arab–Israeli war and therefore shared some responsibility for the OPEC oil embargo in 1973. Its responsibility was still more evident in the case of Iran. The United States backed the Shah's regime, helping to bring him to power in a 1953 coup d'état; the 1979 revolution brought an Islamic theocracy to power, led by Grand Ayatollah Ruhollah Khomeini, whose regime was virulently anti-American. Iranian revolutionaries burned the American flag and effigies of "Uncle Sam" in the streets of Tehran, and they stormed the American embassy, seizing and holding hostages for over a year, until they managed to escape and flee the country. Iranian oil production was seriously disrupted during the upheaval, as it was again during the Iran–Iraq war.

The lesson here is that hegemony is a double-edged sword: In its benign form, it can stabilize international capitalism, but in its predatory form, it can disrupt it. Keynes recognized the importance of a benign hegemon for stabilizing capitalism. Whether he also recognized the dangers of a more predatory one is not clear, although being bested by the Americans at Bretton Woods should have alerted him to this possibility.

Neoliberalism and the Attack on State Capacity

Stagflation created thorny problems for policymakers. By the 1970s, Keynesianism was the playbook with which nearly everyone in the advanced capitalist world managed their economies. Even Nixon, a conservative Republican, remarked to a reporter in 1971, "We are all Keynesians now." But suddenly that playbook did not seem to work. Keynesians assumed that there was an inverse relationship between inflation and unemployment: much like a seesaw, as one went up, the other went down. The idea was that as unemployment declined because of strong economic growth, inflation would increase. When unemployment was low, workers could demand and get higher wages. With more money to spend, demand for goods and services would increase, putting upward pressure on prices. Higher prices meant inflation. Conversely, if unemployment rose in a weak economy, there would be less demand, and therefore lower prices and less inflation. The job of government was to balance the seesaw with prudent fiscal and monetary policy – that is, by fiddling with taxes, spending, interest rates, and the money supply. But, beginning in the early 1970s, all this fell apart. Inflation and unemployment were rising together. The seesaw was broken. The stagflation era had arrived. Suddenly, policy-makers did not know what to do.

Economists offered a variety of explanations and possible policy solutions, but neoliberalism carried the day. Neoliberals believed that stagflation was the result of excessive government intervention in the economy. This was precisely the sort of intervention that Keynesians had advocated for decades and which contributed to the thickening of state capacities. The neoliberal analysis had three parts. First, it held that excessive government spending on welfare programs had made people lazy and sapped their incentive to work hard. Productivity and economic growth suffered accordingly. This argument was personified by President Ronald Reagan's frequent public references to a "welfare queen," sponging off government assistance. Second, neoliberals argued that tax increases had been necessary to pay for this sort of exorbitant welfare spending. The more the government taxed people, the less money they had to buy the things that would sustain economic demand. The more government taxed businesses, the less money they had to invest in the things that boosted productivity. And, to pay higher taxes without cutting profits, businesses had to raise prices. Economic growth went down, and inflation went up. Third, neoliberals believed that complying with environmental, occupational safety and health, and other business regulations promulgated in the late 1960s and early 1970s was expensive – a further reason why businesses had to raise prices. With all this in mind, the neoliberal solution was obvious: to slay stagflation, all you had to do was slash taxes and government spending and deregulate – or, more accurately, reregulate – the economy in ways that unleashed market forces.[9]

Two clarifications are necessary. First, in practice, neoliberalism is not a pure or monolithic whole; it is a bundle of policy options, including free trade, balanced budgets, low debt, and more, from among which policymakers can pick and choose, not always consistently. For instance, they may decide to cut taxes on corporate profits but increase them for personal income – or vice versa. While cutting taxes, they may increase spending for social services or the military – but they may also do the reverse. They may impose trade barriers on the free flow of steel and aluminum but reduce them on soybeans, corn, and wine.

They may cut regulations for environmental protection but increase them for occupational safety and health. These and many other choices are driven not only by the prevailing economic conditions but also by politics. This means that there is no guarantee that the full package of neoliberal policies will be adopted. Second, not all aspects of neoliberalism are necessarily bad. List had argued that free trade is desirable but only under certain conditions, and Keynes had shown that balancing government budgets and reducing national debt are prudent only when the economy is in good shape. We will see that economies have often worked better when some elements of neoliberalism, such as the free movement of goods and labor, were mixed with some forms of redistribution to manage inequality and facilitate economic mobility.

But what matters here is that neoliberalism was a recipe for reducing the state's institutional capacities for managing the domestic economy. For this reason, it was unlikely that neoliberalism would work as advertised.[10] Particularly in the event of an economic crisis, policymakers' hands would be tied. For example, with less tax revenue to spend, it is more difficult to launch an effective Keynesian stimulus to counteract a recession, at least without racking up mountains of debt. Without regulatory authority, it becomes harder for policymakers to prevent capitalists from wreaking havoc with the environment and exploiting workers to the point in which social cohesion disintegrates, and capitalism breaks down. In short, neoliberalism was the antithesis of the thick state capacities that capitalism needed – capacities that were essential for pursuing the double movement that Karl

Polanyi thought society required to prevent capitalism from destroying itself.

The stagflation riddle was not the only problem for which neoliberalism seemed to be the solution; the other was economic globalization and rising international economic competition. Ford, for example, now had to compete against not only other American automobile manufacturers but also Volkswagen, Datsun (now Nissan), Mercedes, Fiat, and Peugeot. Figure 3.2 shows that world trade was rising slowly in the late 1960s but really took off in the 1970s. Much of this activity was concentrated in the so-called triad region of the advanced capitalist world – that is, North America, Western Europe, and Japan.[11] Figure 3.2 also shows that, between 1970 and 1980, the value of exports in the triad region jumped sixfold, from roughly $232 billion to $1.3 trillion, and soared

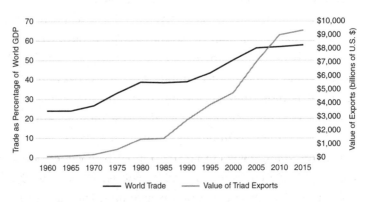

Figure 3.2 World trade and advanced country exports, 1960–2015
Source: World Bank (2019a) for trade; International Monetary Fund (2019a) for exports.

even more spectacularly after that. Something similar was happening with investment. Worldwide foreign direct investment (FDI), such as buying or establishing production facilities or businesses in foreign countries, increased sevenfold between 1975 and 1990. In the advanced capitalist countries, long-term portfolio investment – purchasing foreign stocks, bonds, currency, and other financial instruments – grew at roughly twice the rate of FDI during the late 1980s and early 1990s.[12] From 1997 to 2013, portfolio investment assets jumped from about 25 percent to 63 percent of global gross domestic product (GDP).[13] The problem was that, in this new environment, countries had to compete more aggressively for a share of international markets and investment capital. The question was how best to handle this. Many saw neoliberalism as the solution.

According to neoliberal doctrine, to attract ever more geographically mobile foreign investment and keep domestic investment from leaving, states needed to create an attractive investment climate by cutting business taxes and regulations. This was another reason for reducing state capacities. But the logic was flawed. There are many reasons why firms and investors decide to put their resources in one country rather than another; taxes and regulations are only two, often outweighed by other considerations. Those who have studied the factors affecting FDI decisions find that, in general, taxes and regulations are only a small part of a much more complicated decision-making formula.[14]

Regardless of the naysayers and flawed logic underlying neoliberalism, people believed it anyway, and policymakers often acted accordingly – most notably, in the United

States during Reagan's presidency and in the United Kingdom during Margaret Thatcher's tenure as prime minister. Reagan and Thatcher led their country's conservative parties in the 1980s. However, the rise of neoliberalism was a bipartisan affair insofar as center-left and center-right parties in the advanced countries often jumped on the same bandwagon.[15] Still, the rhetoric did not always align with the action governments took in practice, and their adoption of neoliberalism varied in intensity and form. Anglo-Saxon countries, already more inclined to smaller welfare states and lower taxes, were more apt to embrace neoliberal reforms; countries with Christian democratic and social democratic traditions were more cautious.[16] But even in the Anglo-Saxon countries, there was slippage between practice and rhetoric. Reagan, for instance, slashed tax rates when he first took office, but he then agreed to raise them later once the government's budget deficits ballooned. And, despite the neoliberal call for balanced budgets, the United States' habit of running sizeable deficits never abated. In the United Kingdom, despite her desire to cut back welfare programs, several of Thatcher's efforts were stymied.[17]

When it came to regulation, the story was about eliminating, revising, or writing new rules to set loose market forces. Capital controls mattered most of all.[18] After the Second World War, many countries beefed up their capital controls – an essential institutional capacity that states used to control the flow of capital in and out of the country. Capital controls are especially important for preventing rapid and potentially devastating disinvestment from a country – that is, for preventing capital flight.[19] This can take many forms, such as limiting the foreign assets and liabilities held by domestic financial institutions, limiting the domestic operations of foreign banks, and taxing capital movements across national borders. In 1974, the United States eased many of its capital controls, presumably as another inducement for investors. Other countries soon followed suit, feeling competitive pressure to do so. As a result, beginning in the early 1980s, transnational capital flows such as FDI and portfolio investment began to increase sharply, particularly in the advanced capitalist world. The rise of portfolio investment was particularly important because it was much more liquid and therefore potentially more footloose than FDI. People can move their money in and out of countries much faster if all they have to do is buy or sell stocks, bonds, and currency rather than factories and equipment.[20] According to Harvard political scientist Beth Simmons, "The spread of neoclassical ideas most clearly embodied in the [neoliberal] policies of Reagan and Thatcher provided a clear framework for eliminating [capital] controls."[21] The problem was that investors could find ways around capital controls, and speculation that governments might devalue their currencies could set off massive, destabilizing capital flight.[22] The absence of capital controls amplified these dangers.

For example, in 1992, when capital flow restrictions were being loosened, George Soros suddenly "shorted" the British pound sterling – borrowing vast amounts of the currency from anyone he could and then selling it, based on the assumption that its value was about to drop against other currencies. Other speculators followed suit, forcing the pound's devaluation, at which point Soros bought pounds again at the new lower price, repaid his debt to those from whom he had borrowed them, and pocketed over $1 billion in profit. Corporations have taken advantage of looser capital controls too. Among others, American nonfinancial corporations such as General Electric, Sears, General Motors, and Ford have enjoyed a dramatic increase in earnings through global portfolio investments. These are examples of the increasing financialization of the economy.[23]

It is hard to overestimate the importance of American hegemony in spreading the neoliberal gospel.[24] Neoliberalism was spearheaded intellectually by conservative economists such as Milton Friedman and his University of Chicago colleagues. When stagflation and globalization emerged, they were poised to advise policymakers and proselytize publicly for neoliberalism. The fact that American economists were generally held in high regard around the world afforded neoliberalism an aura of legitimacy. The United States was the intellectual hegemon in the field of economics, often training economists from other countries too.[25] However, wealthy capitalists in the United States also pushed neoliberalism hard. Some of their largesse went to support neoliberal academics in economics departments and law schools.[26] Some of it went to conservative think tanks, such as the Heritage Foundation, American Enterprise Institute, and Cato Institute, which aggressively advocated neoliberalism in Washington, D.C., and around the world, often with great success – another sign of American intellectual hegemony.[27] Neoliberalism also had an international dimension called the Washington Consensus, a set of policies backed by Wall Street interests and the U.S. Treasury, and often foisted on developing countries by the International Monetary Fund (IMF). If countries were in economic trouble, the IMF offered conditionality programs – financial assistance but only if these countries adopted the neoliberal agenda, dropping capital controls, cutting state spending, and balancing government budgets.[28] Finally, neoliberalism benefited from the collapse of communism in Europe. When the Berlin Wall fell in 1989 and the Soviet Union dissolved in 1991, many postcommunist countries adopted shock therapy, which entailed the rapid privatization of state-owned enterprises, the liberalization of prices, trade, and cross-border capital flows, the reduction of expensive government social programs, and the development of Western-style capital markets and tax systems. This was neoliberalism on steroids and an example of the Washington Consensus at work.[29]

Let us pause for a moment to summarize. The rise of neoliberalism was an assault on state capacities. At the domestic level, it called for cutting government spending, taxes, and reregulating the economy to free market forces. At the international level, it favored reducing capital controls. This attack on state institutional capacities was like a rider dropping the reins of their horse, letting it run wherever it wanted, and hoping that they would not fall off.

Globalization and the Assault on Labor

Let us turn from the erosion of state capacities and the predatory shift in American hegemony to the question of social cohesion. Groups toward the bottom of society were losing power, and social cohesion was being undermined as a result. Two different processes were at work – economic globalization and an attack on organized labor – with the first paving the way for the second.

Thanks to the creative use of new transportation and communications technologies, trade and FDI were expanding rapidly at the end of the twentieth century, and challengers to the powerful postwar economies were emerging – notably, the BRICS and a handful of small East Asian countries. Consider India and China, the most successful of the BRICS. Their annual GDP growth rates in the second half of the 1990s averaged an impressive 8.5 percent and 9.1 percent, respectively, which was far better than the European or North American countries. Part of the success of these and other rapidly developing countries was that they provided locations for multinational corporations that wanted to outsource production and build international supply chains.[30] Figure 3.3 illustrates this trend by plotting the VAX ratio in all the exports of forty-two countries from 1970 to 2005. The

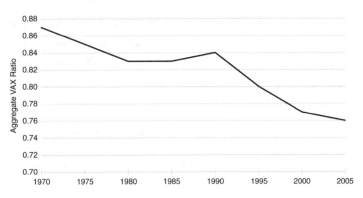

Figure 3.3 Decline in domestic content of exports, 1970–2005
Source: Johnson and Noguera (2012).

VAX ratio captures the value of domestic content in a product.[31] A decline in the VAX ratio, illustrated in the figure, means that less value is added domestically to products during the manufacturing process, and more is added by foreign sources. For example, if Ford used to make steering wheels for its Mustang sports car in the United States but now outsources steering wheel production to Mexico, the percentage of value added domestically to its American product drops, and so does the VAX index, at least a little.[32] To remain competitive, corporations often outsourced production to reduce labor and production costs. However, risks were involved. Firms became vulnerable to disruptions in their international supply chains, especially when they depended on just-in-time delivery systems. For example, a recent labor strike in Mexico forced Ford to build the Mustang with temporary steering wheels and hold thousands of them in parking lots awaiting the right parts.[33] The breakdown of international supply chains became especially glaring during the coronavirus pandemic, when hospitals had trouble buying personal protective equipment and critical medical devices.

Rising international competition, supply chains, and outsourcing represent the sort of disruptive creative destruction that Joseph Schumpeter described. That disruption hit workers especially hard. Outsourcing and increased foreign competition cut the legs out from under traditional manufacturing in automobiles, steel, and other smoke-stack industries. Factories were closed, and workers were laid off. In some cases, workers were forced to accept wage and benefit concessions or else risk losing their jobs to outsourcing. Employment began shifting from manufacturing, where unions were strong and workers had high-paying jobs, to service industries, in which it could be more difficult for unions to organize and workers might not earn as much.[34] Those with skills and education tended to fare better than those without. Furthermore, labor market institutions came under attack. For example, Germany has long been famous for its corporatist system in which labor unions such as *IG Metal* and employer associations such as *Gesamtmetall*, both in the metal-working industry, have bargained over wages and benefits for the entire industry. In the 1990s, small and medium-size producers in the metal industries lobbied for an end to corporatist bargaining to help restrain wage costs that were hurting their international competitiveness. Fearing an end to harmonious labor–management relations, necessary for high-quality production in key German exports such as automobiles and machine tools, larger manufacturers thwarted their efforts. But a two-tier system of wages and benefits emerged anyway, with workers outside the industrial core receiving less generous packages than workers inside it.[35] Similarly, in some Scandinavian countries, centralized corporatist wage bargaining was decentralized. The drift toward these two-tiered and decentralized systems was becoming common.[36]

Labor suffered most in the United Kingdom and in the United States, where the great believers in neoliberalism, Reagan and Thatcher, assaulted unions, both for their own ideological reasons but also at the behest of their capitalist backers.[37] What was involved here was class war – an attempt by capitalists to force the state to do its bidding.

Thatcher's assault on labor is legendary. It began with laws limiting "closed" union shops requiring workers to join the union and secondary picketing, and it culminated in the long and violent coal miners' strike of 1984–1985, triggered by her move to close some of the mines. The government won, delivering a crippling blow to the labor movement. Before the strike, half of all British workers had been trade unionists; a decade later, that number had dropped by a third and the strike rate had plummeted, indicating labor's acquiescence to the new status quo.

The situation in the United States was similar. Reagan fired 11,000 members of the national air traffic controllers' union when they went on strike in 1981, sending a clear signal to the business community that the administration was firmly antiunion and willing to support business in its efforts to weaken the unions. Corporate union-busting strategies flourished. State-level assaults on closed shops, and demands for right-to-work laws that gave workers the right to opt out of joining the union even when they enjoyed the benefits of a union-negotiated contract were just as important.

Figure 3.4 shows that union membership declined as a percentage of the labor force in many advanced countries.

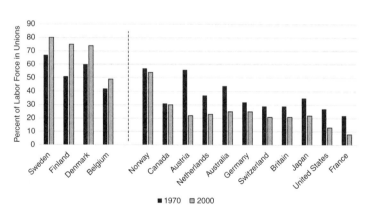

Figure 3.4 Declining union membership, 1970 and 2000
Source: Visser (2009).

The exceptions were some Scandinavian countries and Belgium, with strong prolabor social democratic parties or other protections for unions.[38] Not surprisingly, the percentage of the labor force covered by some sort of collective bargaining agreement declined in several countries in which unionization rates dropped, such as Germany, Australia, Switzerland, the United States, the United Kingdom, and Japan.

All of this began to shake the foundations of social cohesion that had been built up during the Golden Age. The attack on labor reduced working-class voice and influence in economic affairs. By cracking down on organized labor, capitalist societies were becoming less inclusive than they had been during the Golden Age.[39] This was antithetical to Albert Hirschman's view that providing voice to capitalism's stakeholders increased their cooperation and loyalty to the system. Nor was it good, as we have seen, for economic growth. During the 1960s and 1970s, economic growth was strongest where corporatism provided workers a voice in economic decision making.[40] Globalization, outsourcing, and the attack on labor contributed to rising inequality and raised doubts about the possibility of improving one's position in life.

Rising Instabilities

These changes in American hegemony, state capacity, and social cohesion, both nationally and internationally, had destabilizing effects within capitalism. The reduction of capital controls was one source of instability. This occurred in tandem with a flood of money into world markets. The rise in oil prices meant that Saudi Arabia and Russia were making money hand over fist and needed somewhere to invest it. They initially invested their "petrodollars" in advanced capitalist economies, but they soon pushed into developing countries, governments in Latin America and then East Asia eager to borrow to pay for economic development projects.[41] This led to rising levels of debt, which, as we shall see, caused serious problems later and opened the door for the dissemination of Washington Consensus policies in the developing countries. Lending to the advanced countries got an additional boost with the emergence of the BRICS during the 1980s and 1990s. The phenomenal growth of its economy in the 1990s allowed China to become an important source of lending to the world. All of this took place without the Bretton Woods exchange-rate agreement, which had limited how much governments could borrow, and countries could now borrow as much as anyone was willing to lend them.[42] The sky was the limit. This increased the possibility for instability in two ways. One was that levels of national indebtedness rose. Figure 3.5 shows that, beginning in the mid-1970s, the level of national debt for advanced and developing economies doubled by about 1990. Historically, periods of high debt have been associated with dangerous credit bubbles and a rising incidence of default or debt restructuring.[43] The other was that, in the absence of capital controls, if national economies ran into trouble, investors could pull their money out more quickly than ever and move it somewhere else. We will provide examples of both these dangers in a moment.

Looser capital controls also created exchange-rate instability. According to one IMF report, "The liberalization of capital flows in the last two decades [1980s and 1990s] and

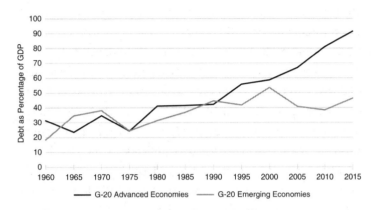

Figure 3.5 National debt, 1960–2015
Source: International Monetary Fund (2019a).

the enormous increase in the scale of cross-border financial transactions have increased exchange rate movements. Currency crises in emerging market economies are special examples of high exchange rate volatility."[44] Of course, exchange-rate volatility depends in part on the nature of the currency regime – whether national currencies are tightly pegged to one another, free-floating, or somewhere in between. From 1970 to 2001, volatility was lowest for currencies with only limited flexibility and highest for currencies that were free-floating.[45] This lends further support to the idea that the Bretton Woods exchange-rate agreement had been a source of stability for capitalism.

There were other forms of instability too. Economic historians have shown that the long-term volatility of prices for manufactured goods and commodities was lower during the Golden Age – a time of exchange-rate stability, hegemonic

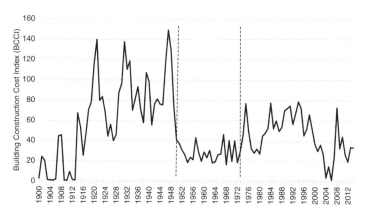

Figure 3.6 Varieties of economic crisis, 1900–2012
Source: Reinhart and Rogoff (2009).

leadership, abundant state capacity, and international social
cohesion – than at just about any time either before or
after.[46] The same trend was true of financial crises. Carmen
Reinhart and Kenneth Rogoff, two well-known Harvard economists, studied eight centuries of financial crises. Some of their
data are presented in Figure 3.6. The vertical axis represents
a composite index tracking the aggregate frequency of several
types of financial crisis in a sample of sixty-six countries. The
larger the figure on that axis, the greater the frequency of crises.
From 1914 to the late 1940s, the frequency of financial crises was
high and volatile, which is not surprising given the tumultuous
international situation we described in the previous chapter. It
declined during the Golden Age. From 1950 until the first oil
shock in 1973, things were rather calm. After that, however,
through to the late 1990s, the frequency of crises trended
upward again. In other words, the Golden Age corresponded

to a relatively stable, crisis-free economic environment, and it was followed by more turbulence in the next three decades, after the Nixon shock and as neoliberalism and the Washington Consensus spread globally. Those decades were particularly susceptible to banking crises.[47] When we add stock-market and other types of economic crisis to the mix, the spike in crises after the Golden Age is even sharper. According to the University of Pennsylvania's Mauro Guillén, an expert on international management, "the number of crises and the number of countries affected has been much larger since the mid-1980s than during any other period."[48]

The trends we have been describing also corresponded to perceptions of economic stress and uncertainty in the advanced capitalist world. Figure 3.7 tracks change in people's perceptions of financial stress in the United States, the world's economic powerhouse in the postwar era, based on a detailed

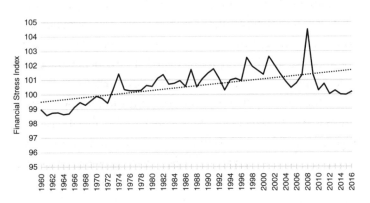

Figure 3.7 Perception of financial stress in the United States, 1960–2016
Source: Economic Policy Uncertainty (2019a).

analysis of economic reports in several prominent American newspapers. The graph begins in 1960, when financial stress started rising following a period of calm after the end of the Second World War, marked by the establishment of the Bretton Woods institutions and the dominance of Keynesianism. The dotted line indicates the general trend. Further inspection reveals that perceptions of financial stress jumped sharply during the stagflation period and continued rising thereafter. Figure 3.8, based on a similar index of international newspaper data, shows that, during the late twentieth and early twenty-first centuries, people in the advanced capitalist countries were becoming increasingly dubious about the prevailing economic policy of neoliberalism. Again, the dotted line represents the general trend.

In short, people's concerns were growing about their own economic situation and about the capacity of

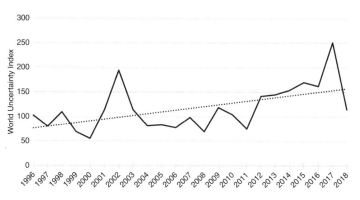

Figure 3.8 Newspaper perceptions of economic policy uncertainty in advanced capitalist countries, 1996–2018
Source: Economic Policy Uncertainty (2019b).

their elites to handle stressful economic times. In the next chapter, we will explain how this helped to undermine social cohesion by fueling a new form of nationalism. But, before that, we need to show how all the trends that we have described so far helped to spark economic crises in the 1980s and 1990s, and then something much larger: the financial catastrophe that began in 2008. They all provide particularly sharp pictures of how, if they tilt in the wrong direction, the sociological forces we have been discussing can undermine capitalism.

Crises of the Periphery

We begin with the Mexican debt crisis. For decades, Mexico's developmental state had been mired in a political system run by industrial oligarchs, corrupt politicians, and privileged labor unions. The state's intellectual capacities in economic policy, rooted in clientelism and cronyism, were quite thin. Moreover, while development improved the lives of urbanites, it marginalized the rural population, who experienced economic stagnation and poverty. As a result, in the late 1960s and 1970s, strikes and demonstrations broke out in the cities, and guerilla movements emerged in the countryside, sometimes put down by military force. Lack of state capacity helped to generate growing economic inequality and therefore a breakdown in social cohesion. The government responded by spending more in the 1970s on economic redistribution and education, and borrowing from foreign sources, including the burgeoning petrodollar market, to pay for it. Mexico's already significant debt continued to climb. For a while, economic growth accelerated, fueled partly by Mexico's new oil discoveries at a time of rising oil prices. But in 1981, when interest rates on Mexico's debt began rising and petroleum prices began falling, concern mounted about a possible devaluation of the peso and capital flight. In 1982, the Mexican government announced that it might default on its debt. Fearing a cascading international financial catastrophe, the U.S. government and IMF arrived with loans and a debt-restructuring deal.[49]

It was then that Mexico turned toward neoliberalism, because foreign aid came with strings attached, including mandates to reduce government spending and budget deficits, to implement fiscal and monetary austerity, to open up to free trade, and to privatize some of the government's largest and most important firms. The government privatized the banks, eliminated their reserve requirements, and deregulated interest rates. Capital controls were loosened for foreign investment – a move that would soon prove to have disastrous consequences. American hegemony was at work here. First, a young cadre of American-trained Mexican economists and technocrats, often from the University of Chicago, stepped into government positions, where they pushed a neoliberal agenda. Second, the IMF, World Bank, and other multilateral organizations, as well as the U.S. government, Wall Street, and international investors, pressed the Mexicans to reform. The Washington Consensus had arrived.[50] Friedrich List believed that free trade and unfettered markets were beneficial if a country was well developed; Mexico was a developing country, far from that status, so the consequences of these moves were terrible.

Following these reforms, Mexico continued to borrow throughout the 1980s, and foreign debt continued to mount, for two reasons. First, although lenders still did not have great confidence in Mexico's ability to manage its finances, they were willing to lend if Mexico would pay higher interest rates. Second, Mexico was to join the North American Free Trade Agreement (NAFTA) in January 1994, which bode well for its economic growth, government revenues, and fiscal stability. In the meantime, however, the peso's value was rising; by December 1994, it had reached a point at which the government felt compelled to devalue. This sparked a vicious cycle: interest rates rose adding to debt, which pushed up interest rates further, adding to debt – and so on. The value of the peso plunged, making it even harder for Mexico to service its debts. Investors headed for the exits, capital flight ensued, a deep recession set in, inflation soared, thousands of businesses went bankrupt, and hundreds of thousands of people lost their jobs. Wages in manufacturing by 1996 were only 64 percent of what they had been in 1980; household incomes dropped, and poverty rose.[51] Social unrest increased. The crisis metastasized to other Latin American countries. Argentina, whose banks had been involved in the Mexican situation, stopped lending and demanded repayment on outstanding loans. Again, the United States came to the rescue, this time with a $50 billion credit line to shore up Mexico's foreign-exchange reserves and assure investors that Mexico would not default on its debts. The World Bank provided $12 billion to Argentina for the same purpose. The crisis was resolved, barely averting an international economic meltdown.[52] But, as Sarah Babb, an astute observer of these events, warned years later, the danger was not over:

> Thanks to neoliberal reforms, today the Mexican economy
> is far more open to free trade and foreign investment than
> it was [in 1980] ... Therefore, although since 1982 the
> Mexican government has followed the prescriptions of
> international financial institutions to the letter, capital
> flight remains an ever-present concern, to which every
> policymaker – no matter how scrupulously neoliberal –
> must attend.[53]

In sum, the Mexican crisis involved several of our key variables. First, rising inequality generated growing social unrest – a breakdown of social cohesion – that then led to greater government spending and more foreign borrowing. Second, borrowing was facilitated by a series of ill-advised neoliberal reforms that weakened the state's capacities for managing the economy. Third, these reforms were driven in various ways by American hegemony and the Washington Consensus. Of course, were it not for the swift intervention of hegemonic power in 1982 and again in 1994, things would have turned out much worse. But American hegemony had been a mixed blessing.

The Mexican crisis paled in comparison to the 1997 East Asian financial crisis, which sent shockwaves around the world. As in Mexico, it can be traced back to a depletion of state capacity – the loosening of capital controls, lax financial supervision, weak regulation, and insufficient expertise in the regulatory institutions. This created the opportunity for "hot money" to move quickly into several Asian countries on the Pacific Rim to finance a variety of projects, many rather risky.[54] This money was "hot" because foreign investors, often betting on local currencies, could just as quickly pull their funds out at the first hint of trouble. This is what happened in Thailand in 1997 as rumors of currency devaluation spread. Investors scrambled to sell the local currency, and it collapsed, sending the economy reeling. Bankruptcies and unemployment soared, wages fell, inequality grew, and hyperinflation gripped the country. Riots and other forms of social unrest erupted, further unnerving foreign investors.[55] Soon, the crisis spread to Malaysia, the Philippines, Indonesia, and South Korea, threatening their banks, stock markets, and economies – and basic social cohesion too. Reverberations were felt as far away as Latin America and Russia, sparking riots and protests there.

In many of these cases, the IMF stepped in with loans to boost the country's foreign-exchange reserves and restore confidence in the financial system. But IMF loans were conditional, attaching demands for much higher interest rates, cuts in government spending, and increases in taxes to balance budgets. According to economist Joseph Stiglitz, "IMF policies not only exacerbated the downturns but were partially responsible for the onset: excessively rapid financial and capital market liberalization was probably the single most important cause of the crisis."[56] Government officials in some countries favored capital controls and other capacities to guard against hot money but did not pursue them, fearing that IMF criticism would scare off foreign investment.[57] This was another example of powerful forces preventing a thickening or building up of state capacity. Some governments were braver than others.[58] For instance, Malaysian banks had nonperforming loans, as did banks elsewhere, but the government had required them to keep enough capital reserves on hand to weather a storm such as this. The government had also prevented banks from borrowing dollars and then using them to finance lending in the local currency – a dangerous practice should the value of the local currency suddenly drop, making it much more difficult for the bank to repay its dollar-denominated debt. Furthermore, the government had limited the amount of foreign loans Malaysian companies could take in the first place, and it froze the repatriation of foreign investment capital for a year. Capital flight was minimized, and Malaysia avoided the worst of the crisis. In effect, the political elite shared List's insight that, until they are fully mature, developing countries should act differently from developed ones, protecting themselves from the vicissitudes of international markets. As a result, the Malaysian political elite had thicker state capacities than many other countries in the region and fared better during the crisis.[59]

Nevertheless, the crisis continued to spread as international credit markets seized up. Russia was one of the biggest to succumb. The state's capacity for financial regulation was extremely limited. The Russians had adopted shock therapy in the early 1990s and followed the Washington Consensus model, with much encouragement from the IMF and the United States. Capital controls were relaxed to encourage foreign investment to flow into the country. However, as the Asian crisis unfolded, investors became wary of putting their money into emerging economies anywhere. Making matters worse, as recessions and depressions developed in East Asia, the demand for oil dropped, and its price on world markets plummeted 40 percent in the first half of 1998. Oil was one of Russia's primary exports and a major source of tax revenue. Russian oil revenues dropped from 4.1 percent to 2.6 percent of GDP from 1996 to 1998, and foreign investment dried up.[60] As a result, it became apparent that the ruble was overvalued and that the government did not have enough foreign-exchange reserves to defend it. Fearing devaluation, the Russian oligarchs converted their rubles into dollars and moved them out of the country. Financial panic set in. Fearing that their banks would soon go bust, regular citizens lined up, demanding their deposits. The IMF worried that devaluation would trigger hyperinflation and crush the Russian economy, which was already suffering from high unemployment and other troubles. The IMF and World Bank teamed up to provide a $22.6 billion rescue package, which the Russians accepted – although the government devalued the ruble anyway and defaulted on its debt. The oligarchs ended up pocketing much of the bailout money, squirrelling it away in offshore accounts and foreign real estate.[61]

Interest rates in emerging markets skyrocketed, and their national economies fell into recession. The reverberations were felt in advanced countries too. Japanese exports of steel and automobiles plummeted – especially those to East Asian countries. Chinese and American exports also declined. According to the IMF, "The Russian default appears to have led to a reassessment of credit and sovereign risks across global financial markets," as measured by increased volatility in global bond markets in both emerging and advanced economies; the IMF argued that, unlike contagion effects seen before, these "seem to have been transmitted across countries with little in common – including countries that don't fit traditional explanations of contagion," such as Russia, Brazil, the Netherlands, and the United States.[62] Bluntly, the capitalist world was becoming increasingly unstable thanks to the globalization and fluidity of finance and trade, itself a product of scaled-back state capacities both nationally and internationally. Instability undermined social cohesion in the process.

Trouble at the Core, or a Crisis Averted

The sociological forces at the heart of our argument were on full display when the 2008 financial crisis engulfed much of the world. The roots of the financial crisis stretch back to the rise of neoliberalism, including reforms weakening the state institutions regulating the banking and financial services industries. In the United States, where the crisis originated, interstate banking laws were relaxed, adjustable-rate mortgages were allowed, and the Glass-Steagall Act, which had separated commercial and investment banking since the Depression, was undone, allowing banks more leeway to engage in all sorts of risky behavior. The local savings and loan banks depicted in Frank Capra's classic Christmas movie *It's a Wonderful Life* were shoved aside by ever-expanding financial service companies such as Citibank and enormous mortgage firms such as Countrywide. To top it off, the Clinton administration passed legislation prohibiting the federal government from regulating markets for mortgage-backed securities (MBSs), particularly those stuffed with risky subprime mortgages, and other complex financial investments that billionaire investor

Warren Buffett warned were financial weapons of mass destruction.[63]

All of this contributed to the booming American housing market of the early 2000s; so did the availability of vast sums of money from China and the oil producers that went to the United States and other advanced countries. In fact, an international capital imbalance had been growing for years. Something similar had been going on in Europe: Germany's huge surplus provided funds that could easily be lent to its neighbors, to Ireland, and especially to the poorer European countries to the south. But when interest rates started rising in late 2006, subprime mortgage defaults piled up, and the housing market began to collapse.[64] Many large Wall Street banks holding risky MBSs faced ruin. Credit markets seized up, stock markets around the world plunged, and national economies headed toward depression as growth stalled and unemployment lurched. The world economy staggered.[65] Echoing what the IMF had said about the Asian financial crisis, Columbia University historian Adam Tooze explained that:

> What made the collapse of 2008 so severe was its extraordinary global synchronization. Of the 104 countries for which the World Trade Organization collects data, every single one experienced a fall in both imports and exports between the second half of 2008 and the first half of 2009. Every country and every type of traded goods, without exception, experienced a decline.[66]

In the United States, millions lost their homes, trillions of dollars of personal wealth evaporated, and many people's life savings shriveled almost overnight. Fed chair Ben Bernanke feared that if dramatic action were not taken immediately, capitalism's financial system would collapse.[67]

Some lifelong proponents of neoliberalism finally realized that the problem had been caused by financial deregulation. Shortly after the crisis, former Fed chair Alan Greenspan, a fan of Ayn Rand's libertarianism, admitted in congressional testimony that his free-market beliefs had been wrong – that it was a "flawed" ideology.[68] Similarly, Hank Paulson, former Goldman Sachs CEO and U.S. Treasury Secretary during the crisis, acknowledged publicly that the absence of regulation of markets for MBSs and other new financial products had been a serious error, saying that now "Regulation needs to catch up with innovation."[69] Their confessions were as clear an acknowledgement of the dangers of thin state capacity as you could imagine. They were also proof that Schumpeter's creative destruction was good for capitalism only if states had the capacities to regulate it.

Thankfully, economic advisors to the Bush and Obama administrations urged massive Keynesian stimulus packages – a dramatic about-face from neoliberalism. The Bush administration pumped billions of dollars into the banking system. The Fed slashed interest rates close to zero and began pursuing quantitative easing – buying up all sorts of assets, including toxic MBSs, to pump even more money into the economy so as to remove these destructive instruments from the markets. The Fed eventually purchased nearly $4 trillion worth of toxic and other assets through its quantitative easing program, aiming to stabilize financial and credit markets, exercising the United States' hegemonic capacity to "print" money to help it to do so. The Fed also served as the lender of last resort not only to the United States but also to many other countries, just barely pulling the international financial system back from the brink of disaster. It provided a total of over $10 trillion to central banks throughout the advanced capitalist world. The largest recipient was the European Central Bank (ECB). Once Obama took over, Congress pumped over $1 trillion more into the economy to save it from collapse and spent additional billions to rescue the real-estate market. At the same time, Obama initiated a major reform of the American health insurance industry that extended coverage to millions of previously uninsured citizens and pumped even more money into the economy. Finally, his administration overhauled the regulations governing the financial services industry to ensure that a similar crisis would not happen again. All of this helped to save capitalism from total disaster.[70] Nevertheless, according to Cornell University's Jonathan Kirschner, the fact that the United States was culpable in triggering the crisis eroded American economic power and influence relative to other countries – raising serious questions about the best way of managing domestic and international money and finance. In other words, the crisis raised serious questions about American hegemony and the dangers of thin state capacities.[71]

The financial crisis hit European countries very hard. Europe had its own capital imbalance problems, as we noted earlier, and these exacerbated the effect. Either directly or indirectly, European banks also began to suffer from the softening American housing and mortgage markets. Tremors were felt first in 2007, when HSBC, the British multinational banking and financial services holding company, announced major losses on its mortgage investments. Swiss megabank UBS closed its hedge fund Dillon Read Capital Management. Two German banks announced major losses. BNP Paribas, France's premier bank, announced it was having liquidity problems and would close three of its investment funds. Northern Rock, one of the United Kingdom's largest and most heavily leveraged mortgage lenders, failed in September 2007. When the financial markets crashed a year later, big lenders in several European countries were in dire straits. New lending plummeted, real-estate prices collapsed, economic growth stalled, and unemployment rose.

As in the United States, the political elites who had adopted neoliberal policies were criticized. Governor of the Bank of England Sir Mervyn King told the BBC that, "With the benefit of hindsight we should have shouted from the rooftops that a system had been built in which banks were too important to fail, that banks had grown too quickly and borrowed too much, and that so-called 'light touch' regulation hadn't prevented any of this."[72] This was a confession much like those of Greenspan and Paulson. Years later, in response to the Trump administration's suggestion that it would unwind many of the new financial regulations passed in the wake of the crisis by the Obama administration, ECB President Mario Draghi told the European Parliament's Committee on Economic Affairs that "The last thing we need at this point in time is the relaxation of regulation. The idea of repeating the conditions that were in place before the crisis is something that is very worrisome."[73] Other European leaders agreed: there was no sense in weakening state capacities all over again.[74]

At least for a short time after the crisis hit, Keynesianism was suddenly back in style as countries doubled down on their states' abilities to rescue their financial systems. We have already explained how the Fed, extending American hegemony, played the leading role – and how the U.S. government moved dramatically to stabilize its own economy. Other central banks and governments followed suit. The integrated Atlantic financial economy committed over $7 trillion in loans to bank recapitalization, asset purchases, and state guarantees of bank deposits, bank debts, and, on occasion, entire bank balance sheets.[75]

The state capacities involved in administering these measures varied considerably and with significant effects. For instance, in Ireland, there was precious little expertise in these matters in either the central bank or regulatory agencies. As a result, policymakers decided to provide a blanket state guarantee to all Irish banks, with little sense of how much this might cost and without consulting the experts elsewhere in Europe, the United States, or even just down the street at Trinity College Dublin. This was a textbook example of a state's thin intellectual capacity. It nearly bankrupted the government and eventually required a massive ECB capital infusion to shore up the state's finances. In contrast, the Swiss central bank had plenty of expertise on hand, and it moved deftly to save UBS and the Swiss financial system from imploding. Later, experts gathered again to devise regulatory reforms designed to prevent another crisis and to deal with it should it nonetheless occur. In Denmark, policymakers heeded the advice of experts from the banks, regulatory agencies, and the Danish central bank, and they accordingly guaranteed bank assets. But, unlike the Irish, the Danes did so on the condition that all money from a private insurance fund financed by the banks themselves be exhausted first; only then would the state step in with additional funds. This was the first of six Danish "bank packages" that relied on expert advice and which constituted a series of wise mid-course corrections in Denmark's crisis management decision making.[76]

Recall Albert Hirschman's call for political voice, necessary for capitalism to function well. The relationship between voice and state capacity in these three small countries is revealing. In Ireland, there was very little input from financial experts or from citizen representatives such as labor unions, business associations, or political parties. In Switzerland, experts ran the show, with politicians sidelined until formal approval was required for the rescue plan. However, the Swiss had a long-standing system in place whereby politicians had agreed that, in the event of a potentially catastrophic national crisis like this, national experts – in this case, those at the central bank and financial regulatory agencies – should be in charge, with minimal political interference. This agreement was not only an artifact of voices being heard previously in planning for crisis management and developing more state capacities for doing so but also a demonstration of Swiss social cohesion. Similarly, politicians relinquished crisis management authority to the experts in Denmark, and virtually all of the political parties agreed to approve the six bank packages. The point is that where state capacities were thick, where citizens' representatives had voice in the process, and where social cohesion was high, things turned out well. The alternative route had proved to be disastrous.

Conclusion

Polanyi and Schumpeter argued that capitalism was prone to instability and disruption, not equilibrium. However, the sources of instability that we have identified for the last third of the twentieth century are entirely novel. These economists did not anticipate capital flight, exchange-rate and price volatility, or the banking crises that we have been discussing. Nonetheless, Polanyi's concern with the state not engaging the economy enough to rectify the deleterious effects of capitalism and Schumpeter's interest in the instabilities associated with technological change – creative destruction – are still relevant. After all, it was new technology such as improvements in telecommunications and transportation – as well as states' moves toward neoliberalism – that created the possibility of these problems in the first place. Crises both in the periphery and at the core regions of capitalism made this very clear. They also underscored the importance of state capacities, social cohesion, and American hegemony for capitalism.

The United States saved capitalism from the financial crisis in an impressive act of benign hegemony. It had little choice if it wanted to avoid another worldwide depression. Whether it would have either the means or the will to do so again remained to be seen – for, in the ensuing years, the state capacities of the hegemon continued to diminish as it shifted toward an even more predatory form of hegemony. But, before we get to that, we need to address the way in which the attack on labor and others on the lower rungs of the economic ladder led to a deterioration of social cohesion that changed politics and capitalism – and not in a pretty way.

4

Nationalism and Social Cohesion

Let us recall three events that challenged the political status quo in the early part of this century. The first took place in 2000, when Danes were asked in a national referendum whether they wished to join the European Monetary Union, abandoning Denmark's national currency, the krone, for the euro. Every element of the political elite – both left and right – as well as most intellectuals and the media were in favor of a "yes" vote. But the vote failed, beaten by a vote of "no" most common among less-educated Danish men living outside metropolitan Copenhagen. This was a harbinger of things to come. The second event saw protestors commandeer Zuccotti Park in lower Manhattan's financial district on a crisp fall day in 2011, setting up a makeshift tent city to protest economic inequality in the United States. The Occupy Wall Street movement had begun. Its signature slogan – "We are the 99 percent" – referred to the fact that much of America's income and wealth was held by the richest 1 percent of the population. Economic inequality had been growing since the 1970s, but the issue peaked in the wake of the 2008 financial crisis that had caused millions of people to lose their jobs and homes, while the big Wall Street banks received multibillion-dollar bailouts from Washington, D.C., and their top executives gained fat bonuses. The third event happened in 2015, when German Chancellor Angela Merkel opened the borders to hundreds of thousands of refugees from the Middle East. Protests erupted, with those opposed to her policy charging that this threatened their national culture, state resources, property values, and the labor market opportunities of German citizens. Two years later, the right-wing, anti-immigrant, nationalist party, Alternative for Germany (AfD), won 13 percent of the vote in a federal election, its strongest showing yet. These events illustrate how social cohesion in advanced capitalism was diminishing.

We have argued that capitalism needs both social cohesion and thick state capacities to prosper, and that the two are intertwined domestically and internationally. This will become especially clear in this and the next chapter, in which we show that the recent deterioration of the two spells trouble for capitalism. Previous chapters treated these things together; now, we separate them out. Our concern in this chapter is with the deterioration of social cohesion, driven by rising economic inequality and hardship that can be traced back to the structural changes and policy decisions we have already discussed. We start by showing how inequality has increased, how it has undermined social cohesion, and how both have hurt capitalism. But we are also interested in explaining how rising inequality and deteriorating social cohesion have transformed politics, blending economic grievances with nationalist animosity to create a new form of nationalist politics – the social dynamite we discussed earlier – whose effects on capitalism are often more indirect and longer in the making than those associated with rising inequality alone. Political elites often forged the links between economic grievance and nationalism by peddling misinformation and false claims through biased media outlets, aiming to garner support from voters and others for their economic agendas. The next chapter will show how these new nationalist politics have hurt capitalism by undermining state capacities for economic management. We have already discussed how capitalism's performance – reflected, for example, in declining rates of economic growth – has worsened since the mid-1970s. We worry that the trends we discuss in these two chapters will make things worse.

As the three examples we opened with suggest, the deterioration of social cohesion has two sides, one looking up at and one looking down upon those people who, rightly or wrongly, are often held responsible for people's economic troubles. On one side was growing anger among the working and middle classes toward the elites. This was nationalism insofar as the anger targeted those who benefited from globalization and the economic rewards it afforded them by virtue of their cosmopolitan profile – especially their high levels of education, linguistic skills, and international experience. It also involved hostility toward the elites who pushed globalization in the first place. This resentment of elites by the rest of society was a feeling that the cosmopolitans had left the rest behind, caged in their nation-states. On the other side was the scapegoating of immigrants whom the caged also blamed for their economic difficulties. This was nationalism too – this time, a desire to exclude others from coming into the country and, in the extreme, to purify the country's population either by throwing out those considered "Other" or by forcing them to assimilate. In several cases, political parties responded to these attitudes by swinging toward the right in an effort to offer disgruntled voters a home and the voice they felt they were being denied.

A few clarifications are necessary. First, there are both right-wing and left-wing variations of these nationalist themes, as illustrated by the AfD and Danish People's Party, respectively. Second, all too often those feeling either caged or resentful of others are blamed for disrupting society and the economy even though they are reacting to limits placed on their lives by globalization, neoliberalism, and the assault on labor described in the previous chapter. We can therefore have some sympathy for them even as we should be repulsed by some of the politics that have resulted from their pain. Third, regardless of whether nationalist ire targets the cosmopolitan elite or others, it is particularly dangerous because it is blended with economic grievance. This is not the type of economic nationalism that List welcomed but the political nationalism that Polanyi feared. This is Gellner's social dynamite, and it is becoming more common. Resentment within countries toward global elites and immigrants has been on the rise in many places, fueling a new nationalist backlash that has poisoned domestic politics. And this sort of resentment has also spilled over into international relations, jeopardizing social cohesion at that level too.

Much of what we are about to describe occurred against a shifting geopolitical landscape. The Cold War and recollections of two world wars provided social cohesion for the advanced capitalist world after 1945. This ensured a basic measure of civility, a refusal to let things get out of control based on living memory of disaster, and a sharp awareness that all liberal capitalist countries needed to stick together to face a hostile world. But, by the dawn of the twenty-first century, these memories – and the lessons learned – had faded, making it all too possible that mistakes would be repeated or new ones made.[1] The Cold War was over. But without the external threat of communism, the risks of political polarization increased.[2] In the United States, for example, Republican senators wrote to Iran's supreme leader in 2015, saying that any deal President Obama made with Iranian negotiators about restricting that country's nuclear enrichment capabilities would be revoked as soon as Obama left office. Such a deep political split over foreign policy would have been unthinkable during the Cold War. European politics became more polarized too.[3] For instance, France, Germany, and the Netherlands banned arms sales to Turkey in 2019 – one of their own allies in the North Atlantic Treaty Organization (NATO) – after Turkey attacked the Kurds in northern Syria, a move that strengthened Russia's hand in the Middle East. This too would never have happened during the Cold War.

Inequality and Its Discontents

Major reductions in economic inequality have been rare, as noted, and are typically driven by extreme events. In the twentieth century, it was mass mobilization warfare that led to the Great Compression in the advanced world – that is, a dramatic reduction in economic inequality. The costs of war are enormous. Soldiers are more likely to fight when promises are made that they will be rewarded, living after the war in what British Prime Minister Lloyd George called "a land fit for heroes." Fulfilling such promises with jobs, pensions, education, and housing is one way of reducing inequality; the more important factor historically in equalizing the distribution of income and wealth is the annihilation of the assets of the rich, through hyperinflation, taxation, and the sheer destruction of their property through war. Peaceful social reforms such as those hinted at by Lloyd George have done less to reduce it.[4]

Not surprisingly, then, the recent decades of peace have coincided with an increase in economic inequality in many advanced capitalist countries. Today, the eight richest Americans, including Elon Musk, Jeff Bezos, Bill Gates, Warren Buffett, and Mark Zuckerberg, own as much wealth as half of all the nation's households combined, while the sixty-two richest people in the world own as much as one half of the world's population – that is, as much as 3.5 billion human beings.[5] Jeff Bezos, Amazon's CEO, saw his wealth increase by about $48 billion in the first six months of the COVID-19 pandemic. Former Microsoft CEO Steve Ballmer's net worth grew by $15.7 billion. They were not alone among billionaires in seeing their wealth increase at a time when the pandemic's economic repercussions saw inequality grow in many advanced countries.[6] French economist Thomas Piketty has shown how important the rise of the super-rich has been to growing inequality.[7] He argues that this is because the returns on capital far outpace money earned from regular employment by the rest of society. This is true. But historian Walter Scheidel has made clear that the rich always know how to protect themselves and are capable in just about every historical circumstance of increasing their slice of the economic pie.

High returns on capital do not come out of some inevitable natural logic; they are often the result of particular taxation regimes, created by the advantaged for the few, not to mention ingenious means of exploiting workers.[8] Indeed, today's super-rich hire professional wealth managers, tax lawyers, and clever accountants to grow and protect their vast fortunes in all sorts of ways.[9]

A common indicator of income inequality is the Gini coefficient, a statistical measure of dispersion. It ranges from 0 to 1. A coefficient of 0 means that the national income is distributed perfectly evenly throughout society – that is, everyone gets an equal share. A coefficient of 1 indicates perfect inequality – one person gets it all, and everybody else gets nothing. Before taking into consideration taxes and government transfers, the average Gini coefficient for twenty-six advanced capitalist countries rose from 0.36 to 0.42 between 1980 and 2010. It also increased after taxes and transfers, but by a smaller amount, which means that, on average, government taxation and spending tended to redistribute income in ways that reduced inequality and slowed, but did not stop, its rise. In fact, there are lots of ways of measuring income inequality, but all of them tell pretty much the same story.[10] The average share of national income going to the top 1 percent of the population in the same twenty-six countries – people such as those whom the Occupy Wall Street movement targeted – jumped from 6.7 percent to 10 percent between 1980 and 2010: almost a 50 percent increase, again indicating a sharp rise in economic inequality.[11]

We need to be a little careful here. First, the level of inequality varies across the advanced capitalist world – even in terms of post-tax, post-transfer disposable income. Figure 4.1 shows that the Scandinavian countries with high taxes and

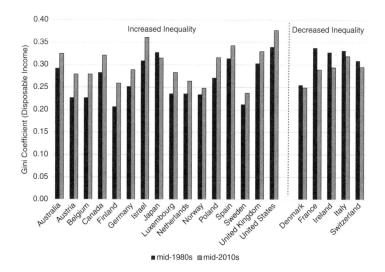

Figure 4.1 Rising and falling income inequality in twenty-one advanced countries

Note: With few exceptions, data are from the mid-1980s and mid 2010s: Australia 1985, 2014; Austria 1987, 2013; Belgium 1985, 2000; Canada 1987, 2013; Denmark 1987, 2013; Finland 1987, 2013; France 1984, 2010; Germany 1987, 2013; Ireland 1987, 2010; Israel 1986, 2014; Italy 1987, 2014; Luxembourg 1985, 2013; Netherlands 1987, 2013; Norway 1986, 2013; Poland 1986, 2013; Spain 1985, 2013; Sweden 1987, 2005; Switzerland 1982, 2013; United Kingdom 1986, 2013; United States 1986, 2013.

Source: Luxembourg Income Study (2019).

large welfare states have much less inequality than countries with lower taxes and less welfare spending, such as the United States and the United Kingdom. Second, in many rich countries since 1980, there has been a significant rise in the household incomes of the bottom 10 percent of the population.[12] Nevertheless, the incomes of the richer deciles have grown faster. So, the key fact remains, as Figure 4.1 also shows, that economic inequality has been rising since the 1980s in most countries, and that it had, by the mid-2010s, reached its highest levels in at least three decades.[13]

There seems to be a vicious cycle here. Economist Branko Milanovic, a seminal figure in the study of international inequality, conducted an analysis of economic inequality in the United States between 1960 and 2000, and he found that growing income inequality tended to spur further income growth at the top of the income distribution but not at the bottom. Put differently, income inequality today seems to produce greater income inequality tomorrow. Like Scheidel, he assumes this is because the rich have political power with which to win policies that benefit their economic interests, such as reduced tax rates.[14] This is especially troubling because of the effects that inequality has on society. One is that it can hurt economic growth; another is that it can undermine social cohesion, which affects both growth and politics. We take each in turn, beginning with inequality's direct effect on economic growth.

Not everyone thinks that inequality is a problem for capitalism. Neoliberals and many other conservatives believe that inequality is beneficial because the wealthy are the principal source of investment. The larger their income share, the more they will invest, and the more economic growth there will be in capitalism. Everyone benefits as the economic pie expands. This was Milton Friedman's justification for why corporations should not siphon off profits toward charitable or other socially responsible purposes.[15] In contrast, the great economists on whom *we* rely – above all, Smith, Keynes, and

Polanyi – stress the opposite, noting the dangers of inequality. Testing these competing propositions is tricky, and there is much debate about it.[16] But we can offer some tentative conclusions.

Sociologist Lane Kenworthy has conducted one of the most rigorous statistical analyses of the economic effects of income inequality in the advanced capitalist countries. He finds that, from 1979 through 2007, "It hasn't reduced economic growth. It hasn't hindered employment. It isn't systematically linked to the occurrence of economic crises. It hasn't reduced income growth for poor households."[17] This view flies in the face of some very prominent economists. Joseph Stiglitz has argued that income inequality hurts economic growth, because it will diminish demand in society, as Keynes had warned.[18] Other economists have found that it is inequality growth in the bottom half – rather than the top half – of the income distribution that inhibits economic growth.[19] This is also consistent with Keynes's argument about underconsumption stifling aggregate demand and growth. Following a similar logic, others have shown that, even when growth does occur, it does not last as long when there are high levels of inequality as it does when there are low levels of inequality – that is, that inequality tends to shorten spells of growth.[20] Although Kenworthy finds only limited evidence for the Keynesian argument, he concedes that the logic makes sense and that inequality probably has not grown extreme enough yet for this effect to show up statistically in his data.[21] Inequality has not yet reached the critical tipping point that Keynes believed it had during the interwar period and Great Depression – but it is moving in that direction.

For the sake of argument, even if inequality does not directly affect economic growth in these ways, it still undoubtedly plays at least an indirect role. Stiglitz, among others, identifies several mechanisms.[22] To begin with, high levels of inequality tend to undermine public investment in infrastructure, education, and basic research, because "the more divided a society becomes in terms of wealth, the more reluctant the wealthy are to spend money on common needs."[23] The association between inequality and educational attainment is particularly important, because contemporary economies need increasingly well-educated workers. Recall that Smith attributed the wealth of nations to a well-trained labor force, which is why he advocated public funding for education. So it is worrying that countries with greater income inequality tend to have worse educational outcomes in terms of test scores and dropout rates.[24] More inequality also means that medical services are unequally distributed, which can undermine the general health of society, as the COVID-19 pandemic has shown in the United States, where poorer communities have been hit the hardest by the virus.[25] Of course, sicker populations are less productive populations, and this also hurts the economy.[26] Finally, societies with greater inequality tend to have lower levels of taxation, which undermines not only the ability of government to provide some of the public goods we already mentioned but also sufficient regulation of the economy to guard against serious market failures, such as those that led to the 2008 financial crisis.[27]

More importantly in terms of our core argument, inequality can ruin social cohesion, with knock-on effects for capitalism. A 2013 Pew Research Center survey of thirty-nine countries found that most people agreed that the economic system favored the wealthy, and that the gap between rich and poor had increased after the 2008 financial crisis. These attitudes were particularly prevalent within the advanced capitalist countries. Moreover, 53 percent of people surveyed in the advanced countries, and even more in the emerging and developing countries, said that the gap "is a very big problem."[28] Perceptions like these can lead to protests and other forms of political instability – a deterioration of social cohesion. The Occupy Wall Street movement was one example. The widespread and sometimes violent protests that occurred throughout Chile in late 2019 and 2020 was a more dramatic illustration in which the president needed to declare a state of emergency and dispatch the army to quell the unrest. Even China's authoritarian political leaders worry about the political instability that inequality can cause. Political instability can have serious economic consequences too. The International Monetary Fund (IMF) found that rising inequality can spark political and economic instability that hurts economic growth insofar as it scares off investment necessary for growth and undermines the ability of countries to cope effectively with economic shocks. Other researchers agree.[29] Indeed, this is exactly what happened in the Mexican and East Asian crises, as we saw in the last chapter.

Kenworthy warns that inequality can undermine social cohesion for another reason too. He finds that, in the United States, income inequality has reduced residential mixing. This is important. Less residential mixing among different classes means that communities live in segregated silos with relatively little interaction across classes. People living in gated communities rarely meet those who live in impoverished ghettos. Social scientists have demonstrated that the less contact different groups have with each other, the more likely they are to be prejudiced against and distrustful of each other.[30] It is too early, Kenworthy notes, to tell from his data whether income inequality affects interpersonal trust, but he acknowledges that reduced or sluggish income growth has contributed to the rise of new nationalist movements and parties in the advanced capitalist countries during the twenty-first century – precisely the sort of political instability and deterioration of social cohesion the IMF worried about.[31] Other research finds that low levels of trust are associated with poorer national economic performance. Political scientist Peter Katzenstein, for example, showed that smaller European countries tended to outperform larger ones during the 1970s and 1980s in part because they enjoyed more social solidarity, which made economic policymaking more consensus-oriented, flexible, and effective.[32]

Inequality undermines social cohesion and economic performance in yet another way. Several studies of advanced and developing countries find that those with greater income inequality have less intergenerational income mobility. In other words, the odds that your child's future income will be significantly greater than your own are worse if you live in a country with more inequality than they are if you live in a country with less inequality. Relatively inegalitarian countries such as the United States, Argentina, Brazil, and Chile have less upward mobility than the more egalitarian Scandinavian countries, Germany, and Canada.[33] Unfortunately, it is not clear how mobility may have changed in these countries, because historical cross-national data are not readily available for most of them. However, data on educational mobility are at hand, and educational mobility is highly correlated with income mobility: as one increases, so does the other. The World Bank reports that educational mobility, which had been rising at various rates in much of the world after the Second World War, tended to stall in the developing countries among cohorts born in the 1970s and 1980s, and it declined for these cohorts in the advanced countries.[34] It follows, then, that something similar has probably happened with income mobility: it has likely slowed, stalled, or declined in many countries after the 1970s – particularly in the advanced ones. The World Bank stresses that stifled or declining mobility can have deleterious consequences for capitalism. One is dashed hopes for the future and thus greater political instability, which, as we have already seen, can undermine investment and economic growth.[35] Another, we would add, is the erosion of people's work ethic and therefore economic productivity.

The connections between rising inequality, economic performance, and social cohesion were clear in the 2008 financial crisis. Since the late 1970s, rising inequality in the United States coincided with a prolonged period of wage stagnation and declining purchasing power for many Americans.[36] To compensate, they began to borrow, especially for housing, which in the early 2000s increasingly took the form of risky adjustable-rate subprime mortgages.[37] This pumped up real-estate prices, creating an enormous housing bubble. But when interest rates began to rise, people could not keep up with their subprime mortgage payments, and the bubble collapsed in

2007 and 2008. Some of the biggest mortgage companies and banks in the country were caught holding lots of subprime mortgages and went bust. AIG, one of the largest insurance companies in the world, had insured them against such an event, and it too almost went bankrupt. As a result, credit markets froze, and the country was suddenly plunged into the worst financial crisis since the Great Depression. In short, as a congressional committee concluded, inequality was a root cause of the financial crisis, which spread rapidly to other countries.[38]

The results were twofold. First was a deterioration of social cohesion. The Occupy Movement was one example. Mass protests also erupted across Europe, including in France, Greece, Italy, Ireland, and Latvia, often in response to how national governments pursued neoliberal austerity to cope with the unemployment and sluggish growth that accompanied the crisis. Tens of thousands of demonstrators congregated in Brussels around European Parliament buildings. Labor unions in many countries took to the streets as unemployment skyrocketed: an estimated 28 million Europeans lost their jobs as a consequence of the financial crisis. Spain suffered a general strike, often marked by violent clashes between police and protestors. In Dublin, a man rammed a cement truck covered with antibank slogans through the gates of the Irish parliament.[39] Second, economic hardship continued for a decade. As of May 2019, unemployment was still over 6 percent in the European Union and 7.5 percent in the eurozone. It was considerably higher in some countries, as was the potential for further political turmoil.[40]

A quick review is in order. We have argued so far that capitalism can suffer from too much inequality and not enough social cohesion. The two are intertwined, with excessive inequality likely to reduce economic growth as well as social cohesion, which itself can hurt growth. Government investment in infrastructure, education, health, and public goods necessary to sustain economic growth can suffer. This stands in obvious contrast to the emphasis on human capital as the source of progress that lies at the heart of the work of Adam Smith. Mention of the Enlightenment political economist suggests something more. If it becomes generally known that the odds are completely stacked against those at the bottom of society, they will come to feel that they have no foot on the societal escalator – no chance to catch up with those above them. Such a development would remove the key source of cohesion within capitalist society.

One caveat is necessary. We are talking about tendencies, not inevitabilities. Rising inequality does not automatically undermine social cohesion and cripple capitalism. First, when the less fortunate have political voice, dissent may be limited, as Hirschman realized, allowing for social cohesion to be maintained. In this regard, it is worth noting that the Occupy Movement began in the United States, where inequality was high relative to other advanced countries, and where there was no social democratic or labor party to give voice to the grievances of the working and middle classes. It did not start in Scandinavia, where there were less inequality and strong social democratic parties. Second, the belief that one can progress on the societal escalator has not completely disappeared, especially in the United States. Francesco Duina found that one of the reasons the poorest people in the United States felt a very strong sense of devotion to their country was that, despite their own economic misfortunes, they still believed it to be the land of opportunity, and they clung to the idea that hard work and a little luck could take you far.[41] Finally, even with high levels of inequality, there may still be enough consumption to preserve social cohesion and keep the economy going, at least if the country is rich enough. People with a smaller share of a richer pie in a rich country may still have enough to remain relatively content and to spend enough to keep capitalism on an even keel. A poor kid in the Bronx or the suburbs of Paris might be able to scrounge up enough money for a fancy pair of basketball shoes even if this is not possible in South Sudan or Somalia. The proceeds of growth may not be distributed evenly, but the result may be anxious discontent rather than full-blown disaster.[42]

But tendencies may yet go in the opposite direction. Even where most groups have enjoyed political voice for decades, there are no guarantees that this will continue. We have seen that, since the 1970s, institutionalized channels for middle- and working-class voice have gradually been reduced in Scandinavia: Unionization rates have declined, corporatism has grown weaker, and even labor and social democratic parties have shifted in more conservative directions. In the United Kingdom, Tony Blair's Labour Party embraced a more conservative "third way" ideology, and the Danish Social Democratic Party moved in a more conservative direction as well. In fact, neoliberalism gained traction in varying degree among center-left as well as center-right political parties in many member countries of the Organisation for Economic

Co-operation and Development (OECD).[43] Perhaps it is no surprise, then, that in 2020 demonstrations sympathetic to the Black Lives Matter movement in the United States emerged in dozens of countries around the world. These were the voices of those who had been ignored by politicians for too long.

Nationalist Anxieties

Deteriorating social cohesion stemmed not only from economic grievances but also from nationalist concerns. Polanyi had insisted that "society" seeks to protect itself from the ravages of capitalism and that the move toward protection is driven by class politics, the poor against the rich. But, under recent conditions, "society" has involved more than just class conflict; it has also involved nationalist conflict. Class-based tensions and conflicts matter, but the mixture of class and nationalist grievances identified by Gellner is far more powerful.[44] Economic historian Barry Eichengreen explains that "The populist [nationalist] temptation is greatest when economic forces fuse with identity politics and when the two are inadequately addressed by mainstream parties," adding that the danger is exacerbated when citizens lack the sort of political voice to which Hirschman referred, thereby coming to believe that political elites are ignoring their concerns about inequality and tough economic times.[45]

This was evident in the United States when, in the midst of the coronavirus pandemic and unemployment crisis that hit Black communities hardest, Black voices were raised in protest, organizing under the Black Lives Matter banner, sparked by the murder of George Floyd, a Black man, by

Minneapolis police. In several places, counterdemonstrations occurred, often violent, led by white nationalist groups that were as anti-Black as they were anti-immigrant. Both groups were motivated in part by the belief that their voices and grievances had not been heard through normal political channels. In many places, police responded with tear gas and rubber bullets, underscoring the extremes to which political polarization had grown.

Nationalism sometimes comes from the top, as in elite desire to develop the power of the state along the lines prescribed by List, and sometimes from below, when a secessionist movement seeks escape from an empire. The nationalism that concerns us now also comes from below, but its character is entirely novel: it is all about seeking to maintain and confirm membership inside the state. As noted earlier, there are two sides to this story. On the one hand, members of the nation-state may want to rein in or cage the cosmopolitans – resenting the ambitions and restricting the behaviors of global elites who feel fewer and fewer commitments to the nation of which they are part. Great resentment is felt, for example, toward cosmopolitans who avoid paying taxes by using offshore tax havens or who can relocate to low-tax countries, as wealthy French actor Gérard Depardieu did when he was granted citizenship in Russia, a country whose flat 13 percent income tax rate is far below what he would have paid in France. On the other hand, there is a growing insistence among the caged that the nation-state, with all its rights, privileges, and benefits, must be reserved for the "native" population – those who are imagined to share some common ethnic, religious, and linguistic features – by controlling entry

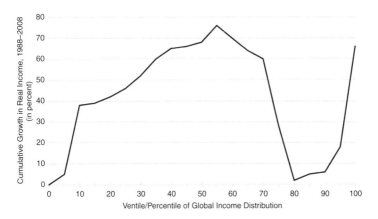

Figure 4.2 The Lakner–Milanovic "elephant curve"
Source: Adapted from Lakner and Milanovic (2013).

to it and, at times, forcing expulsion from it. This side of the
story is about immigration. Both sides of the story are linked
to the issue of inequality, so first we need to say a few things
more about that.

We have focused to this point on inequality and opportunity *within* advanced capitalist countries. But our argument
can benefit from considering inequality *across* a broader range
of countries. Here, things are different, insofar as the last few
decades have witnessed a dramatic decline in inequality across
a wide range of capitalist countries. Consider the famous graph
summarizing many of the findings of Christoph Lakner and
Branko Milanovic. Their so-called elephant curve (Figure 4.2)
illustrates the cumulative gains in real household per capita
income between 1988 and 2008 – the period of intense economic globalization – across various points of the global
income distribution. It shows that the income gains increased

gradually through the bottom half of the global income distribution, but then suddenly and dramatically dropped, bottoming out at the 80th percentile and remaining low, until suddenly shooting up at the very top of the global income distribution. Income growth from about the 40th to 60th population deciles – the top of the elephant's back – went predominantly to people in the emerging Asian economies – notably, in China, but increasingly also in India, Thailand, Vietnam, and Indonesia. In contrast to this high-growth area, the shockingly low-growth group in the 80th to 90th decile range – the bottom of the elephant's head – was made up mostly of people in Western Europe, North America, and Japan. Finally, those in the top 2 or 3 percent of the global income distribution – the end of the elephant's trunk – enjoyed almost as much income growth as the emergent Asian group. In other words, the graph shows that a new global middle class was emerging in Asia; the old global middle class of the advanced capitalist countries was suffering income stagnation – that is, in effect, suffering increasing inequality in global perspective – and a super-rich global elite, mostly in the rich economies, but also a few in places such as China, Brazil, South Africa, and Russia, were getting phenomenally wealthier.[46]

Opening up to free trade, one part of the neoliberal package, has lifted millions of people out of poverty in India, China, and some other emerging economies. But what is important about Lakner and Milanovic's finding here is the stagnant position of the "middle classes" in the advanced countries. Suffering can be either absolute, such as when you lose your job, or relative, like the feeling that your children may no longer have decent life chances in the future.

What matters in both cases is the sense that globalization has diminished the hopes and dreams of the middle classes in the advanced capitalist world. Some believe that others have cut in front of them on the societal escalator; others are coming to believe that they no longer have a place on it at all.

Harvard University economist Dani Rodrik has proposed another way of thinking about what is at stake in terms of a trilemma. He notes that there are three essential institutional goods in today's global political economy: democratic politics, national sovereignty, and global economic integration. He argues that a country can possess only two of these at any one moment. Most importantly for us, countries must forsake their sovereignty if democratically elected political elites in a globally integrated world want to remain in power. This is because the assertion of sovereignty by imposing regulatory restrictions on transnational capital will likely undermine the global trade and investment required to fuel economic growth and prosperity in a country – something political elites need to sustain to win reelection in a democracy. So, in a global economy (Smith's international trade), people must give up either some democracy (Hirschman's voice) or some element of national sovereignty (Gellner's nationalism).[47] However, nationalism today is all about curtailing globalization so that the benefits of national sovereignty and democracy are preserved. As a result, in advanced capitalist countries today, objections to globalization are being expressed in nationalist form – a revolt that threatens capitalist prosperity to the extent that prosperity depends increasingly on international trade and other forms of global economic integration.

This brings us to the global elites. One target of nationalist revolt is the cosmopolitan actors who can navigate successfully beyond their nation-states in the larger world. Wealth certainly helps such navigation. But there is more, including high levels of education, proficiency in English, technical skill, and the ability to switch from one job to another, sometimes even in different countries. This new global elite is also determined to make sure that their children learn how to succeed in this larger world by attending the finest schools and universities possible. This elite is cohesive in other ways too: Marriage now occurs more frequently within the elite, with divorce being rare, and both partners now tend to have important jobs.[48] So, we have here the emergence of a class likely to remain on top at least partly for meritocratic reasons. These are the global elites – globalists, not nationalists. They have left their less-fortunate compatriots behind, trapped within the boundaries of nation-states. Those left behind – particularly the middle and working classes, who have suffered increased economic pressure and limited economic opportunities since the 1970s – are particularly resentful of this turn of events.

There are several indications of this new anti-elite/ antiglobal nationalism. For instance, there is anecdotal evidence of dislike for cosmopolitan members of the political elite who maneuver successfully in the larger world. In Denmark, the nickname given to Prime Minister Helle Thorning-Schmidt – trained in the European Academy, Commissioner to the European Union, and cosmopolitan to a degree – was "Gucci Helle." Similar sentiments were held in the United States against Hillary Clinton, massively reinforced when knowledge leaked out of the exorbitant fees that she received for speeches given to Wall Street's international bankers.

More systematic and direct evidence of resentment toward global elites is not available, but there are data pointing in that direction. To begin with, sentiment against political elites in general is widespread. In twenty-one of twenty-seven advanced and emerging capitalist economies surveyed in 2018 by the Pew Research Center, less than half of the respondents believed that their political elites care what ordinary people think. Respondents viewed these elites with disdain. Moreover, Pew found that Europeans who held unfavorable views of the European Union also tended to be those who were more supportive of what they called right-wing populist political parties, typically anti-elite and antiglobalization.[49] Most respondents in several EU member states also said that they wanted at least some powers returned to their national governments from Brussels – another indication of anti-elite/antiglobal attitudes. Pew's populist groups were especially emphatic about this.[50] Finally, Pew found that anxiety about the economy in several European countries – stemming from rising inequality, wage stagnation, and unemployment – was another concern that attracted people to anti-elite/antiglobal populist parties.[51]

What all this boils down to is that those who were opposed to the European Union had economic concerns and wanted alternative national choices that would afford them the chance to elect new politicians less supportive of Europeanization and globalization than the current crop of political leaders. Here, then, is a vivid example of nationalism and class mixing into a potentially explosive form that threatens economic integration within one of capitalism's largest markets.

Anti-elite/antiglobal nationalist resentment often has a rural base directed against metropolitan centers housing the global elite, such as London, New York, Paris, and Brussels. For this base, the technological revolution of our time is not producing high levels of employment, let alone employment in lucrative and secure jobs, as was the case in previous historical periods of dramatic technological change. Perhaps the most striking general characterization is provided by sociologist Robert Wuthnow's painstaking work chronicling the economic troubles of America's rural communities – particularly their sense of being abandoned by what they perceive to be the nation's morally bankrupt leaders. All of this makes the rural United States fertile ground for right-wing nationalism.[52] Although racial and ethnic minorities have endured economic hardships more than whites, especially in rural areas, Anne Case and Angus Deaton have demonstrated that non-Hispanic white Americans are now suffering too; in addition to their economic woes, they are often wracked by drugs and face increasing morbidity.[53] An opioid crisis, for instance, has hit the rural United States particularly hard.[54] But Wuthnow's story lacks something important – namely, the central finding of Duina's excellent ethnography.[55] The economic suffering may be real, but this does not mean that these people somehow lack moral substance – that is, they still believe in the societal escalator, and that hard work and perseverance will pay off. In this regard, Hillary Clinton made a terrible mistake during her campaign for the presidency when she called middle- and working-class people who supported Donald Trump "the deplorables" – an offensive comment that added to her image as a condescending global elitist.

The rural dimension of antiglobal/anti-elite resentment is not restricted to the United States. Recall that the referendum on Denmark's entry into the eurozone was defeated in part by Danes living in more conservative rural areas outside metropolitan Copenhagen. In France, right-wing nationalism has long been found in southern areas known not only for their wine but also for reactionary politics, stretching back to the days of Vichy during the Second World War. Right-wing nationalism has deep roots in other European rural regions too. The anthropological fieldwork of Agnieszka Pasieka in Poland is particularly interesting, because that country never suffered from recession during the financial crisis and its aftermath, unlike so many other European countries. Yet it too has witnessed a significant rise of right-wing nationalism – notably, the Law and Justice Party, which has strong rural support. The various far-right groups that Pasieka studied demonstrate superb solidarity with those who suffer from the effects of globalization.[56] The broader point, however, is that the rural dimension of right-wing nationalism in Europe is tied closely to the interplay of class and antiglobal/anti-elite feelings, because globalization has taken a severe toll on agricultural regions. As a result in large measure of globalization during the last decade, 100,000 small-scale farms have vanished in Germany, 300,000 in Bulgaria, 600,000 in Poland, and 900,000 in Romania. The number of full-time farmers in the European Union fell by over a third.[57]

Although globalization and the hardships it brought to the middle and working classes spawned nationalist ire targeting global elites, the new nationalism also zeroes in on outsiders from the lower ranks of society – that is, it is hostile to immigrants and other racial and ethnic minorities. With the advent of globalization, advances in international tele-communications and transportation, and the rapid spread of information around the world, popular awareness of global inequality has been heightened. In particular, the awareness of people in poor countries of the quality of life in richer countries has grown, making them mindful that emigration can give them a better life.[58] Not surprisingly, net migration to the OECD countries increased, often in response to deterior-ating economic and political conditions in the home coun-tries. In the late 1960s, immigration added about 0.1 percent annually to the OECD population; in the mid-1980s, that number began to rise. By the mid-1990s, immigration was adding roughly 0.33 percent each year to the OECD popula-tion, and by the first part of this century, it had risen to nearly 0.5 percent each year. By 2000, there were just over 75 million foreign-born people living in OECD countries. A decade later, that number exceeded 100 million.[59] Put differently, while the number of immigrants had hovered at about 3 percent of the world population since 1960, the percentage of immigrants living in the advanced countries more than doubled from about 5 percent to 12 percent between 2000 and 2010.[60] When it comes to refugees rather than all immigrants, the numbers are smaller. For example, since 2000, Sweden – the most welcoming of the advanced capitalist nations – experienced an annual refugee inflow of only about 0.4 percent of the population. The United States was even stingier, admitting only 0.04 percent.[61]

There is a great deal of variation across countries. According to the OECD, immigration growth in Germany has been especially large as a consequence of people coming from the East and Central European postcommunist countries, as well as but to a lesser degree from southern Europe. By 2012, Germany was the second largest recipient of immigrants after the United States, receiving over 10 percent of all permanent immigration in the OECD area that year. By then, France, Sweden, and Finland were also experiencing substantially higher immigration flows. But the United States accounts for the largest influx of immigrants in absolute terms – over a quarter of all permanent flows to the OECD area.[62] The point is that immigration was on the rise. Figure 4.3 shows that, for the OECD countries for which data are available, most countries received more permanent immigrants in 2015 than they did a decade earlier.

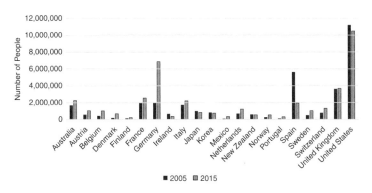

Figure 4.3 Annual permanent immigrant inflows, 2005 and 2015
Source: OECD (2019b).

The Second World War saw genocide and ethnic cleansing homogenize European countries to a significant degree along linguistic, religious, and ethnic lines. Immigration has the opposite effect: since the late twentieth century, it has contributed to rising cultural heterogeneity. Good cross-national historical data measuring this are very difficult to access. Most research provides only a snapshot of heterogeneity across countries at a single point in time. In earlier work, however, we collected data and constructed measures of ethnic, linguistic, and religious heterogeneity for each of the OECD countries in years as close to 1985 and 2000 as possible.[63] This work was painstaking, but its results were clear: Between 1985 and 2000, ethnic and religious heterogeneity increased, on average, by about 10 percent in the OECD countries; linguistic heterogeneity increased by about 5 percent. On average, then, the OECD countries became noticeably more diverse.

Regardless of how many immigrants there actually were in a country, what mattered was the perception that they posed some sort of a threat – a perception cultivated by some conservative politicians and right-wing figures peddling half-truths and misinformation in service of their own economic and political agendas. Donald Trump's baseless claims to white voters that an influx of immigrants was threatening their economic interests was just one example; similar claims were made by political entrepreneurs in Poland, Hungary, Denmark, Sweden, and other countries. As a result, immigration seen in these terms has had immediate and serious political consequences. Among people worried about the impact of increased cultural diversity within countries, hostility

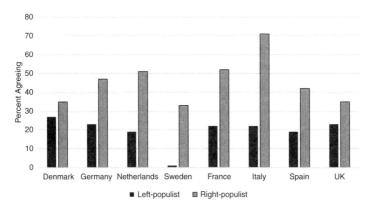

Figure 4.4 Are immigrants an economic burden?
Source: Pew Research Center (2018b).

toward immigrants has increased in recent years, and it has fueled right-wing nationalist movements in several countries.[64] Figure 4.4 represents Pew Research Center data from 2017 showing that right-wing populists are far more anti-immigrant than even left-wing populists, because they believe that immigrants are an economic burden on their country. In some cases, anti-immigrant sentiment has reached shocking levels.

The war in Syria illustrates the point. The war caused about 5 million people to flee in search of safety and economic opportunity. As their numbers grew, countries began to balk at giving them passage, let alone at receiving them. Hungary, for instance, closed its border with Serbia to keep the refugees out. Hundreds of thousands of refugees ended up in Germany, as noted, causing a major political crisis for Prime Minister Angela Merkel. Concerns were voiced in other countries too, particularly about the possibility that the Syrian

exodus would facilitate the spread of Islam and Islamic terrorism, since Syria is predominantly Muslim. Similar concerns, including movements aiming to limit immigration, had
manifested themselves in Europe in the 1990s long before the
refugee crisis.[65] As the post-communist states were admitted
to the European Union, Ireland, Sweden, and the United
Kingdom threw open their doors to East and Central
European workers seeking economic opportunities, while
others refused to do so, invoking a seven-year escape clause
permitted under EU rules.[66]

Meanwhile, in the United States, concern mounted
during the twenty-first century over immigrants entering
from Mexico and Central America, also seeking better economic prospects or asylum. As in Europe, many Americans
believed that immigrants were taking jobs away from them
and depressing their wages. Some worried that this influx was
a source of drug trafficking, crime, gang violence, and huge
demands on welfare and educational services – and they
believed this in part because of elite-led misinformation campaigns. Many were concerned that immigration was threatening American culture, particularly insofar as it diluted the
percentage of Americans who were non-Hispanic whites.
Forecasters projected that, by 2045, whites would be only
a minority of the American population.

Some caveats are in order here. First, one's admir-
ation for Angela Merkel's determination to allow refugees
into Germany needs to be tempered by remembering the
unpleasant deal she made with Turkish President Recep
Tayyip Erdoğan to provide billions of euros in return for
him keeping the vast majority of refugees in Turkey, outside

the borders of the European Union. Second, one must always draw a distinction between those who are determined to stay in their adopted country, given the genuine horrors and poverty back home, and those whose migration is temporary, likely to end when economic and political conditions improve there. Remember that Italian, Irish, and Spanish migrants ceased traveling to other EU member states, and Irish migrants to the United States, when the economies of their own countries improved. The same is now true of Mexicans in the United States.[67] Finally, we should treat with skepticism the assertion that the United States will soon have a minority white population. Much depends on the official U.S. Census Bureau classification: Irish Americans were once considered to be black; Hispanic Americans may yet be classified simply as white.

We also need to reiterate a crucial distinction between fear and reality – or, perhaps, between different senses of the real. People worry that immigration will depress wages and take jobs from native-born workers. Their concern is overblown. For instance, most immigrants to European countries have at least some post-secondary education and so have not depressed wages or otherwise exacerbated income inequality. Immigrants also help to make up for labor scarcities in many countries where aging populations and low birth rates have slowed or stopped the growth of the labor force. Although immigrants use public services, they typically compensate for that by paying more in taxes than they receive in public benefits.[68] But objective reality is often irrelevant; what people believe to be real, as sociologist W.I. Thomas put it, is real in its consequences.[69]

The irony in all this is that the immigrant minorities targeted make up only a tiny fraction of the population. Yet let us never forget that anti-Semitism convulsed Germany in the middle of the twentieth century even though Jews comprised only a little more than 1 per cent of the population. The same is true of Islamophobia in Quebec, with that sentiment peaking in areas that have virtually no Muslim presence, and of Brexit (coined to refer to the United Kingdom's exit from the European Union), with peak support coming in the northeast of England, where there were few foreign workers. Muslims constitute only about 5 percent of the Danish population: Most are first- or second-generation immigrants, and about 70 percent are citizens.[70] Yet the anti-immigrant Danish People's Party (DPP) has played an oversized role in national politics, punching far above its weight for years. Again, what matters is perception not reality. Here, we have the politics of fear and resentment, seeking to expel or exclude "Others" from the nation, or from the benefits – such as jobs, welfare, and education – that it delivers to citizen insiders.

The Politics of the New Nationalism

Feelings of being abandoned by the elite from above or suffering because of immigrants from below are often inchoate and poorly focused. As a result, people feeling these things are easy prey for politicians like Donald Trump, Boris Johnson, and Viktor Orbán, able to manipulate those feelings for their own political advantage. We should not too easily blame those who fall under the spell of such opportunists. Nevertheless, these concerns have changed the political landscape. In

France, Jean-Marie Le Pen founded the National Front in 1972, a right-wing nationalist political party. During the 1980s, the National Front wanted to restrict naturalization, tax employers for hiring foreigners, and expel foreigners who had engaged in criminal activities. But the party struggled to win much political support nationally until the 1988 presidential election, when Le Pen won over 14 percent of the vote. As the debate about immigration grew, the party's base expanded. Between 1973 and 1997, the National Front's share of first-round votes in elections for the National Assembly rose from less than 1 percent to nearly 15 percent, and by 1995, Le Pen's share of the vote in presidential elections jumped from virtually nothing to 15 percent. His daughter, who succeeded him as party leader, stunned Europe by making it to a second-round run-off election for president in 2017, which she lost – but notably gained 34 percent of the vote.

In Denmark, the DPP won slightly more than 7 percent of the vote and thirteen seats in parliament in the 1998 elections. In 2014, it won the most votes of any party in Denmark's election for representatives to the European Parliament. Aside from immigration, the DPP was a typical center-left Danish political party, supporting the Danish welfare state so long as it did not cater to immigrants. Here, we have what some might call national socialism – that is, universal welfare benefits for the Danish-born – although otherwise vastly different from the German Nazism of a previous era. The DPP lost twenty-one seats in the Danish parliamentary election of 2019, but it held on to 8.7 percent of the total, which still made it the third largest party in parliament. Meanwhile, the Swiss People's Party, established in 1971, became known for its right-wing, anti-immigrant, and anti-EU nationalist agenda. Its influence grew slowly, but under the leadership of Christoph Blocher, by the 1999 national elections, it had become the strongest party in Switzerland, garnering over 22 percent of the vote and 44 of the 200 seats in the National Council. In contrast to the DPP, Blocher's party was less supportive of the welfare state, but it was just as concerned about immigration as its Danish counterpart. Hungary's Prime Minister Viktor Orbán – who based his political campaigns on anti-refugee and anti-immigrant sentiment – has warned that if Hungarians do not begin procreating, the nation will disappear. His counterparts in the Czech Republic, Poland, and Serbia have made similar remarks, and they have put their governments' money where their mouths are, offering financial incentives for Czech, Polish, and Serbian nationals to have children.[71] But the most shocking case was Golden Dawn, a party founded in Greece in 1980 and growing to prominence in the 1990s, which espoused racist, xenophobic, and strong anti-Islamic ideologies. This ultranationalist party has been known to praise Nazism and advocate the expulsion of Greece's Turkish-speaking Muslim minority – a touch of fascism that has now been punished in the courts.

The 2008 financial crisis also helped to fuel nationalist sentiment and the deterioration of social cohesion within the European Union, especially in Portugal, Ireland, Italy, Greece, and Spain (the so-called PIIGS). Spontaneous protests targeting banks, corporate greed, and economic injustice broke out in 2011.[72] Greece is the most egregious example, where calls within the country to exit the eurozone grew on both the left and right as the grip of the European Central Bank (ECB) tightened over Greece's fiscal affairs, forcing the government to lay off thousands of workers, cut public pensions, and reduce public spending in other ways. Unemployment soared beyond 25 percent of the labor force, increasing economic hardship throughout the working and middle classes. Nationalist outrage was palpable as demonstrations erupted in the streets and eventually brought a socialist government to power on the basis of a promise to push back against the ECB and perhaps to abandon the euro – a blow that some believed would jeopardize the eurozone itself. Although not as extreme, similar grievances were being expressed in the other PIIGS too. Here, again, was social dynamite, this time pitting southern European countries against those more prosperous ones on the rest of the continent.

The overall trend is clear. Figure 4.5 shows that, in many European countries, nationalist parties have emerged

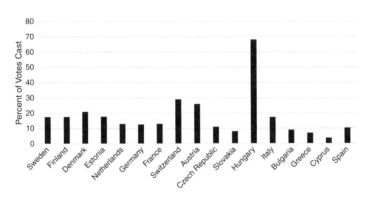

Figure 4.5 Votes won by nationalist parties in the most recent national election
Source: British Broadcasting Corporation (2019).

and, in some cases, won a significant proportion of the vote in recent national elections. In many countries, they fared even better in elections for the European Parliament.[73] This is important because, when combined with the antiglobal/antielite sentiments discussed earlier, it is a recipe for conflict in the European Union that threatens social cohesion at the heart of world capitalism.

Despite all of this, however, rising nationalism in Europe cannot be reduced simply to the consequences of the fiscal crisis and ECB austerity policies. Poland, for example, escaped the worst of the financial crisis and did not require ECB aid. Economic growth in Poland never dipped below zero, yet in the 2000s it has had several governments dominated by right-wing nationalist, anti-immigrant, and occasionally anti-Semitic parties. Similarly, in Hungary, although the economy fell briefly into recession, since 2012 it outperformed the OECD economic growth average, and its government was in the hands of a right-wing nationalist party. In both cases, nationalist governments posed threats to democratic institutions. In 2018, Viktor Orbán's government in Hungary moved to shut down the Central European University, funded by George Soros, a Hungarian-born billionaire and liberal critic of the Orbán regime. This move was widely condemned as an attack on academic freedom and free speech. The same year, Poland's fervently nationalist President Andrzej Duda named twenty-seven new likeminded justices to the Polish Supreme Court, sparking a lawsuit in the Court of Justice of the European Union charging that he was dismantling the rule of law. He was reelected in 2020 by a slim margin. And, when the coronavirus pandemic hit, Orbán convinced the Hungarian parliament to grant him the ability to rule with a free hand, including by ignoring old laws and creating new ones without parliamentary approval for as long as the national state of emergency continued.

Of course, the two most important manifestations of the forces we have been discussing are the election of Donald Trump as president of the United States and the United Kingdom's decision to leave the European Union. Both have disrupted social cohesion internationally and have thrown a monkey wrench into the workings of capitalism. Trump won the U.S. presidency in 2016 by raising alarms about the dangers immigrants posed to the United States and railing against corporate elites who outsourced jobs and manufacturing to other countries. Thanks to decades of middle- and working-class wage stagnation coupled with diminished opportunities for upward mobility, many Americans were fed up with politics as usual. Struggling to make economic ends meet under these conditions, household debt had been rising, creating an illusion of prosperity as the average American borrowed more and more money to sustain the standard of living to which their family had grown accustomed during the Golden Age. Debt was the mechanism with which to keep one's place on the societal escalator. Inequality had been rising since the late 1970s, and millions had suffered during the 2008 financial crisis. Moreover, growing numbers of non-Hispanic whites blamed minorities and immigrants for their misfortunes, believing, for example, that immigrants were competing for their jobs and depressing their wages. Trump capitalized on all this. His was a campaign that pandered to Americans' economic fears and anxieties with rhetoric full of nationalist and racist language. He threatened to stem the tide of immigration from Latin America and the Middle East, and he pledged to abandon American commitments to several international trade, defense, and climate agreements – moves that eventually jeopardized social cohesion internationally by alienating the United States' allies.[74]

As for the United Kingdom, it had long been ambivalent about the EU project. After joining the forerunner to the European Union, the European Economic Community (EEC), in 1973, the United Kingdom was often a cantankerous partner in European deliberations. The political elite never accepted the loss of its empire. Victory in the Second World War made it reluctant to acknowledge the importance of new institutions on the continent designed to sustain peace and economic prosperity.[75] All this came to a head in June 2016 when, in another blow to international social cohesion, 51 percent of voters in a national referendum decided that the United Kingdom would "Leave."

The UK Independence Party (UKIP), a right-wing nationalist party founded in 1993, had led the "Leave" campaign. The vote turned on issues of ethnic nationalism, economic protectionism, and sovereignty. Conservative Prime Minister Theresa May captured much of this sentiment after the referendum in her disparaging remark about EU membership, saying "If you believe you are a citizen of the world, you are a citizen of nowhere." This is a classic statement of hatred for globalization. Furthermore, Brexit supporters from the middle and working classes, often hailing from either semirural areas or those in industrial decline, feared for the future of their children and worried about the loss of national cultural traditions.[76]

Those in favor of Brexit also tended to be less educated, older, retired, Christian, and either manual workers or unemployed – a profile resembling Eurosceptics in other countries too.[77] Those backing the "Leave" campaign were likely to see globalization and immigration as forces for ill.[78] They often worried that immigrants were competing with them for jobs, and rising economic inequality, driven in part by huge neoliberal cuts to welfare spending, added fuel to the campaign.[79]

However, none of this would have happened without equally strident antiglobal, anti-EU nationalist sentiment among the right-wing political elite. For instance, former Conservative Party member Nigel Farage, an ambitious political entrepreneur from southeast England, former Member of the European Parliament, and two-time UKIP leader, was instrumental in pushing the Brexit issue for years. Also, on the far right was Boris Johnson, one-time Mayor of London, and Conservative Party member of Parliament whose outlandish public persona and nationalist ideology were often compared to those of Donald Trump. Both Farage and Johnson touted Brexit as a panacea for just about everything ailing the United Kingdom. Many in the Labour Party supported Brexit too: Jeremy Corbyn, the party's leader at the time of the referendum, had long been a Eurosceptic, fiercely opposing Britain's initial membership in the EEC and later the eurozone project. His failure to support the "Remain" campaign was arguably its death knell. In sum, economic and nationalist trends came together, creating the same sort of social dynamite we saw in Trump's United States.[80] In both cases, this was nationalism bolstering the kind of reactionary, right-wing impulses that Polanyi abhorred.

Immigration does not automatically trigger nationalist hostility. Canada, for example, has received large numbers of immigrants: 25 percent of the population are first-generation descendants of immigrants, and 25 percent are immigrants. For several reasons, it has done so with enthusiasm and without resentment. These numbers make many Canadians aware of the immigrant condition, and they are equally aware that immigrants have helped to build a country that is still sparsely populated relative to its geographic size. Furthermore, immigrants to Canada tend to apply for citizenship as quickly as they can, thereby ruling out the sense that they are somehow different from those born in the country and mitigating the sort of "us vs. them" conflict seen elsewhere. Moreover, Canadian immigration policy is not blind: it privileges skill and the needs of the economy, thereby making immigration seem acceptable and necessary. The desire of millions to move that remains a huge issue in much of the world is less so in Canada than it is in the European Union and United States, where millions of refugees and asylum seekers have arrived or are waiting to do so. Yet even in Canada the sensible and humane policies under which this has happened previously are beginning to lose out to reactionary forces, such as the issuing of temporary labor permits, restricted residency cards, and limiting of access to health care and social services that establish immigrants as "others," that points to the real viciousness of the new nationalism.[81] In Montréal, Quebec, where one of us works, the Parti Québécois played a xenophobic card during its last period in power that seems to be directly related to a rise in hate crimes – a direct threat to people's lives; hate crimes have also been on the rise in the United States since Donald Trump won the White House on a nationalist platform.[82]

Conclusion

Our argument in this chapter has been that rising economic inequality and hardship undermines capitalism in several ways. As social cohesion has deteriorated, it has given rise to a new form of nationalist politics that mixes economic griev-ances with growing animosity toward the cosmopolitan elite and immigrants, both of whom are held to be responsible for working- and middle-class troubles. This mixture of class-based resentment and nationalism is precisely the sort of social dynamite that concerns us – particularly when it is exacerbated by a lack of political voice. Worse still, the effects of this resentment are not restricted to national politics; they have spilled over into international relations, generating con-flict among countries within Europe and North America, jeopardizing social cohesion at that level too. Examples include Brexit, Trump's disregard for various international agreements, anti-European animosity among the PIIGS, and Poland and Hungary's flouting of EU principles and law. Such destructive forces seem to be spreading. The question is whether it will explode – and with what effects for capitalism. There may be a brief ray of hope insofar as the European Union has unanimously agreed to raise €750 billion ($883 billion) in bonds backed collectively by its members to help stimulate those European economies hit hardest by the coronavirus pandemic – an unusual moment of international solidarity. Perhaps Joe Biden's presidency will improve the situation in the United States, although we are not terribly optimistic in that regard. Nevertheless, the ability of states to handle the economy under the current political conditions is becoming increasingly difficult.

5

State Failure

The rise in social inequality and the emergence of the new nationalism place us in a new world. The postwar system of social cohesion is gone; the potential for new disruptions to capitalism has grown. So we write this chapter with a good deal of fear and trembling for two reasons. First, the capacities of many advanced capitalist states to effectively manage their economies continue to diminish. We will show how this has happened at capitalism's core – the triad region – focusing on the United States, the European Union, and Japan. Second, the international architecture of capitalism is changing rapidly owing to the rise of Asian economic power – notably, China – as well as a dangerous shift in American hegemony from a relatively benign form to one that is markedly more predatory. The United States is becoming a disruptive presence within the capitalist world – a change that has jeopardized international cohesion and the capacity of states to cooperate as they did in the early postwar years.

Before we explain all this, some background is necessary. Recall that our sympathy is for those in the advanced world who have been left out and are no longer on the societal escalator. Are the nationalist politicians they elected serving their interests? The answer is "yes," insofar as to be taken seriously by these politicians makes those left out feel part of a single nation. But the answer is also "no," insofar as these politicians are doing very little to address the material grievances of those left out who elected them in the first place. No one exemplifies this sort of politician better than British parliamentarian Jacob Rees-Mogg, an ardent Brexiteer but also part-owner of Somerset Capital Management, a $7 billion fund with most of its clients' money invested outside the United Kingdom.[1] The absence of EU regulations on British businesses following Brexit may allow him to prosper personally, but exiting the European Union will hurt those left out and caged inside the United Kingdom. Similarly, Donald Trump, whose real-estate interests span the globe, promised to "Make America Great Again" for those left out, then signed off on huge tax cuts that did nothing to reduce inequality. The point is that these Janus-faced politicians often attack the capacities that provide states with tools for better economic management, including those that could jump-start economies for those left out.

That state capacities have diminished since the Golden Age is clear. Some might object to this claim, citing the fact that, within the Organisation for Economic Co-operation and Development (OECD), average revenues and expenditures rose steadily from the 1970s on. This is true.[2] But these are crude measures of state capacity that disregard, for example, how those revenues were collected and how they were used. More refined indicators are available that bear more directly on a state's capacities for affecting economic activity. For example, the period from 1980 to 2006 was characterized by dramatic liberalization and privatization throughout the OECD – notably, in electricity, gas, railways, and telecommunications – led in the early 1980s by the United States and followed quickly by the United Kingdom, Canada, New Zealand, the Nordic countries, and Japan. Most other European countries followed suit from the mid-1990s onward.[3] Remember that this was the period during which economic growth slowed in the OECD, and the frequency of economic crises increased. In the late 1990s, the OECD urged further reform to get rid of "regulations which impede innovation or create unnecessary barriers to trade, investment, and economic efficiency."[4] The OECD's dream came true. The regulatory constraints imposed on business declined in most OECD countries as the neoliberal move toward regulatory reform continued. The World Bank rates the burden of government regulation on business using a seven-point scale in which 7 is the lightest burden and 1, the heaviest. Between 2008 and 2018, the years for which data are available, the median score for North America, Western Europe, and Japan increased from 3.2 to 3.8, with three-quarters of these countries reducing their regulatory burdens. Some of the largest economies showed the biggest reductions – notably, Germany, the United Kingdom, and the United States.[5]

It is hard to overstate the effects of state capacities on economic performance. Figure 5.1 plots the quality of national institutions against gross domestic product (GDP) per capita for forty-nine countries in 2018. Institutional quality is a World Economic Forum (WEF) composite index measuring the quality of security, property rights, social capital, checks and balances, transparency and ethics, public-sector performance, and corporate governance – virtually all of which reflect the state's rules, regulations, and other institutional capacities. The higher the score, the better the institutional quality. Gross domestic product per capita is a proxy for economic prosperity. The figure reveals that more prosperous countries are associated with higher-quality institutions. Of course, a correlation such

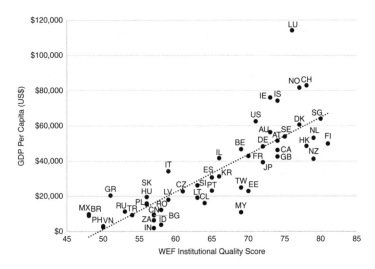

Figure 5.1 Institutional quality and economic prosperity
Note: Australia, AU; Austria, AT; Belgium, BE; Brazil, BR;
Bulgaria, BG; Canada, CA; Chile, CL; China, CN; Czech Republic,
CZ; Denmark, DK; Estonia, EE; Finland, FI; France, FR;
Germany, DE; Greece, GR; Hong Kong, HK; Hungary, HU;
Iceland, IS; India, IN; Indonesia, ID; Ireland, IE; Israel, IL; Italy,
IT; Japan, JP; Latvia, LV; Lithuania, LT; Luxembourg, LU;
Malaysia, MY; Mexico, MX; Netherlands, NL; New Zealand, NZ;
Norway, NO; Philippines, PH; Poland, PL; Portugal, PT;
Romania, RO; Russia, RU; Singapore, SG; Slovakia, SK; Slovenia,
SI; South Africa, ZA; South Korea, KR; Spain, ES; Sweden, SE;
Switzerland, CH; Taiwan, TW; Turkey, TR; United Kingdom,
GB; United States, US; Vietnam, VN.
Source: World Economic Forum (2019b).

as this does not reveal a causal relationship. But development
economists have long known that good institutions improve
economic performance, mainly by providing the right incentives and reducing uncertainty.[6] The question, then, is what

leads to good and bad institutions? One important factor is social cohesion. More cohesive societies tend to build thicker institutions with a wider array of policy tools and expertise to guide their use. For example, countries with long histories of vulnerability, such as a small domestic market and dependence on foreign trade, often develop a strong sense of national cohesion and, in turn, thick state capacities, which provide the necessary flexibility for meeting economic challenges.[7] This was the story of Denmark and Switzerland, whose abundant state capacities served them well in dealing with the 2008 financial crisis. Ireland was not so fortunate, having had a history of divisive nationalist conflict within society, including a brief but bloody civil war from 1922 to 1923 stemming from its fraught relationship with England, which stifled the development of many state capacities until the late 1980s.[8] However, the growth of inequality, the erosion of social cohesion, the rise of neoliberalism, and the ascendance of the new nationalism are undermining state capacities in many countries and creating serious problems for capitalism.

We proceed now in two stages, concentrating first on the domestic political economies of the advanced capitalist countries, and then on the architecture of the capitalist system as a whole. The greatest dangers lie in the second of these arenas.

Core Concerns

The United States

Let us begin at the capitalist core – with the workings of capitalism within the United States. We start by considering the two faces of the Obama years and the Trump era, before offering initial notes about the presidency of Joe Biden – whose general prospects are considered in the next chapter, where we speculate on likely developments.

Barack Obama became president at the height of the 2008 financial crisis. He took dramatic steps to pull the economy back from the brink of disaster, and he improved some of the state's capacities for managing key sectors, including financial services, real estate, and health care. But long-term forces continued to erode the state's capacities. First, the elite continued to turn away from Keynesianism toward neoliberalism. Second, the American corporate leaders became less unified and less concerned about the national political economy than they were with the interests of their individual corporations. They had been a moderating force in American politics during the Golden Age, but that now diminished. In turn and thanks partly to changing campaign finance laws that allowed more money to flow into politics from corporations and wealthy donors, right-wing elements came to the fore in politics.[9]

As a result, Republicans and Democrats in Washington, D.C., disagreed about almost everything. The state's capacity to tackle even the most basic problems deteriorated. For example, the government was shut down several times when Congress and the president could not agree either on a budget or whether to raise the debt ceiling – that is, the legal limit on government borrowing. Failure to raise the ceiling could cause the government to default on its debt, thereby jeopardizing the country's credit rating. In fact, the United States' credit rating was downgraded anyway in 2011, even though Congress did raise the ceiling, because concerns were mounting that the United States' capacity for keeping its economic house in order was slipping. In the midst of one debt ceiling battle, Christine Lagarde, then head of the International Monetary Fund (IMF), warned that failing to raise the ceiling and then defaulting would result in "massive disruption the world over" and undermine the world's "trust in the U.S. signature."[10]

All of this pales next to the Trump administration's effect on the state's capacities. The deterioration of intellectual capacities was especially worrying.[11] Trump's transition team did little to prepare for taking office.[12] Once in office, Trump appointed people at the highest levels who often had little or no experience appropriate to their posts. Furthermore, many highly qualified bureaucrats were not invited to stay, as they normally are during a transition, nor were well-qualified replacements found for them.[13] Making matters worse, an unprecedented number of Trump's top-level appointees either quit in disgust or were fired because they dared to contradict the president.[14] The same is true of many government researchers. As a former government climate scientist told reporters, "Regulations come and go, but the thinning out of scientific capacity in the government will take a long time to get back."[15]

Even when expertise was available to him, Trump often ignored it.[16] He insisted on deep tax cuts against the advice of some of his aides and of the nonpartisan Congressional Budget Office (CBO).[17] He rejected advice on climate policy. He also disregarded advice on trade policy, choosing instead to launch trade wars with China, Mexico, Canada, and the European Union. Trump's National Economic Council director, Gary

Cohn, quit as a result and said that nobody was left in the White House to stabilize economic policy by standing up to the president and insisting that policy be made on the basis of factual analysis.[18] The same was true of foreign policy.[19] In addition, Trump's restrictions on immigration ignored data showing that immigrants were unlikely to take away American citizens' jobs or reduce their wages, and that they were a vital part of certain sectors of the American economy. Finally, he scaled back financial regulations and their enforcement, which had been designed to prevent another financial crisis.[20] All of this constituted a withering attack on the state's intellectual and institutional capacities.

It is time to make some judgements about what all this means. First, recall the analysis by French economist Thomas Philippon that we discussed in the introductory chapter. By reducing the state's capacity for regulating competition, Philippon showed that "state capture" by capitalists hurt the American economy by restricting competition and creating the world that Smith inveighed against – one of high profits and low wages. If America continues to implement tax cuts favoring the wealthy and less regulation of the economy, these problems will persist. It will also deepen economic inequality, thereby weakening the cohesion that can come when all feel they are at least on Smith's societal escalator.[21]

Second, the imposition of import tariffs on Chinese products hit American manufacturing hard, forcing American manufacturers and consumers to pay billions of dollars more for imported products. Another result was what *Fortune* magazine called a "trade-driven malaise." Manufacturing exports declined to levels not seen since the Great Recession.

Agricultural exports fell by nearly 20 percent as countries countered American tariffs with tariffs of their own. As a result, the administration spent nearly $28 billion in aid for American farmers hurt by the trade war.[22]

Third, despite all this, Trump claimed that the economy was doing better than ever. In fact, the stock market had soared to new heights. But the wealthiest 10 percent of the population owned over 80 percent of that stock, so most Americans did not benefit.[23] Indeed, by 2019, inequality hit a fifty-year high, most of the benefits of economic growth going only to the richest 20 percent of the population.[24] This flew in the face of Keynesianism, which held that this would hurt consumption, economic demand, and employment. Indeed, the employment rate on Trump's watch rose only by about 1 percent before plummeting when the coronavirus pandemic hit. And the official unemployment rate – including underemployed and part-time workers seeking full-time jobs – was nearly 7 percent in 2019.[25] The Brookings Institution reported that "there [was] still a considerable amount of underutilized labor and many people for whom the labor market [was] not providing adequate opportunities."[26] Finally, although average wages were beginning to rise, Americans were borrowing to make ends meet: household debt reached an all-time high of nearly $14 trillion in 2019.[27] It is also important to remember that most of the positive economic trends during Trump's presidency were not new but rather continuations of trends that began during the Obama administration.

Fourth, the state's insatiable appetite for borrowing created the potential for more economic trouble. The federal

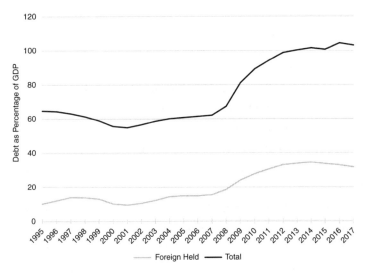

Figure 5.2 U.S. federal debt, 1995–2017
Source: U.S. Federal Reserve Bank (2019a, 2019b).

government's debt ballooned from about 60 percent of GDP
to 100 percent between the onset of the financial crisis and
2017 (see Figure 5.2).[28] By then, American debt was among the
highest in the developed world. So far, that had not been
a problem for the economy. Indeed, it was consistent with
Keynesianism insofar as much of that debt was incurred to
combat the Great Recession. However, on Trump's watch, the
economy was growing again, so in a Keynesian world it was
time to begin reducing that debt, as the Clinton administration had done during the 1990s. Thanks partly to Trump's tax
cuts, the fiscal year 2020 budget, released before coronavirus
hit, would have added between $7 trillion and $10 trillion to
the national debt over the next decade.[29]

The dangers this debt poses require explanation. Put simply, the U.S. government incurs debt by borrowing money. It does so by selling Treasury bonds, which are a very safe investment and therefore particularly attractive during rocky economic times. Because investors must use dollars to buy these bonds, foreigners who want them must convert their currency into dollars. So, when economic times are tough, the demand for both dollars and bonds increases. This is where the dangers emerge. One is that rising demand for dollars causes the dollar's value to appreciate against other currencies. As it does so, American goods and services become relatively more expensive abroad, and foreign goods and services become relatively less expensive in the United States; hence American exports decline, imports rise, and the trade deficit increases. This is what happened following the 2008 financial crisis. Furthermore, as we explained in Chapter 3, one way in which the government covers the cost of issuing these bonds is by "printing money." Some economists worry that this will eventually spark inflation.[30]

For us, the most serious problem of mounting national debt is that the fiscal conservatives – deficit hawks – in Washington, D.C., can use it as an excuse to cut government spending and attack other state capacities, such as the budgets for infrastructure, business regulation, science, health care, and education. Deficit hawks also target social programs, exacerbating inequality and further threatening social cohesion. This undermines the double movement Polanyi felt was essential to sustain capitalism. Hinting at such a move, chair of the Federal Reserve (the Fed) Jerome Powell, among many others, has warned that the United States has not been on a "sustainable" fiscal path for a while, because the nation's debt is growing faster than the economy.[31] The implication is that either taxes must increase, or spending must be cut. In today's political climate, raising taxes does not seem to be in the cards. Indeed, beginning in mid-2020, Senate Republicans invoked the debt excuse in delaying, for seven months, passage of additional coronavirus spending – the House of Representatives' HEROES Act – unless House Democrats agreed to reduce the size of the package.

The coronavirus pandemic shed new light on the dangers of the Trump administration's propensity toward weakening state capacities.[32] Consider intellectual capacities first. Once in office, the administration disbanded the Obama administration's Global Health Security and Biodefense Unit, which had been responsible for pandemic preparedness.[33] Moreover, in September 2019, the Council of Economic Advisors warned the administration that a pandemic could kill 500,000 people and severely damage the economy. The administration ignored the report and similar warnings that followed once the virus surfaced in the United States. Public health advisors to the White House were constantly at odds with the president and his economic advisors as they tried to urge bolder and swifter steps to prevent a major public health and economic catastrophe. But it was not until March 13, 2020 that Trump declared a national emergency. Dragging his feet cost many thousands of lives.[34] It also exacerbated the economic crisis.

Insofar as institutional capacities are concerned, prior to the COVID-19 crisis and in keeping with neoliberalism, the administration reduced spending for emergency management and pandemic research, and it allowed the national stockpile of emergency medical equipment to dwindle. The administration left it to the private sector to provide the necessary equipment for fighting the virus. This sparked a chaotic competition among states, municipalities, and hospitals scouring the world for supplies that proved to be inefficient and expensive.[35] The federal government also left it up to individual states to determine when to lock down their economies when a nationally coordinated response was needed. As a result, despite having the world's most expensive healthcare system, the United States soon became a world leader in COVID-19 morbidity and mortality.

The effect of all this was devastating for the economy, which shrank by 9 percent in the second quarter of 2020 – the steepest single-quarter decline on record. The official unemployment rate (excluding underemployed and part-time workers seeking full-time jobs) skyrocketed from 4 percent to about 13 percent – a height not seen since the Great Depression; although then declining, it remained 7 percent by October.[36] By the beginning of September, an estimated 164,000 small businesses had closed permanently as a consequence of the crisis, and tens of thousands were in jeopardy.[37] Gross domestic product was expected to have declined by as much as 8.5 percent by the end of the year.[38] The crisis pushed even large firms in the retail, apparel, petroleum, hospitality, entertainment, and travel industries into bankruptcy. The government's response was sweeping. The Fed cut interest rates nearly to zero, but they were already so low that, even before the crisis hit, Fed chair Powell had admitted that this would do little to stimulate the economy.[39] So the Fed resumed quantitative easing to pump more money into the economy. The United States' ability to "print money" helped to cover the costs. How long the United States could continue doing this remained an open question. The Fed's balance sheet had already ballooned from about $878 billion in assets in late 2007 to $4 trillion by the beginning of 2019 because of quantitative easing during the financial crisis.[40] According to the Brookings Institution, "The Fed's powers and tools, as impressive as they are, aren't sufficient to cope with the economic harm of the COVID-19 crisis."[41] Powell himself acknowledged that the Fed alone did not have the capacity to handle the crisis.[42] This is why Congress scrambled to pass four massive stimulus packages in 2020, totaling $2.4 trillion for businesses, state and local governments, and individuals, an amount predicted to push the federal debt to 136 percent of GDP by year end – the highest level in American history.[43] To finance the spending, the Treasury borrowed by selling bonds, and again the Fed "printed money." But the point is that the thinning of state capacities, including the lack of expert-based policymaking, enabled the pandemic to hit the economy harder than it would have otherwise – and harder than it hit nearly all other advanced countries.

Perhaps surprisingly, none of this rattled investors' confidence in the American bond and stock markets, which, despite a brief hiccup, continued to do well even though unemployment was so high, and the economy was in tatters. This was because the vast bulk of the spending by the Fed, Treasury, and Congress went to corporations, with few of the strings attached that would have forced them to use it to stimulate the economy and reduce unemployment. In particular, the Fed purchased mountains of corporate debt and lent money to corporations, thus bailing out lenders in the private bond market. The fact that all this was necessary to prop up the stock market is a stark illustration of how capitalism is not as self-regulating as neoliberals claim. This was not Keynesianism designed to increase demand and employment but rather a move that propped up the bond markets. It also increased inequality by boosting the wealth of American billionaires by about 9 percent.[44] In short, the cosmopolitans won, the middle and working classes were left out, and the economy continued to languish.

Some of this will change for the better. It seems clear that U.S. President Biden will enhance state capacity, especially in relation to the COVID-19 catastrophe. Restoring social cohesion will be much harder. Giving voice to the discontented will help, and serious attempts look likely to be made in that direction. But the structural changes needed to make those left out feel that they are included will be much harder to accomplish. Such changes would require determined major policies to equalize conditions between the nationally bounded and the more cosmopolitan members of society. We have worries on this account, addressed in the concluding chapter.

Europe

Nationalism and deteriorating social cohesion were exacerbated in Europe by the 2008 financial crisis. State capacities suffered too. Recall from Chapter 4 that austerity contributed to the erosion of social cohesion in several EU member states, where nationalist parties experienced a renaissance. We presented evidence of this in Figure 4.5 for seventeen European countries. However, another look at those countries reveals a connection between rising nationalism and a deterioration in the quality of their institutions. Figure 5.3 shows the change between 2008 and 2018 in the WEF rankings of the quality of these countries' institutions: two-thirds of those seventeen countries experienced a decline in their institutional ranking. The quality of these institutions is one key to a country's economic success. Although nationalism is a double-edged sword – it can be either a source of social cohesion or division – the nationalism represented in Figure 5.3 involved parties that tended to divide rather than unify their countries. So, although this evidence is not definitive, it lends support to our argument that a rise in divisive nationalism – Gellner's social dynamite – is associated with a deterioration in the state's institutional capacities for economic prosperity.

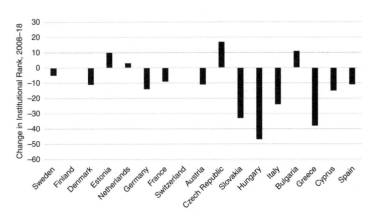

Figure 5.3 Deterioration of institutional quality
Source: World Economic Forum (2019a).

Additional evidence of the deterioration of state capacities in Europe comes from the World Bank burden of business regulation index mentioned earlier. Between 2008 and 2018, excluding the postcommunist members that lacked much capitalist-style business regulation to begin with, the index among EU members rose from a median of 3.1 to 3.5, indicating that these states were loosening their business regulations. The decline was particularly sharp in the United Kingdom, whose index rose from 3.2 to 4.0. This brings us to Brexit – that is, the United Kingdom's decision to exit the European Union: the most important European example of the relationship between the social dynamite of nationalism, the deterioration of state capacity, and the terrible effect it can have on economic performance.

The United Kingdom was the bedrock of neoliberalism in Europe. Beginning with Margaret Thatcher, British state capacities had been under siege for decades. Insofar as the Brexit vote is concerned, the British state's intellectual capacity was notably thin. Brexit supporters in parliament were badly informed about Brexit's implications. Then not yet prime minister, Boris Johnson promised that Brexit would lead to a massive increase in funding for the National Health Service (NHS), an easy trade deal with the European Union, and greater economic prosperity. Other Brexiteers claimed that if the United Kingdom were to remain in the European Union, she would be swamped by Turkish immigrants once Turkey joined. But experts inside the government and most academics outside considered these claims to be nonsensical, warning that the economic impact of Brexit would be horrible.

For instance, a 2016 report by the Treasury warned: that the United Kingdom would be permanently poorer if it were to leave the European Union; that tax receipts would drop, leading to either more government borrowing and debt, large tax increases or major cuts in public spending; and that trade would suffer. The Treasury also advised that much foreign investment would be lost, because most of it located to the United Kingdom in the first place to access the EU market. The report also estimated that the United Kingdom would lose between 4.6 percent and 9.5 percent of its GDP over the next fifteen years and that millions of jobs would be at risk.[45] The OECD agreed that tighter financial conditions and weaker investor confidence, coupled with higher trade barriers and restrictions on labor mobility, would significantly diminish British GDP. Labor productivity and technological innovation would suffer as a result of a fall in foreign direct investment (FDI) and a smaller pool of labor skills.[46] Finally, reducing immigration, a central pillar of the "Leave" campaign, would prove disastrous for a country that faced continuing labor shortages as the population aged. It would also become harder to pay for services for an aging population without those additional foreign workers paying taxes. The Brexiteers paid no attention.[47] But these negative forecasts are already coming to fruition.[48]

Relevant state capacities were also in short supply after the Brexit referendum. Consider the government's Department for International Trade (DIT), a critical agency for an island nation dependent on trade. Maritime UK, the trade association representing British shipping, ports, and marine services, warned in late 2018 that the DIT had "far too few industry experts," noting that it was in worse shape now than it had been when it was established two years earlier. This did not bode well for the United Kingdom's maritime sector, which moves 95 percent of the country's international trade, employs 185,000 people, and supports 932,000 jobs. However, the association's chair worried that the problem transcended his part of the economy: "We, and countless other sectors, are falling victim to the lack of strategic vision and ambition that seems to be rife in the Department for International Trade." Efforts to beef up expertise in the DIT were insufficient, because most of those hired by the department were career civil servants with no experience in the industry. Yet this is the department responsible for renegotiating current trade deals and striking new ones with the rest of Europe, as well as promoting British exports worldwide. The European Commission was also deeply concerned about DIT's incompetence and inexperience. This is just one example of the fact that business leaders are increasingly worried about the lack of state capacity for handling Brexit.[49] Making matters worse, Brexit itself will weaken the United Kingdom's state capacities. Over the years, the country had become heavily dependent on more than forty EU agencies for expertise and guidance, including, for instance, the European Investment Bank, the European Food Safety Authority, and the European Centre for Disease Prevention and Control. By relying on these agencies, the United Kingdom had effectively offloaded some of its state capacity to the European Union – capacity that it will lose entirely unless it negotiates new agreements with each agency.[50] Insofar as policymakers in Westminster rely on information and guidance from these and other EU agencies, this is a real danger for the United Kingdom's economic policymaking.

Brexit is one of the worst decisions in British history for additional reasons. Besides alienating its European allies, Scotland's interest in secession has been reenergized, while amicable relations between Northern Ireland and the Republic of Ireland may change dramatically as well, perhaps for the better. But Brexit will have awful effects on the rest of Europe too. In addition to weakening European cohesion and cooperation in dealing with things such as Russian aggression and the climate crisis, it will likely reduce economic growth in the European Union and fragment financial markets at a moment when market uncertainty is already fragile in the global economy, particularly in the throes of the COVID-19 pandemic.[51] Trade barriers will go up, cross-border financial accounts will be more difficult to reconcile, and it will be hard to craft and enforce cross-border financial regulations.[52] None of this is good for the stability of either European or global capitalism.

Brexit aside, the eurozone faces problems of its own associated with weak state capacities at both the domestic and European levels. Euro member states can no longer devalue their currencies to boost exports during economic downturns. Furthermore, members must abide by the Stability and Growth Pact, which limits the size of their budget deficits and public debt to no more than 3 percent and 60 percent of GDP, respectively. Exceptions to the Pact have been made in the past, but if these were to become widespread, they would devastate the euro, throwing European capitalism into turmoil. The inability to devalue or spend much to stimulate the economy means that eurozone members have forsaken monetary policy and deficit spending, two important Keynesian-style economic crisis management tools.

This also means that eurozone members depend on the European Central Bank (ECB), which has its own problems of intellectual capacity, as the 2008 financial crisis revealed. Thanks to the recession, tax revenues dropped, unemployment benefits soared, and budget deficits and debt increased in some eurozone countries, who then turned to the ECB for help. But the ECB was committed to neoliberal austerity despite much evidence suggesting that it was a terribly misguided approach.[53] So recipients of ECB bailouts were forced to cut government spending to reduce deficits. The idea was that this would restore business confidence and spark economic growth. It did not work. Recession persisted, yet the ECB stayed the course, demonstrating remarkable inflexibility and an inability to learn from the past – shortsightedness indicative of thin state intellectual capacity at the European level. The rationale for austerity was wrong, particularly as it applied to Portugal, Ireland, Italy, Greece, and Spain (the so-called PIIGS), which had been hit hardest by the crisis. The belief was that these states suffered deficits and debt because their politicians were corrupt, unable to refuse the demands of their constituents, and consequently could not stop spending. This is a common neoliberal trope. In fact, Figure 5.4 shows that debt grew dramatically after the 2008 crisis. But this had more to do with these states having to absorb toxic bank assets and doing whatever else it took to avoid another Great Depression than it had to do with corruption and

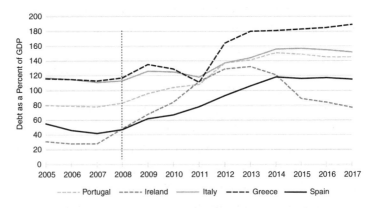

Figure 5.4 Rising national debt in the PIIGS, 2005–2017
Source: OECD (2019e).

a lack of political will. The problem was risky bank behavior enabled by inept financial regulation – that is, flawed state capacity.[54] The consequences were long-lasting.

Figure 5.5 shows that, after the financial crisis and the adoption of ECB austerity policies, all the PIIGS suffered dramatic declines in economic growth. As late as 2014, all but Ireland were still struggling to rebound from recession.[55] Figure 5.6 tells a similar story for unemployment, which rose in all of the PIIGS after 2008. Ireland and Portugal had recovered by 2017, but at that time – nearly a decade later – the rest still had unemployment rates far above what they had been just before the crisis. None had fallen below 5 percent. A seasoned investment banker summarized the European situation and laid blame squarely at the feet of foolish policymakers: "An alarming percentage of the political leadership in the developed countries have flirted with or have outright implemented fiscal austerity policies. Nothing could be more damaging . . . ."[56]

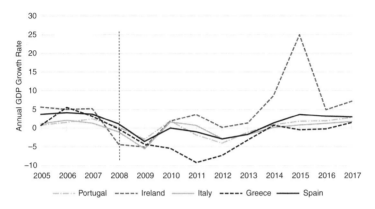

Figure 5.5 Economic growth in the PIIGS, 2005–2017
Source: OECD (2019d).

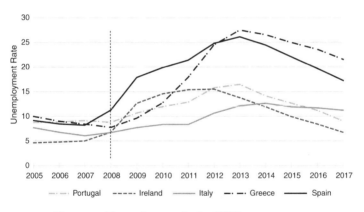

Figure 5.6 Unemployment in the PIIGS, 2005–2017
Source: OECD (2019c).

In short, this was a story of thin state intellectual capacity at the ECB and among eurozone members. But such foolishness had its causes. First, the ECB, as well as the IMF and European Commission, sought to protect politically powerful eurozone banks and investors. Second, the troubled countries were hemmed in institutionally. They could neither print money nor devalue, because they did not have a sovereign currency; they could not deploy extensive Keynesian-style stimuli, because they were constrained by the Stability and Growth Pact; and they could not default, because that would destroy the banking system. State capacities were limited; the only option left was austerity.[57]

Ten years later, these problems persisted. As of late 2019, seasonally adjusted unemployment in the European Union (6.3 percent) and eurozone (7.5 percent) was significantly higher than in the United States (3.6 percent) or Japan (2.2 percent).[58] Furthermore, serious financial imbalances remained within the European Union. In 2018, EU public debt averaged 80 percent of GDP; for the eurozone, it was 85 percent. But it was twice as high for some countries, including Greece, Italy, and Portugal, as it was for others such as Germany, Finland, Ireland, Austria, and especially the Baltic countries. Economic growth in the high-debt countries is likely to remain sluggish, because their debt service and borrowing costs are high. Moreover, it has been hard to maintain a strong euro when some eurozone members have such high debt.[59] This is reflected in the value of the euro against the dollar, which peaked in early 2008 at $1.59 and then slid gradually to $1.10 in 2020. The problem can again be traced back to thin state capacities. The high-debt countries were unable to keep their spending under control. Besides, the temptation to borrow was overwhelming given the fiscal imbalance within the eurozone: Germany's huge surplus had to go somewhere.[60]

Two final points reinforce how important state capacities are for European economic prosperity and crisis management. One is that the countries typically topping the list of the world's most competitive economies are those with thick state capacities – notably, small countries such as the Nordics and Switzerland. The other is that state capacities influenced how well European countries handled the COVID-19 crisis. Figure 5.7 shows that, during the first eleven months of the pandemic, countries with better-quality institutions suffered

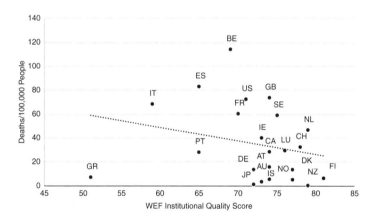

Figure 5.7 Institutional quality and coronavirus mortality in twenty-three advanced capitalist countries through November 9, 2020

Note: Australia, AU; Austria, AT; Belgium, BE; Canada, CA; Denmark, DK; Finland, FI; France, FR; Germany, DE; Greece, GR; Iceland, IS; Ireland, IE; Italy, IT; Japan, JP; Luxembourg, LU; Netherlands, NL; New Zealand, NZ; Norway, NO; Portugal, PT; Spain, ES; Sweden, SE; Switzerland, CH; United Kingdom, GB; United States, US.

Source: World Economic Forum (2019a) for institutional scores; Johns Hopkins University and Medicine (2020) for mortality rates.

lower coronavirus-related mortality rates. The contrast between Denmark and the United Kingdom illustrates why.

Denmark is not a eurozone member, and it therefore has more fiscal and monetary tools at its disposal than member states. It enjoyed low national debt and huge savings prior to the crisis. Denmark moved swiftly to contain the virus, closing universities, schools, public offices, restaurants, museums, and cinemas. It also sealed the border and forbade all gatherings of more than ten people. Furthermore, by mid-May 2020, it had twice the testing capacity per capita of the United States and a much lower mortality rate. Another reason why containment was so effective was that costs did not deter people from getting tested: everyone is covered by the national health insurance system. The Danish government also launched a massive program to save the economy, planning to spend as much as 13 percent of GDP in three months. It agreed to pay the salaries of workers in firms who stayed home on furlough. It guaranteed 70 percent of new bank loans to firms to keep the credit markets functioning, extended unemployment benefits indefinitely, and agreed to pay 75 percent of most workers' salaries if they were laid off. If a firm's profits sagged, the government agreed to compensate it for fixed expenses such as rent and other contractual obligations, as long as the firm agreed not to pay dividends, buy back its stock, or use offshore tax havens to avoid paying taxes. Taxes were postponed until the autumn. Even though the Danish People's Party had introduced a divisive form of nationalism into politics, the decision-making process behind all this was based on a high level of social cohesion – nearly unanimous consent by all ten parties in parliament – and thick state capacities, including Keynesian deficit financing and tripartite negotiations between unions, employer associations, and the state – another example of Hirschman's voice.[61] The results were impressive. Unemployment in the United States was 13.3 percent in mid-May, while in Denmark it was 5.5 percent, although the gap narrowed by September when the American economy experienced a mild economic improvement.

In contrast, despite plenty of warnings from experts, the United Kingdom responded more slowly. It was only in late March that the government shut down schools, pubs, and restaurants. Why the lackadaisical response? First, the government was distracted by Brexit. Second, leadership did not believe the pandemic was really serious. Third, several ministers did not want to hurt the economy. Finally, the United Kingdom's winner-take-all electoral system meant that the Conservative Party in charge did not have to listen to other voices. Making matters worse, despite warnings for years that the NHS faced a shortage of intensive care capacity, critical care nurses, ventilators, and protective equipment, the government had paid little attention. Once the crisis began, it missed an EU procurement deadline for ventilators, and it then ordered only half as many as the NHS requested.[62]

The results were horrifying. By November, the COVID-19 mortality rate in the United Kingdom was among the highest in the world and, although it is hard to parse the effects of the pandemic from those of Brexit, the economy took a huge hit, shrinking by 20 percent in the second quarter, with GDP forecast to shrink anywhere from 11.5 percent to 14 percent by the end of 2020.[63] Unemployment claims skyrocketed, but because the government provided subsidies to employers who furloughed workers rather than firing them, the unemployment rate hovered around 4.3 percent in July.[64] In short, the United Kingdom's limited state capacities – both intellectual, in terms of policymakers' unwillingness to heed the advice of experts, and institutional, particularly its unique system of governance – were largely to blame for the country's poor response to the pandemic compared to those of other countries. Even the limited trade deal between the United Kingdom and the European Union – effectively all that was possible given the dilatory character of the negotiations – will badly hurt the economy. The deal benefits the European Union because of the agreed provisions on trade in goods, in which EU member states have a surplus; it hurts the United Kingdom because there is no agreement on services, in which the United Kingdom has a surplus.

Japan

The third pillar of the capitalist triad has long been Japan, one of the largest advanced capitalist economies. Japan was a tremendous success story after the Second World War. The country's remarkable state capacities – notably, the Ministry of Finance and the Ministry of International Trade and Industry (MITI), working closely with business leaders – allowed Japan to rebuild its economy through a variety of state-led export-oriented industrial policies, which included subsidies and trade protection for selected firms that the government felt would lead the way toward economic prosperity. Tariffs like these were just what List prescribed for developing economies – including, we would add, those rebuilding from war. The government also had very particular policy tools to allocate investment and credit – notably, that most people deposited their money into postal savings accounts. Because the state ran the postal system, it was able to use these monies for economic development. MITI, as well as other state agencies, constituted what political scientist Sven Steinmo calls a "highly sophisticated interventionist elite bureaucracy," staffed through a competitive meritocratic process connected to the universities that channeled the best and the brightest into elite positions in government and industry. Capacities such as these were augmented by routinized channels of communication between the state and business community that produced a "politics of reciprocal consent" featuring the sort of voice that Hirschman favored. This fueled not only economic growth but also the creation of excellent public health, education, and low economic inequality, all of which contributed to social cohesion and political stability.[65]

In the 1990s, Japan ran into trouble. Global economic competition was increasing, and the demographic pressures of an aging population were growing. Japan's tax burden had long been among the lightest in the advanced capitalist world and its welfare state one of the smallest, thanks to Japanese firms providing generous insurance benefits and pensions for their employees. As businesses began to lose their global competitive edge, the government urged banks to continue extending credit to keep them afloat: it could not let these "zombie" firms fail, given their central role in the Japanese welfare system. The government also began spending more on infrastructure to provide jobs and keep unemployment down. Spending on social programs also increased as economically stressed firms cut back on their benefits to workers. Japan had been an exception to Polanyi's double movement insofar as the private sector, not the state, had assumed responsibility for many tasks performed by welfare states elsewhere; now, true to Polanyi's theory, the state began to shoulder those responsibilities. But all of this stoked the business community's fear that higher taxes were on the way, which led them to embrace neoliberalism and push for administrative reform. Beginning in 1995, successive governments accepted neoliberalism and began cutting taxes. This did not stimulate economic growth, but it did cause budget deficits to soar, and it undermined public confidence in the government's ability to manage the economy.[66]

Compounding these problems, the prosperity and growth of the 1980s generated real-estate and stock-market bubbles, financed largely by increasingly speculative bank loans. The risk-averse restraints on Japanese banking had changed in the face of neoliberal reform. Under pressure from the United States and some business leaders, the state had forsaken much of its institutional capacity for prudential financial supervision. Sensing trouble, the Bank of Japan began raising interest rates in 1990 to slowly deflate the bubbles. But in 1991 stock and land prices began a steep decline, losing 60 percent of their value in only a few years. This brought a sharp drop in investment, consumption, and demand. Economic growth slowed, and companies began shifting to part-time workers – a move that the government facilitated by easing labor market regulations. The result was increased economic inequality, which, following Keynesian logic, reduced aggregate demand further and weakened macroeconomic performance.[67] The government cut interest rates to zero to stimulate demand, but that did not work. Next, it turned to spending and deficit financing. According to Paul Krugman, that too failed because the government was too cautious, not spending enough to permanently reenergize the economy. The problem was that policymakers were unwilling to heed economists' advice. A reluctance to pursue politically unpopular policies that could have caused short-term economic pain was to blame.[68] Such inflexibility is a sign of the state's thin intellectual capacities, perhaps diminished too by neoliberalism's ascendance in policymaking circles. When investors saw that the budget deficit was projected to hit 10 percent of GDP, private capital markets began to tighten. To loosen them, the government put together a $500 billion bank stimulus plan. This too failed. In the end, it was growing exports – to the United States and China, whose economies were booming – that did the trick.[69] Japan's "lost decade" of the 1990s came to a close in 2002, but the country never regained its full economic strength.[70]

Some might wonder how a country as successful as Japan had been could so suddenly run into such serious problems. How could Japanese state capacities deteriorate so quickly? Just to be clear, although it is unusual, it is not unheard of for states to quickly change their institutional capacities. The Trump administration did just that in the United States in less than a single term in office. More to the point, this did not happen overnight in Japan; it unfolded gradually over more than a decade.[71]

The chipping away of state capacities continued to facilitate more market-oriented behavior. Yet Japan's economic problems persisted. Employment insecurity and economic inequality kept rising. Corporate governance reforms allowed firms to engage in practices that did not always improve their performance. The potential for risky behavior in the financial sector remains, especially now that the postal service has been privatized, which means that more savings are channeled through private profit-oriented financial firms. Moreover, the government transferred its authority for setting accounting standards to the private sector. Some now suspect that Japan has gone too far in cutting back its state capacities. For example, acknowledging that Japan has lost its competitive edge in information technology as a result of its shift toward a more market-based approach, the Ministry of Economy, Trade and Industry has advocated a return to old-style Japanese industrial policy – a renewal of state capacities.[72]

The emergence of new players in the region – first, the Asian Tigers (South Korea, Taiwan, Hong Kong, and Singapore), and more recently, Vietnam, Indonesia, Malaysia, Thailand, the Philippines, and, of course, China – has compounded Japan's competitive problems. Firms are outsourcing heavily to these countries and making investments there in infrastructure, industry, and technology. Supply chains within the region, especially for Asian manufacturers, are becoming common. Furthermore, extensive trading relationships now link these countries, also diminishing their dependence on American and European exports. Political leaders in these countries tend to use a similar developmental formula: export-oriented state-capitalism *plus* special economic zones to attract foreign capital *plus* capital controls to prevent short-term capital flight *plus* Listian protectionism for key sectors *plus* industrial policy to stimulate those sectors. This has involved building up state capacities for economic regulation, Keynesian macroeconomic management, and Smithian human capital formation. All of this is a world away from neoliberalism.[73]

Singapore is a prime example. In 2018, the WEF ranked Singapore the third most competitive economy in the world, and it has been in the top five for the last decade. Although it is an autocratic state, it is also a technocratic one, with a meritocratic system of recruitment and advancement that ensures competent leadership and a rigorous approach to policymaking, often involving long-range planning by a highly trained professional civil service. Under their direction, the state has spent billions of dollars on infrastructure and public goods to attract FDI and promote local innovation, particularly in high-tech sectors such as biomedical research. The government has also minimized ethnic and religious tensions both coercively and benevolently, such as by equitably distributing various government benefits among the country's ethnic groups. And it has worked to reduce income inequality and facilitate intergenerational mobility, albeit with mixed results. In short, success has stemmed from both abundant state capacities and political efforts to facilitate social cohesion that help to counterbalance the lack of citizens' voice in this autocratic system.[74]

Singapore's thick state capacities enabled it to respond quickly and effectively to the coronavirus pandemic. It coordinated the response across all levels of government.

It imposed restrictions on anyone who had recently been to China and mandated strict quarantine rules for those possibly infected, backed up with a sophisticated text-based mobile communications system to ensure compliance. It also possessed excellent epidemiological surveillance and contact-tracing capacities, as well as ready-made quarantine facilities, including a national center for infectious disease management.[75]

Other countries in the region benefited from their own thick state capacities. Taiwan and Hong Kong were especially vulnerable to the virus, given their extensive travel connections with mainland China, where the virus originated. However, both remembered the SARS crisis of 2003 and learned that the faster the response, the more effectively such an outbreak could be controlled.

The ability of policymakers to learn is an important part of state capacity. In Taiwan's case, it also helped that the vice-president was an expert epidemiologist. Taiwan swiftly established an outstanding testing and contact-tracing system. Hong Kong moved early to enforce quarantine and to require social distancing and masks. South Korea's response was also impressive. The government met with medical suppliers as soon as the virus appeared, getting them to mass produce test kits, which were quickly deployed for large-scale testing. The region's results were impressive: By November 2020, Singapore's coronavirus death rate was 0.5 per 100,000 cases; Taiwan's was 0.03; South Korea's was 0.93; and Japan's was 1.4. This was far better than the United Kingdom (73.9), the United States (72.6), and even Denmark (12.82).[76] Moreover, these East Asian countries also fared better economically during the pandemic. By late summer, forecasters had predicted that

Singapore's economy would contract by 5.4 percent of GDP in 2020; Taiwan's, by 0.5 percent; Japan's, by 4.9; and South Korea's, by 1.1 percent. This was much better than predictions for the United Kingdom and the United States, as noted earlier.[77]

The pandemic underscored just how interconnected and fragile global capitalism had become. Change in one place could reverberate quickly throughout the rest of the world, upsetting life everywhere – depending very much on state capacities. This brings us to the changing architecture of capitalism.

Transforming the Architecture of Capitalism

In the introduction to this book, we explained that capitalism prospers when the international community is cohesive and enjoys transnational state capacities that coordinate their activities and mitigate conflict. We also argued that this is more likely in the presence of a benign hegemonic power. Absent that, as Keynes understood, capitalism runs into trouble. We also explained that state capacities and social cohesion within countries can influence international capacities for economic management and cohesion. In particular, change in the hegemonic state's capacities can spark change in the architecture of international capitalism.

The architecture of postwar capitalism was established by the United States at Bretton Woods, and it survived in muted form even after the link between the dollar and gold was abandoned in 1971. The United States remains the hegemonic power: Most trade is conducted using the dollar; interest rates are lower for the United States; the consequences of "printing money" are less onerous for the United States than most countries; and the United States' allies tend to support rather than attack the currency of the country on which their defense depends. But that architecture is changing, and so too is the behavior of the country that had done most to create it.

While not everything about capitalist society has turned sour during these recent decades – as we noted earlier, inequality across countries, although not so much within them, has declined – serious worries remain. At the center of them are the facts that China has emerged as an economic powerhouse and that the predatory behavior of the United States has increased. Each has much to do with the other's changing state capacities.

The Rising Asian Power

China's rise as a world economic power means that the center of the world economy is shifting toward the East. By some measures, China has the largest economy in the world, accounting for roughly 18 percent of world GDP in 2018, followed by the United States, with about 15 percent. Adjusting for exchange-rate differences, the Chinese economy is only about two-thirds that of the United States. Between 2008 and 2018, China's average annual economic growth rate was an eye-popping 7.9 percent compared to a paltry 1.4 percent in the United States.[78]

There are many reasons for China's phenomenal success, but improvements in its state capacities are a very important part of the story. Figure 5.8 charts changes in the quality of public institutions in China and the United States

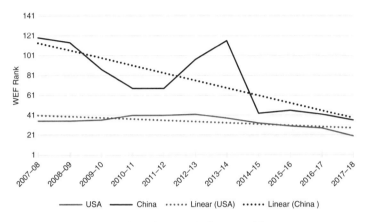

Figure 5.8 Quality of U.S. and Chinese public institutions, 2007–2018
Source: World Economic Forum (2019a).

based on their WEF rankings over the last decade. The lower the number, the better the institutional rank. The solid lines represent actual fluctuations in the rankings, while the dotted lines are the general trends. China has been catching up to the United States. How did this happen?

To begin with, the Chinese state has upgraded its intellectual capacities. It sends teams of bureaucrats and experts to other countries to identify and then import policy best practices from abroad. It has also improved its educational system, not only because it is a source of innovation and productivity – a move consistent with Smith's thinking – but also because the state needs a steady supply of well-educated officials and technocrats. Government spending per capita on urban education more than doubled between 2006 and 2016. As a result, China's WEF educational quality ranking rose from seventy-eight to forty-seven over the last decade.[79] China has also sent students abroad in increasing numbers, especially for graduate education.[80] So, although China is a country based on one-party rule, its system is one of meritocratic authoritarianism.

China has also fortified its state capacities by accumulating wealth. Thanks to its rapidly expanding exports, the state has amassed vast reserves of hard currency and related assets, primarily in dollars but also in euro, yen, and other currencies; these assets grew from less than $250 billion in 2000 to over $3 trillion by 2013. Moreover, Chinese workers and businesses have saved money at an unprecedented and increasing rate, rising from 37 percent of GDP in 1988 to 53 percent of GDP by 2012. Much of it was deposited in state banks, but some of it went to the state as tax revenues, which doubled between 1998 and 2011. As China became richer, the state's fiscal capacities thickened. It put these capacities to good use investing in infrastructure, energy, and education. But it also invested outside the country.[81]

In the last forty years, Chinese political leaders have been smart, strategic, and disciplined in facilitating China's rise as a world economic power – a clear sign of intellectual capacity. They have exercised great patience in their strategic planning, often taking the long view. For example, China has purchased more than $1 trillion of U.S. government debt in part to keep the value of the dollar strong relative to the yuan – a ploy that boosts Chinese exports to the United States by keeping them inexpensive for American consumers.[82] More impressive is China's Belt and Road Initiative, scheduled for completion in 2049. This is a massive land and sea infrastructure project, funded partly by Beijing, designed to link dozens of countries around the world, from Asia to Europe, Russia, and parts of Africa. When finished, it will constitute a vast network of railways, energy pipelines, highways, and streamlined border crossings, with more than fifty special economic zones along its routes. It will be the largest infrastructure project in history. Closer to home, China has put its capacities to work building an East Asian regional political economy that may eventually rival that of the North American–West European part of the triad region. Chinese investments throughout the East Asian region have been extensive and have helped to fuel economic growth among its neighbors. Some observers think that even if China does not become some sort of global hegemon, it will at least anchor a pan-Asian political-economic mega system.[83] It has also taken steps to build new financial systems that may eventually rival those of the American-led ones.

Of course, China is not without its problems. One is rising inequality, particularly between rural and urban areas, which can undermine social cohesion to the detriment of economic growth and stability. A second is the possibility of institutionalized corruption in an enormous state with many levels of government spread across a vast area – something that can compromise the state's institutional capacities for tax collection, spending, and decision making. Third is state authoritarianism and repression, particularly when it runs into demands for human rights and democracy. The state has had no qualms about jailing dissidents, much to the dismay of international human rights groups, although it initially exhibited surprising restraint in dealing with the current protests in Hong Kong. The government recently stepped up its repression of 13 million Turkic Muslims in the northwestern Xinjian region; its repression of social action in Tibet is well known. This is repulsive and echoes the European pattern of forcible assimilation discussed earlier. It is too soon to know whether such coercion will create rather than destroy social cohesion. But, so far, the threats to social cohesion within China have been contained, because most citizens trust the state's technocratic expertise and other capacities, which have managed to keep the economy flourishing to most people's benefit.[84] Smith's societal escalator seems to be successfully in place.

China is also becoming a global military power. Further, it has blended its economic and military capacities by encouraging Chinese firms to pirate and reverse engineer technology from the United States. While *The Economist* recently suggested that China and the United States are now engaged in a new technological cold war, it is too soon to make such a clear statement. It is certain, however, that China is challenging both U.S. military and economic power in ways that inject more uncertainty and risk into the world, particularly because the United States has responded aggressively.[85] That is the important point: firms and investors hate uncertainty and balk at doing things that would promote economic growth if the uncertainties they face were to get out of hand. Growing tensions between the United States and China brings us to the issue of American hegemony.

American Hegemony in Question

Maintaining thick state capacities is especially important for the hegemonic power that serves as the cornerstone of global capitalism. If they begin to deteriorate, hegemonic power can change, with significant consequences for the stability and prosperity of capitalism. State capacities have certainly thinned in the United States, and this is affecting its role in the world. In the immediate postwar decades, the United States was a relatively benign hegemon, willingly taking a leadership role in the world and showing some respect for its allies and trading partners. Nowadays, it is more predatory: a leader acting like an unpredictable tyrant in ways that disturb the international architecture of capitalism. How this happened is a story of geopolitics and the erratic policies of the Trump administration.

We begin with the geopolitics of war. The Second World War and Korean conflict established the United States as the world's principal defender of capitalism. But the Vietnam War was a fiasco that raised questions about whether the United States was acting as a benign hegemon or a more predatory one. These doubts grew after the terrorist attacks of September 11, 2001. The Bush administration's response was to invade Afghanistan in 2001 and Iraq in 2003. The goal was to root out the terrorists and their supporters and, in Iraq's case, to take down Saddam Hussein, allegedly in possession of weapons of mass destruction. But the United States lied to justify its actions and elicit support from its allies.[86] Saddam Hussein did not have weapons of mass destruction nor was there much evidence that he did. And, contrary to American predictions that the wars would be short and that the invasion would help to democratize the region, they ended up being long; they were costly financially, culturally, and in blood; and they spawned further terrorism around the world.[87] The

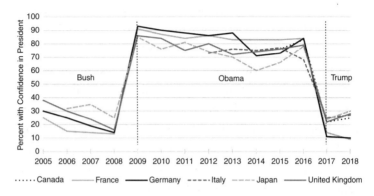

Figure 5.9 Percent saying they have a lot or some confidence in the U.S. president, 2005–2018
Source: Pew Research Center (2018a).

disconnect between the administration's predictions and these outcomes reflected the state's thin intellectual capacities. As a result, surveys showed that the United States' international reputation deteriorated sharply after the invasion of Iraq, recovering only during the Obama administration, as, for example, Figure 5.9 illustrates.[88]

The predatory shift in American hegemony worsened during the Trump administration. This was the United States trying to bully and extract rather than lead. This was partly a problem of diminishing expertise at the State Department.[89] To begin with, the president ignored diplomatic protocol, embarrassing and insulting the leaders of many American allies and lavishing praise on authoritarian adversaries such as Russian President Vladimir Putin and North Korea's Kim Jong-Un. He also turned his back on multilateral treaties, such as the Paris climate accord. He also refused to confirm

American support for allies in the North Atlantic Treaty Organization (NATO) if they were attacked; he abandoned Kurdish allies in the Syrian conflict; he pulled back from the World Trade Organization; and, in the midst of the coronavirus pandemic, he withdrew U.S. funding from the World Health Organization. Condemnation of these moves was widespread. German Chancellor Angela Merkel exclaimed, "I can only say that we Europeans must really take our fate into our own hands." Others worried that "the United States is less interested in leading globally than has been the case for the last 70 years," and that the country "has forgotten why [its] leadership is important and is flushing its power – and its reputation – down the drain."[90]

But most critical to the stability and prosperity of world capitalism was the Trump administration's disregard for international trade agreements. Soon after taking office, the president announced that the United States would not participate in the Trans-Pacific Partnership and would abandon the North American Free Trade Agreement (NAFTA). Then, in 2018, ignoring advice from some of his top economic advisors, he imposed tariffs on $250 billion worth of Chinese imports. He naively thought this would reduce the trade deficit with China.

This was List's theory in reverse: the desire of a great power to stay on top by protecting its industrial strength with tariffs as opposed to a developing country using them to grow its economy. It made little sense to target tariffs at a large, secure state with its own enormous internal market. China retaliated with tariffs on $110 billion of American imports and blacklisted certain American firms so that they could no

longer work with Chinese companies. China also began looking for markets elsewhere. At a 2019 meeting of the G20
countries, world leaders warned that Trump's predatory
trade policies were threatening the global economy. France's
finance minister worried that a full-blown trade war might
soon break out – a "situation [that] would lead to an economic crisis, to a lack of growth, and to a slowdown everywhere in the world."

In fact, even before the coronavirus pandemic, signs
of a slowdown were evident. German automobile manufacturers, for instance, feared the possibility of tariffs on their
imports to the United States, and they cut back on spending
and investment as a consequence. The World Bank, the IMF,
and the ECB all lamented that Trump's trade war with China
and others had cut demand for exports and upset the global
economy.[91]

According to some of Trump's own intelligence and
economic experts, these and other unilateral trade moves
strained traditional alliances and prompted foreign partners
to seek trade relationships elsewhere.[92] Many firms began
reorganizing their international supply chains.[93] The United
States could have managed China's rise in a less antagonistic
way and in a way that did not alienate America's allies.
Evidence that it did not can be seen in the fact that several
European countries have joined the Chinese-sponsored Asian
Infrastructure Investment Bank despite American objections.
Furthermore, to date, only a few of the United States' thirty-
five European and Asian allies have agreed to its request to
ban Huawei, the Chinese telecommunications giant, from
building 5G telecommunications systems in their countries.

Fed chair Powell expressed dismay in September 2019 about the ongoing trade war with China, stating that "uncertainty around trade policy is causing some companies to hold back now on investment . . . We've been hearing quite a bit about uncertainty . . . they want some certainty that the demand will be there."[94] Adam Posen, president of the Peterson Institute for International Economics, was more blunt: "This is now the post-American world economy . . . The world is a riskier place, where access to markets is a lot less sure . . . In a world in which there is arbitrary use of commercial regulation by the United States, no cross-border investment looks to be as safe and useful as it used to."[95] Amplifying this uncertainty was the fact that the Trump administration had arbitrarily wielded tariffs to gain concessions from countries for things that had nothing to do with trade, for example threatening Mexico, its largest trading partner, with tariffs unless it stopped its own nationals from migrating to the United States.

Many of the administration's trade moves stemmed from a sheer lack of competence in international trade – another indication of the state's diminishing intellectual capacity. The administration was wrong to obsess over Chinese merchandise imports to the United States, because they constituted only a small fraction of the American current account deficit with the rest of the world.[96] Furthermore, most independent economists warned that imposing tariffs would neither open the Chinese market for American products nor force China to refrain from subsidizing their exports. Indeed, China responded with tariffs of its own on American products. Economists also cautioned – despite Trump's promises – that tariffs would not be paid for by the Chinese but rather by

American firms and consumers buying imports from China. For example, the imposition of duties on steel and aluminum raised the prices for cars and washing machines produced in the United States. The cost of products assembled in China – most obviously, the Apple iPhone – rose too.[97]

The uncertainty that Trump's tariff policies created translated into volatility and instability in world capital markets. Since the administration ended tariff exemptions for imports from the European Union, Mexico, and Canada in 2018, then began imposing tariffs on Chinese imports, major American, Chinese, and Mexican stock markets have become increasingly volatile.[98] Moreover, the American and Chinese economies both slipped significantly in the world competitiveness rankings as a result of the increased uncertainty their companies faced as a result of the trade war.[99]

There is another way in which the United States has become a more predatory hegemon. Because the dollar is the world's reserve currency, it is the preferred currency of central banks and capital markets, and it is the favored form of foreign-exchange reserves. Most international transactions are cleared in dollars through New York corresponding banks. The United States holds sway over the Society for Worldwide Interbank Financial Telecommunication (SWIFT), the dominant payments-messaging system that banks around the world use to transfer funds. The problem is that, since the September 2001 terrorist attacks and especially during Trump's presidency, the United States has weaponized this system by threatening firms and individuals that they would be shut out if they were not to bow to its wishes. Being shut out of SWIFT would be a crippling financial blow. For instance, Trump threatened to deny Europeans access to Wall Street if they were to trade with Iran after the United States imposed new sanctions on that country. Similarly, the ability to blacklist a company such as Huawei ultimately rested on punishing those who did business with it through the dollar-based banking and payments system.

Weaponizing the financial system in this way further upsets the architecture of international capitalism, especially if countries create alternative systems.[100] This is already happening. After the 2008 financial crisis, China began to reduce its dependence on the dollar by promoting bilateral currency swap agreements with other countries and by allowing trade deals with Japan to be settled without using dollars. The rest of the BRICS countries (Brazil, Russia, India, and South Africa) did the same. The Bank of Japan opened swap lines with India and the ECB.[101] Additionally, the IMF added Australian and Canadian dollars to its list of the world's safest currencies – a list that already included four others, including the euro, pound sterling, and yen, as well as the dollar.[102] More recently, it appears that China, India, and other countries are considering a jointly run alternative to the SWIFT system. And the European Union has tried to find a way to allow its banks and firms to continue trading with Iran despite American sanctions against doing so.[103]

Thanks to policy moves such as these, according to the Wharton School's Mauro Guillén, "The dollar and the country whose government issues it, and stands by it, is showing clear signs of fatigue." Not only is the dollar becoming less important as an anchor for other currencies, says Guillén, but also its share of world currency reserves have dropped from close to 100 percent in the 1950s to roughly 60 percent today.[104] Some economists go further, arguing that the dollar-centric system and therefore American financial hegemony will not last.[105] In fact, this is still an open question. For the power of the United States is still present, and it is very hard to predict the tipping point. It is clear that the international reputation of the United States has plummeted. Its botched handling of the coronavirus damaged its reputation among allies even further as majorities in many European countries lost faith in the United States as a global leader. Chancellor Merkel summed it up in 2020 when she told reporters that the world could no longer assume that the United States still wanted to be a global leader. That the United States under Trump brought more disorder than order to the world suggested that the tipping point might come sooner rather than later. Europeans in several countries warmed to the idea of more cooperation within the European Union.[106]

President Biden is changing this picture. The United States has rejoined the Paris climate accord and the World Health Organization, and it wants to restore new relationships with Iran. Cordiality and civility have been restored with allied powers. This development matters, albeit not always in the best ways: it is likely to undermine European determination – never strong in the first place – to take greater charge of their own military affairs, although that will not stop the United States from insisting that they make greater financial contributions to NATO. That last comment points toward a fundamental feature of foreign policy – namely, the fact that its contours often remain the same across party or regime change. By and large, the U.S. Democratic Party has signed on to a view that China is a threat, with Biden championing a campaign to "buy American." Although there may be some changes in the relationship between the two greatest powers of the contemporary world, little indication is present of sophisticated plans to manage the relationship between them with imagination and skill. Trouble in this arena still lies ahead.

Conclusion

Our first conclusion, surprisingly, stresses continuity. If we were writing this book a few years ago, we would have had to discuss the BRICS countries as rising economic powers.[107] However, other than China, these countries have languished for reasons involving their state capacities, which are thin compared to those of many other countries. All of them have been hampered in varying degree by corruption, scandal, lax regulation, nepotism, cronyism, and government inefficiency.[108]

But our second conclusion, summarizing the contents of this chapter, stresses change. The capacities of many states within the OECD have diminished, while China's have improved with dramatic effect. More important, however, is another point. Thomas Hobbes famously declared that without a sovereign – a Leviathan state – able to establish order, life would be nasty, brutish, and short. That was true internationally of the era of the two world wars, with order established in 1945 thanks very much to the United States' benign hegemony, which helped capitalism to prosper. But one must remember John Locke's response to Hobbes: what if the

Leviathan behaves badly, using power for entirely self-interested, predatory ends? That is what has happened as the architecture of the world economy has been subjected to threat. This raises the obvious question: what will happen next?

6

What Next?

We began this book by presenting the ideas of great economists that have been unduly neglected. Smith recognized that capitalism works best when people seek to catch those above them on the societal escalator. That requires a sense that they are at least on the escalator – something stressed too by Polanyi, who was well aware of the dangers that could follow if people were to feel themselves to be left out altogether. Keynes wanted the state to smooth out capitalism's instabilities – notably, persistent unemployment – which often stemmed from the creative destruction that Schumpeter described. Hirschman understood that another way of ensuring that capitalism worked for everyone was to provide voice to all of its stakeholders.

We have extended these insights so as to highlight two elements necessary for capitalism to function. Thick state capacities, both intellectual and institutional, are crucial. The former involves thoughtful political leadership and policy-making based on the best expertise available; the latter involves a wide array of policy tools and the authority to use them. Together, they enable policymakers to respond flexibly to whatever challenges capitalism presents. This is important not only at the domestic level but also at the international level, where transnational organizations that have developed these capacities have benefited capitalism. So too has been the presence of a relatively benign hegemonic power willing to provide international leadership for the capitalist world.

The second way in which we have extended the insights in question is by showing how important social cohesion is for capitalism. When people believe that they can improve their lot in life, when they see that inequality is limited, and when they do not resent the class or nationalist differences between them, they will live their lives within the limits of the system. The possibility for social cohesion is enhanced when institutions provide all groups in society with adequate voice in policymaking and economic decision making. But when voice is absent, when belief in the possibilities of mobility and egalitarianism disappears, and when class and nationalist differences become politicized, especially when they overlap, capitalism runs into trouble.

All of the economists discussed echo and amplify the hopes of Adam Smith for a world of commercial sociability resting upon social cohesion and substantial state capacity. That point of view is morally powerful and sociologically astute. Capitalism prospered in the Golden Years after 1945, because it had these two elements. Several factors increased social cohesion. The Second World War helped to brutally homogenize national populations in Europe, with reductions in economic inequality resulting everywhere in the advanced world as the result of mass military mobilization. Unions gained strength, corporatist institutions were created, capital–labor accords were forged, and wage increases were pegged to productivity increases. The Cold War boosted social cohesion nationally and internationally. State capacities increased too. The Keynesian revolution went hand in hand with state building, including welfare state expansion, greater capacities for raising revenues, and the growing importance of economic expertise for policymaking. Finally, the United States emerged as the capitalist world's hegemonic power, spearheading the creation of an international architecture for capitalism at Bretton Woods.

But times have changed, and the Golden Age has gone. Globalization led to outsourcing, deindustrialization, and job loss in many advanced capitalist countries. Immigration increased, and national homogeneity decreased. Inequality grew. Unions became less important, corporatist bargaining came under attack, capital–labor agreements were abandoned, and Adam Smith's societal escalator broke down for many people, leading to the emergence of nationalism. The Cold War ended. For all these reasons, social cohesion started to deteriorate nationally and internationally. State capacity was undermined too when policymakers turned away from Keynesianism toward neoliberalism. The role of the United States became a problem rather than a solution. What seems to be emerging now is a more unstable, often nationalist, and cold-hearted form of capitalism.

So we begin this conclusion in a state of depression. This is not because we lack a sense of what needs to be done. We agree with the World Bank, for example, when it insists that states should aggressively implement policies to reduce inequality and increase economic mobility:

> The state can play a proactive role in "compensating" for differences in individual and family starting points to level the playing field in opportunities ... The state also has a prominent role to play in making markets work more efficiently and equitably, given that discrimination,

anticompetitive behavior, and market concentration are likely to constrain [economic mobility]. Fiscal policy is the most effective public policy tool for realizing many of these objectives, by raising resources for investments in public goods and reducing inequality through redistribution.[1]

Investments in early childhood education, labor market policies, and human capital formation also come to mind.[2]

But Karl Marx made us realize that a decent theory needs practical means of implementation if it is to become effective. This problem – combining theory and praxis – is daunting. Consider the recent work of French economist Thomas Piketty, who suggested that raising taxes on the wealthy up to 90 percent, giving a one-time "public inheritance" of $130,000 to every 25-year-old, and limiting shareholders' influence in corporate decision making would improve capitalism. His analysis of need is splendid, but the mechanism of correction is totally absent. Remember that the "Great Compression" in income and wealth that Piketty described came on the back of world war. Is a similar equalization of economic resources really possible during peacetime? That is a question without an easy answer. Yet it is a question well worth pondering, especially in light of the powerful social forces that would try to block this from happening.

Of course, other analysts have recognized some of the problems that we have identified, so we turn to them first in the hope that they may offer remedies. Some progress may come from what they show to be morally desirable, but we will review their proposals with the problem of praxis in mind. Next, we will highlight three entirely new and terribly dangerous problems facing contemporary capitalist society; they show that what capitalism needs now, perhaps more than ever, is state capacity and social cohesion. We finish by exploring the politics necessary for resolving these problems.

What Is to Be Done?

Perhaps the most original set of proposals can be found in economist Fred Hirsch's *Social Limits to Growth*.[3] This is an extraordinary book, in part because the title has two meanings – each of which suggests a distinctive thesis. First, Hirsch notes pessimistically, but correctly, that growth cannot solve our problems, because some goods are "positional" – that is, they are in limited supply, so only a few in the top positions of the social hierarchy can obtain them. Furthermore, the efforts of everyone to rise to the top is also self-defeating. Not everyone can afford to have a house on a small, quiet lake, but if they could, so many people might move there that the bucolic lifestyle and environment everyone wanted in the first place would be destroyed. This view has, as we will soon see, great relevance, given climate change. Hirsch's second thesis is very different. He suggests that a change in our current social arrangements might allow growth – seen now in a positive light – to resume after all, but free of conflict and with greater possibilities for equality. He notes, for example, that the best jobs, those with inherent interest, are also those with the highest rewards. Would it not be possible, he asks, to uncouple this mixture – to pay less for the more interesting jobs? Doing so would release funds with which to raise wages for other less-fulfilling jobs in the hope that this would lessen inequality, and therefore lead to less class conflict and more social cohesion. The idea of uncoupling economic rewards from status and self-satisfaction is very original, and there may be something to it. After all, academics have high status and rewarding occupations, but in many places their remuneration has fallen. In fact, we would both have been prepared to work for less, given the pleasure of research.

But, as sensible as this argument sounds, we are not convinced of its general viability. Hirsch does not really face the problem of power. How would it be possible, as a matter of policy, to remove the privileges of those prepared to defend them?

Political sociologist Colin Crouch is well aware of this when he writes that "the logic of politics is the logic of power, not that of the coherence of arguments."[4] He does not think that social democracy can change advanced capitalism and solve its problems, because the electoral base of social democratic parties has shrunk: trade unions are smaller and far less representative of the labor force than they used to be. In his view, we need instead to build up institutions in civil society – that is, to bolster social cohesion – not only rejuvenating social democratic parties and trade unions but also engaging churches, nonprofit organizations, nongovernmental agencies, volunteer organizations, and civic groups. Only organization can create an effective countermovement to corporate power.[5] Such a movement would seek to establish a new set of social priorities.

In this matter, Crouch is joined by economist Paul Collier, who insists that contact and dialogue among diverse groups in society is needed, so that they can learn from and become familiar with each other.[6] We certainly applaud and endorse the desire for political dialogue, but we are skeptical of some parts of Collier's position. He argues, for example, that better electoral systems are necessary – specifically, ones that encourage compromise and mitigate the influences of extremism, such as proportional representation. This is a tall order to fill. Proportional representation often comes on the back of political disaster, and efforts to introduce it in the United Kingdom and Canada failed. That said, it was introduced in New Zealand in peacetime, so there is at least a little room for hope. But the fact that the struggle to achieve new electoral systems will be hard also leads us to reject the views of Torben Iversen and David Soskice, who are extremely optimistic about the ability of democratic politics to respond to pressure from below and seem too to think that changing electoral systems will be relatively easy.[7] The world is simply a harder place to change than they are willing to admit, as is perhaps most apparent in the United States thanks to the influence of excessive amounts of money in politics, gerry-mandering, voter suppression efforts, and attacks on the judiciary – another example of obstructionist power in politics that even Crouch's civic groups might not be able to overcome.[8]

Economic sociologist Fred Block sees a deeper problem – namely, cognitive obstacles to meaningful reform. In his view, "virtually everybody – left, right, and center – believes both that our economy is capitalist and that the economy is autonomous, coherent, and regulated by its own internal logics ... [and] that if we pursue policies that conflict with the imperatives of capitalism, they will inevitably backfire and produce slower growth and fewer jobs."[9] He wrote these words before the coronavirus pandemic, so some people may have changed their minds. Nevertheless, he writes that if we can pierce this illusion, we will realize that we can build institutions, particularly at the global level, to better regulate capitalism. This is a call for thicker state capacities and greater social cohesion internationally. Block may be on to something here.

The Business Roundtable, an American lobbying organization of nearly 200 chief executives from some of the largest firms in the world, including Apple, Pepsi, Walmart and J.P. Morgan Chase, announced recently that its corporate members would no longer simply kowtow to the interests of their shareholders but would invest in their employees, deliver value to their customers, deal fairly and ethically with their suppliers, and protect the environment. Regardless of whether this was a response to a cognitive shift in corporate thinking or pressure from below in the form of consumer and stakeholder movements, the announcement was a dramatic break from decades of corporate orthodoxy driven by increasing social and political discontent over income inequality, dangerous products, lousy working conditions, environmental degradation, and global warming. This too was recognition of the need for greater social cohesion – sensitivity not only to the interests of shareholders but also to those of all stakeholders.

The obvious question is: How much of this was serious, and how much of it was just rhetorical window dressing? The Business Roundtable provided no specifics on how it would do these things. Further, the president of the Ford

Foundation remarked that the notion of short-term profit maximization and the pursuit of shareholder value "is so embedded in the psyche of investors and legal theory and the C.E.O. mindset. Overcoming that won't be easy."[10] As Block concedes, changing minds and rhetoric is fine, but it needs to be backed up with political muscle to affect substantive change – so we are back to our worries about praxis.

Not every analyst of capitalism's current troubles is able to propose reform. Political economist Wolfgang Streeck warns that contemporary capitalism is "collapsing from internal contradictions . . . What comes after capitalism in its final crisis, now underway, is . . . a prolonged period of social entropy, or disorder (and precisely for this reason a period of uncertainty and indeterminacy)."[11] What we are fast approaching, he believes, is a world in which individuals have to fend for themselves or occasionally work together in an ad hoc and unstable fashion, because neoliberal capitalism has "cleared away states, governments, borders, trade unions and other moderating forces" that used to provide the integrative source of social cohesion in capitalist societies around the world.[12] In other words, state capacities and social cohesion have been dangerously eroded. Streeck says that all of this is driven by the cumulative effects of three structural crises: the global stagflation of the 1970s, the explosion of public debt in the 1980s, and the rapidly rising private debt leading to the 2008 financial crisis. Economic stagnation, growing inequality, and rising debt became mutually reinforcing to the point in which nothing seems likely to break these trends – a perfect storm relentlessly blowing capitalism toward the abyss. Making matters worse, he says, capitalist countries are now facing a fourth crisis – very cheap money and deflationary pressures – which threatens to collapse the gigantic pyramid of debt that has been built up over the years, so as to finally crush capitalism. At the same time, Streeck says that democracy has been unravelling as political party membership has declined, parties have fragmented, and populism – especially right-wing populism – has risen. This has undermined the traditional democratic institutions that once spurred economic growth, moderated inequality, and guarded against these other destructive trends. Moreover, the growing political power of the financial sector now constitutes a kind of international private government riding roughshod over national governments at the expense of everybody else. The result of all this, he says, is a long list of maladies: prolonged economic stagnation; persistent and worsening inequality, which further undermines growth; plundering of the public domain through underfunding and privatizing government programs; rampant fraud, corruption, and greed; and, finally, the lack of a center – a hegemon – to stabilize the international monetary regime, act as an international lender of last resort, and guard against global anarchy.

Unfortunately, there is a good deal of truth in this analysis; it has obvious resonance with some of the arguments we have made. But we do not completely follow Streeck. He is too extreme: collapse is far less likely than instability, crises, and a system likely to benefit the few rather than the many. He is a pessimist – one who looks for problems and difficulties, and who thrills us with despair. We see immense difficulties too, but at least look in the opposite direction, grabbing onto such shreds of hope as are available, even though we appreciate the cognitive, normative, and institutional obstacles that must be overcome to bolster the state capacities and social cohesion necessary for capitalism to prosper – or, in Streeck's terms, to save capitalism from itself.

Sociologist Lane Kenworthy offers a far more optimistic view based on the idea that institutions are sticky and difficult to undo. He observes that, within the advanced capitalist world, state capacities have thickened incrementally: Tax burdens have become heavier; government spending has increased; and welfare states have grown.[13] He acknowledges that this is not a perfectly linear process; sometimes, conservative forces delay or even momentarily reverse these trends. But in the long run it continues – two steps forward for every step back. There may be some truth to this, but Kenworthy's optimism stems, ironically, from the same problem that plagues Streeck's pessimism: both assume a certain inevitability to change. In our view, this is too deterministic, because the politics behind economic inequality and mobility, social cohesion, state capacities, and American hegemony are contingent and very much up for grabs, especially in today's increasingly competitive capitalist world.

New Dangers

There are three new dangers to twenty-first-century capitalism – namely, the coronavirus pandemic, cyber threats, and the climate crisis. None can be resolved without substantial social cohesion and thick state capacities.

We have already discussed the pandemic, but a few things are worth reiterating. Containing, let alone eradicating, the virus requires substantial state capacity. States must heed the advice of public health and medical experts, be able to provide sufficient medical capacities to treat those infected, and coordinate a national response to prevent the spread of the virus. Containment also depends on the level of cohesion in a society. In the United States, to take an extreme example, wearing masks, social distancing, and to some extent even believing that there *is* a pandemic became politically polarized. The virus spiraled out of control as a result. In Denmark, by comparison, a small country with a high level of social cohesion, adhering to virus-related government mandates was unquestioned, and the country handled the crisis much more effectively. In contrast, Belgium, another small country, enjoyed much less social cohesion given its lack of strong national identity, and hence its unwieldly national bureaucracy was slow to respond to the crisis. Belgium consequently registered very high morbidity and mortality rates compared to those of other advanced countries.[14]

An effective vaccine will end this health crisis eventually, although the speed with which this happens will depend on the capacities of states and the level of cohesion within their societies. But this will not be the last pandemic, and we will do well to remember how easily zero-sum politics came to the fore during the COVID-19 crisis. Many of the steps that governments took to stop the pandemic were nationalist in character. Trump's frequent racist description of the virus as the "Kung Flu," a ploy to rally his electoral base, signifies this attitude. But other national leaders, including Hungary's Viktor Orbán and Poland's Andrzej Duda, also played the nationalist card during the crisis, aiming to enhance their power by invoking fear of "Others."[15] Some observers argue that if the European Union fails to organize an effective collective response to the economic crisis caused by the pandemic, the most devastated parts of Europe may succumb to right-wing nationalism or worse, further weakening the Union itself.[16] This form of nationalism is antithetical to capitalist prosperity.

Digital technology poses an entirely different threat to capitalism. Everyone knows how the digital age, computerization, and information technology have transformed our daily lives. There are certainly benefits. But there are downsides too. The first is market manipulation. Artificial intelligence and Big Data allow technology firms to develop and tap consumer markets. Giant tech-based companies such as Facebook, Alibaba, Oracle, Amazon, and Google have managed to use their information advantages to strengthen their market power, create ever more formidable barriers to market entry, and stifle competition.[17] They also use computer algorithms to shape people's market preferences by recommending things they might like to buy. In this regard, it should come as no surprise to readers of this book that if you bought it on Amazon, the next time you visit that website, you will probably find recommendations for other books on similar subjects. Market valuation algorithms do the same thing. For example, TripAdvisor is a website that more than 260 million people visit each month and which receives seventy new reviews every minute. It operates websites in thirty countries and posts information about 2.7 million travel-related businesses, including more than 725,000 hotels in 125,000 destinations worldwide. Based on the reviews it receives, its proprietary algorithm rates and ranks all the hotels in a region.

You might think that this is good for capitalism, because it provides information to consumers and weeds out good products from bad ones. But roughly one third of all online reviews are fake, and many are inaccurate, so the rankings you see may be terribly misleading, thus driving out the good products and leaving the bad.[18] Schumpeter never mentioned technologically driven creative destruction like this – especially insofar as it undermined, rather than improved, capitalist performance.

Cyber technologies also have the capacity to destabilize markets. For instance, automatic trading algorithms paired with high-speed computers and fiber-optic networks can now buy and sell vast amounts of stock in milliseconds, sending stock prices tumbling or soaring almost instantly and sometimes crashing financial markets. This happened on May 6, 2010, when the Dow Jones Industrial Average plunged nearly 1,000 points in only a few minutes. This "flash crash" wiped out nearly $1 trillion in shareholder value, only for the markets to rebound just as quickly.[19] Markets can also be destabilized by computer hackers that plant malware, launch web crawlers, and sabotage national banking systems, stock markets, communications networks, electric utilities, and nuclear power plants. For example, Iranian hackers have attacked some four dozen American financial organizations, including J.P. Morgan Chase, Bank of America, and the New York Stock Exchange, not to mention Saudi Arabia's enormous state-owned oil company Aramco. In 2014, the Russians hacked Ukrainian computer systems, causing temporary failures in automatic teller machines (ATMs), television broadcasts, software companies, local shops accepting credit cards, and virtually all business throughout the country.[20]

Hackers compromised hospital computer systems in the United States during the coronavirus pandemic.

The new digital technologies can also destabilize politics in ways that hurt capitalism. At the international level, revelations by Edward Snowden and others that the United States used technology to spy on its allies undermined the mutual trust upon which these long-standing alliances rested.[21] This can also upset traditional trade relations and other forms of international cooperation and commerce. The United States, for instance, has threatened China with trade sanctions over its use of Huawei and TikTok for purposes of data piracy and espionage. At the national level, digital technologies have helped to generate the social dynamite we mentioned earlier that can be so destructive to capitalism. Modern social media have helped to cage people within ideological echo chambers in which they are exposed only to the opinions, data, and information that confirm and reinforce what they already believe. Sometimes, this is the result of people's own choices, such as clicking on the same websites or Twitter feeds every day. But this is also something that is done to us by others.

For instance, Facebook uses algorithms to track our Internet clicks to identify our interests and political inclinations, so as to then feed us information that fits our digital profiles. More insidiously, organizations try to shape our opinions for politically partisan purposes. For example, Cambridge Analytica, a now defunct British firm specializing in mining and analyzing vast amounts of Internet data, helped to turn the tide in favor of both Brexit and Trump's presidential victory. Internet trolls and bots also disseminated misleading information to sway these events. As a result in large part of cyber activity such as this, our exposure to heterogenous information and opinions that give us the chance to reconsider our views and consider those of others is disappearing.[22] This erodes the civility, moderation, and social glue that plays a powerful, but neglected, role in holding society together.

The danger is compounded when foreign sources do these things deliberately to disrupt domestic politics. For example, Sweden has long been a paragon of social democratic capitalism. But Swedes are beginning to believe that immigration is threatening public safety, the social safety net, and their national culture. As a result, a new nationalist political party, the Sweden Democrats, has emerged, rooted in the neo-Nazi movement. It won nearly 6 percent of the vote in the 2010 elections – enough to enter the Swedish parliament for the first time. Since then, its popularity has increased. It has benefited enormously from an international cyber misinformation campaign that has been traced back, ironically, to both Putin's Russia and American right-wing extremists. Both provided support for websites, Facebook pages, and digital content that spread all sorts of nationalist propaganda, inflammatory claims, and fake news stories that often went viral. Counteracting these problems requires nation-states and corporations operating in this digital environment to develop very sophisticated technological capacities for monitoring the Internet, as well as a willingness to censor deceptive information and inflammatory rhetoric. Given their different constitutional and other legal capacities, some countries, such as Germany, are more likely to do this than others, such as the United States.

The climate crisis is a far more serious threat to capitalism, not to mention humanity. Global warming is causing sea levels to rise, as glaciers, polar ice sheets, and snow covers melt, and seawater warms and undergoes thermal expansion. This is already happening at an accelerating pace. Between 1992 and 2011, ice loss from the Greenland Ice Sheet increased sixfold, and Antarctic ice loss more than quadrupled. The rate of sea-level rise is also increasing. State-of-the-art scientific research predicts that the mean global sea level could rise as much as 6 feet by 2100. The consequences would be catastrophic. Some 680 million people (10 percent of the 2010 world population) live in low-lying coastal areas. In the United States alone, nearly 40 percent of the population lives in high population-density coastal areas where rising sea levels play a role in flooding, shoreline erosion, and storm hazards, such as the deadly and destructive storm surges associated with Hurricanes Katrina and Sandy. Short of that, rising sea levels entail more "nuisance flooding" that damages infrastructure such as roads, bridges, subways, sewage treatment plants, water supplies, and oil and gas wells. It increases the salinity of coastal wetlands and aquifers, and it worsens marine and freshwater ecosystems. Eight of the world's ten largest cities are near a coast and increasingly susceptible to these dangers.[23] Furthermore, global warming also increases the risk of drought, marine heatwaves, ocean acidification, land degradation, desertification, food shortage, and famine. It also contributes to devastating wildfires, landslides, avalanches, and ground destabilization.[24] Not surprisingly, then, the World Bank warns that "Climate change is an acute threat to global [economic] development and efforts to end poverty.

Without urgent action, climate change impacts could push an additional 100 million people into poverty by 2030."[25] In our view, the action required needs three elements in response: social cohesion and the capacity for political cooperation at the international level, and hegemonic leadership by the United States, one of the world's biggest polluters, to set a positive example for other countries to follow. Obviously, these needs are not being met with the requisite solutions.

The economic problems associated with the climate crisis are twofold. First, economic development will stall in countries currently trying to raise their standards of living. The World Bank estimates that the cost of extreme natural disasters is now equivalent to an annual loss of $520 billion in consumption. Second, as poverty increases, those affected will inevitably seek better economic opportunities elsewhere. The World Bank also predicts that, by 2050, there could be as many as 143 million people across three developing regions who will become climate migrants. That means a rise in immigration from poorer to richer countries. As we have seen, rising immigration is one of the reasons why anti-elite/ antiglobalization right-wing nationalism has been emerging in the advanced capitalist countries and undermining social cohesion.[26] Given the explosion likely in the number of climate migrants, things may get much worse.

We two authors now live in a world very different from that in which we began our own careers. Then it seemed automatic that growth was good, and that success could be measured in the increasing size of national product. That remains the case, but the problems of cleaner growth – growth that does not diminish the life expectations of later generations – are very considerable: an area of immense concern for us. It is the importance of the subject that makes us feel that Hirsch's discussion of positional goods is relevant. In his view, the individual pursuit of positional goods can wreak havoc on the environment as well as the economy. It is indeed true that if everyone wants a peaceful and healthy life in the countryside and buys a house there, the countryside eventually gets crowded, and the bucolic environment people sought in the first place is destroyed by suburbanization.

But we can go beyond this to make two slightly contradictory points. The first is obvious and pessimistic. Most of the people alive in the world today have not benefited from the standards of living of the advanced world; they will not be nor should they be denied the chance to achieve them. Thus this is an international problem requiring international cohesion, cooperation, and coordination, and the political capacities to achieve it. The Kyoto Protocol was established in 1995 to strengthen the international response to climate change – an agreement that bound the developed countries to emissions reduction targets for greenhouse gases. Eventually, 192 countries signed on to the deal; the United States refused to do so. In 2015, the Paris Agreement was reached whereby countries pledged to keep the global temperature rise to no more than 2°C above the preindustrial temperature levels. The rich countries agreed to help developing countries to reach that goal, and 186 countries ratified the Agreement. This time, the United States was on board – until, in 2017, Trump announced that it would withdraw because, as one who denied that global warming is caused by human activity, he believed that participating would hurt the American economy. Joe Biden has reversed this policy.

The second point goes in the opposite, more optimistic, direction. Considerable popular mobilization around the climate crisis has been evident in recent years in the advanced world, at times headed by Swedish teenager Greta Thunberg. Might it be the case that green politics will start to have a substantial political impact? There is talk within the Democratic Party, for example, of a "Green New Deal" for the United States. And green parties have recently made electoral inroads in Germany, France, the United Kingdom, and several other European countries. Whether their voices are heard in the halls of power depends on political pressure.

What Lies Ahead?

We began this conclusion affirming that changes in capitalism in the last forty years justify feelings of depression. Those feelings are reinforced in light of the three challenges just described. The pandemic, cyber threats, and the climate crisis pose dire threats to capitalism that can be managed effectively only in the presence of social cohesion and thick state capacities, both nationally and internationally. We have also made clear that we have serious doubts about the extent to which various remedies – breaking the link between status and reward (Hirsch), organizing civil society (Crouch), changing electoral systems (Collier), relying on democratic renewal (Soskice and Iversen), promoting cognitive epiphany (Block), and banking on institutional inertia (Kenworthy) – can change the structural patterns we have identified. Yet we are more hopeful than Streeck, and we support efforts made in those directions. We certainly believe that movements from below – whether among the general population, environmentalists, or those who feel painfully left behind – should not be scorned: they are the essence of democracy and need to be accommodated. Politics should not try to muzzle them but rather find ways of hearing them and take them seriously. In other words, we cannot return to the past but need policymakers, civic leaders, business, and the public to think more about what the future politics of capitalist societies may look like and how well they might address capitalism's challenges.

In this regard, we can make two fundamental points. First, capitalism has always come in different national forms, and the same has been true of its politics. That will not change. Second, the nation-state is not dead; very much to the contrary, it has proved its resilience even as the social bases of its support have changed. With this in mind, we offer a perspective on the politics of contemporary capitalism and the possibilities they offer for addressing the challenges to capitalism that we have identified. We summarize this perspective in Table 6.1. The horizontal axis comprises the traditional politics of the left and right. The vertical axis captures the politics supporting and opposing globalization – a relatively new dimension of politics that complicates the traditional left–right political divide. Note that the latter axis needs to be and will be interpreted generously, with immigration and environmental matters being mixed with more obvious economic concerns. This introduces some complexities to the discussion, but this complexity is inevitable. We do not pretend to completely capture the politics of the future; merely to point to pressures that will lead in different directions, all of which contain tensions of their own.

Table 6.1 *Today's comparative political landscape*

| | | Political Inclination | |
		Left	Right
Globalization	For	**1** *Social Democracy* Denmark Sweden Norway	**2** *Globalized Capitalism* England Switzerland
	Against	**4** *Democratic Populism* Bernie Sanders Podemos	**3** *Claustrophile Capitalism* United States Poland Hungary India

The first quadrant represents the traditional pro-welfare politics of the left combined with the more recent politics of pro-global market exchange. Denmark exemplifies this position. Here, we have considerable social cohesion and impressive state capacity, including a large welfare state, geared toward an open economy highly dependent on international trade. Nationalism here has long been a cohesive force allowing the country to swim in the global capitalist sea on which its prosperity has been based. Concern for environmental protection and climate change is also a central feature here – another indication of the country's pro-globalization location insofar as Denmark is an advocate for international cooperation in this area. A red–green political alliance between leftists and environmentalists is entirely possible here. But the most striking recent change, amounting to at least a temporary new equilibrium, is slightly different. The Social Democrats came to power, moving to the right, prepared to impose restrictions on immigration and to endorse or create policies for forcible assimilation, thereby regaining working-class support at the expense of the populist People's Party. But this move alienated the highly educated cosmopolitan voters of Copenhagen, who abandoned the Social Democrats, becoming either red or green. Stability results from the fact that the red–green alliance in fact supports the Social Democrats – albeit that its hands are clean, because they are outside the government. It may well be that there is now a general acceptance of anti-immigration policies. Not all good things go together, and it may be that limited openness to others may be the price paid if social democracy in general is likely to succeed, especially if an open international trading regime remains in place, not least as a result of high levels of human capital, infrastructure development, and other forms of extensive state support in these countries.

The second quadrant, globalized capitalism, exemplifies right-wing suspicions of welfare spending and too much state interference in the economy, with a strong preference for pro-global market exchange. Historically, the United Kingdom has fallen into this quadrant, particularly since the days of Margaret Thatcher. Although it is too early to be sure, it is very likely that the United Kingdom – or perhaps only England – will remain there insofar as it remains heavily dependent on international markets. However, things get more complicated in that hostility is shown to immigration and rather little is spent on the environment. We believe that the British approach will fail: Social cohesion will not increase, especially in the crucial area of human capital formation, and the intellectual and institutional capacities of the state look set to decline. But it is just possible that there may be a second, more successful, economic outcome in this quadrant. Switzerland is another complex case that is well integrated into the global economy and which ranks among the world's most competitive economies. It is conservatively corporatist, with labor unions playing only a minor role as compared to Scandinavia or Germany. It is smaller than the United Kingdom and has a much smaller welfare state, but it still benefits from its historical legacy of social cohesion, moderate state capacity, and environmental concern. It has also been open to and dependent on foreign workers, although it has recently become more hostile to immigration. Swiss attempts to change this pattern failed spectacularly: the country is small and vulnerable, and accordingly not prepared to engage in the illusions of the Brexiteers that will so deeply hurt the United Kingdom.

Politics in the third quadrant is also on the right, but it combines with antiglobalization in every way – a dislike of immigrants, resistance of free and open international markets, and disavowal of green policies. This is the world of rapidly diminishing state capacity in combination with domestic cultural wars in place of social cohesion. Countries here are nationally inward-looking: keen to be locked in and protected – that is, claustrophile. Poland and Hungary represent this quadrant, but the crucial case has been that of the United States under Trump. Of course, the United States is unique. The comparison with Denmark is instructive. The United States is very large, possesses a vast domestic market, and therefore is less reliant on the rest of the world for trading purposes – so this huge continental power at least has a decent chance of shutting itself off from the world. But there are unique problems here too. In particular, any increase in interest rates needed to fund borrowing may diminish the competitiveness of American goods overseas. Crucially, an increase in the power of money in politics may continue to diminish state capacity, increase political polarization, and undermine social cohesion. We do not believe that this mixture is stable or prone to economic success in the long run. That this is so in the United States carries grave implications for the rest of the capitalist world. One of the questions of the age is how much President Biden wants or is able to move the United States out of this quadrant.

The final quadrant, democratic populism, is leftist in seeking to protect people with expansive welfare programs. It is also antiglobalization in the sense that it wants to protect people from global economic interactions by means of tough trade agreements, and it finds huge multinational corporations to be anathema to equality and social justice. This is the world that Bernie Sanders advocated in his 2020 campaign for the American presidency when he railed against global corporations for taking jobs away from American workers, and it stands at the heart of Podemos, Spain's left-wing populist political alliance. There is complexity here too, because these politics are not hostile to immigration and are positively welcoming to green issues. It is also a quadrant that positions the state's role in the economy as very important. We are skeptical that social cohesion will come from this mixture nowadays or that the capacity of the state to achieve it is likely, at least in the United States. The crucial question however is simple: will there be votes for this option? Empirical evidence suggests not: Sanders's bid failed, and so too did the attempt of the Labour Party's Jeremy Corbyn – who offered something similar – to become prime minister in the United Kingdom.

These quadrants represent logical possibilities signified by prominent figures – Denmark's Prime Minister Mette Frederiksen, the United Kingdom's Boris Johnson, and Donald Trump and Bernie Sanders in the United States. Of course, life does not always fit neatly into a box; our intention in Table 6.1 is simply to encourage thought. We can move in this direction immediately by noting the particular complexities of fitting countries into our four quadrants. Germany is a good example. For one thing, Angela Merkel's decision to welcome immigrants was distinctively leftist and pro-globalization, especially as Germany has been committed to green politics and open markets. But she hails from the Christian Democratic Party, with more loyalty to rightist economic policies than many on the left would tolerate. For another, we should also be mindful of how countries may move within and sometimes between quadrants. Germany's reaction against the sudden surge of refugee immigration that Merkel allowed has moved that country somewhat closer to Trump's United States, although with the potential for greater stability given the possibility of a black–green political coalition between the Christian Democratic Union/Christian Social Union and environmentalists.

But it is what happens to the United States that matters most, given its hegemonic position in the world. Four factors suggest that it will not be easy for Biden to place the United States permanently on a better and secure footing. First, despite the fact that Biden promises to bring Republicans and Democrats together after years of gridlock and stalemate, it is hard to imagine that the polarization that has engulfed politics over the last few decades will suddenly disappear. Economic inequality persists; social mobility remains stalled for many people; and systemic racism still pervades many aspects of American life. The moneyed interests underlying political polarization have not disappeared either. Under these conditions, it will be hard for the Biden administration to restore social cohesion. The restoration of civility to public life will be a great blessing, but it is structural change that is needed. It is hard to see how it can be achieved.

Second, we are a bit more optimistic, as noted, about the Biden administration's chances of improving state capacities. Biden has moved swiftly to appoint people to his administration who are smart, have experience, and are inclined toward fact-based policymaking. Within a week of his election, he appointed a COVID-19 task force comprising leading scientists and public health officials to figure out how best to contain the further spread of the virus. Biden will try to chart a new course in health care, tax, and immigration policy, and in environmental, climate, and financial regulation. However, success will depend on whether Congress agrees to his proposals. It will also depend on how sympathetic the courts are to his administration's arguments when conservatives try to stop him. Trump's success in elevating three justices to the Supreme Court, thus locking in a conservative majority, will be a major hurdle for the Biden administration. In short, we expect marginal, but not sweeping, improvements in state capacities.

Third, American hegemony will shift back toward a somewhat more benign form on Biden's watch. The United States' allies breathed a sigh of relief when he was elected, because they knew that Biden was well versed in foreign policy and understood the importance of cultivating cooperative relationships with the country's allies. They also expected the United States to reject isolationism and resume at least some of its leadership roles in the world. In the short term, then, the United States' reputation and status in the world will improve. But the world will not soon forget how Trump moved aggressively in a predatory direction, turned his back on many of the country's allies, and walked away from a variety of treaties, agreements, and international organizations, thus destroying faith in the United States' word. One election will not soon restore that trust.

Finally, it is always possible that another version of Trump might come to power again, especially if the Biden years are not marked by substantial success. Remember that Trump still won more than 70 million impassioned votes in 2020. That danger is particularly acute when one considers that some of the Republican politicians whom Trump defeated to win the party's nomination in 2016 share many of his views, are likely to run for the nomination in 2024, and are politically smart and experienced. Put differently, the struggle over social cohesion, state capacities, and the United States' role in the world is not over.

All of this mandates a final reflection. Many may wish to slow down globalization, reduce political polarization, eliminate the sort of vicious nationalism we have described, and live in a world with greater chances for individual advancement and fulfillment. Many may hope that the state can facilitate these things. In other words, many may yearn for a better version of capitalism than that which we have now. We certainly do. Whether it is possible remains an open question. Capitalism is with us for the long haul, like it or not. Based on the insights of some of the greatest economists of all time, at least we know what capitalism needs to do better.

NOTES

Preface

1. Jones et al. (2020).

1 Sociology from Economics

1. Both Smith (2012, Book IV) and List (2005a, 2005b) used this terminology to describe their work and the work of their contemporaries.
2. Hodgson (1988); Philippon (2019); Piketty (2014).
3. Fourcade (2010); Yonay (1998).
4. Friedman (1962).
5. Stiglitz (2010), p. 289.
6. Krugman (2009), p. 10.
7. Drezner (2017), ch. 4; Stiglitz (2019), p. 20.
8. Smith (2012), p. 260. See also Smith (2016), p. 162.
9. Smith (2016).
10. Smith (2016), p. 44.
11. Smith (2016), pp. 104–106.
12. Smith (2016), pp. 159, 187, 217–218.
13. Smith (2012), p. 148; also pp. 49–56, 62.
14. Smith (2012), pp. 148–149.
15. Smith (2012), book I, ch. 8.
16. Smith (2012), pp. 80, 148–149.
17. Friedman (1978).

18. Hirschman (1992), p. 151.
19. Hirschman (1970), p. 19.
20. Hirschman (1970), pp. 33–43.
21. Hirschman (1970), p. 53.
22. Keynes (1964), p. 249.
23. Keynes (1964), p. 104, chs. 8–10.
24. Keynes (1964), pp. 372–373. A few contemporary economists have started to realize this too, including Joseph Stiglitz (2012, p. 83) who wrote that "[w]idely unequal societies do not function efficiently, and their economies are neither stable nor sustainable in the long run." See also Hirsch (1976).
25. Keynes (1964), p. 104.
26. Keynes (1964), p. 219; Keynes (1926), pt. IV.
27. Hirsch (1976), p. 123.
28. Keynes (1926), pt. IV; Keynes (1964), pp. 153–162, 220–221, 254, 378.
29. Hirsch (1976), p. 120.
30. Keynes (1964), p. 374.
31. Schumpeter (1942), pp. 31, 83.
32. See Schumpeter's speech, "Can Capitalism Survive?," in Swedberg (1991), ch. 8.
33. Schumpeter (1942), p. 134, ch. 12.
34. Rogan (2017), p. 61.
35. Polanyi (1944), pp. 29–30.
36. Polanyi (1944), p. 241.
37. Rogan (2017), pp. 83–91.
38. This is not to deny that war industries can stimulate capitalist innovation, production, and even state capacities. Our point is simply that prolonged prosperity throughout the capitalist world requires peace.
39. Alpert (2013), pp. 242–245; Skidelsky (2009), pp. 180–181.

40. This is not to say that the United States was ever a completely innocent hegemon. It certainly exercised plenty of soft diplomatic power in international affairs, particularly in its dealing with allies and advanced capitalist countries, but it was not averse to threatening and sometimes using brute force in other cases – notably, in Latin America, Africa, South East Asia, and the Middle East – especially when the Soviet Union was involved. Our point is simply that, since the middle of the last century, the United States has always vacillated between being a benign or predatory hegemon but with the balance shifting recently more toward the latter.

41. Philippon (2019).

42. Philippon (2019), pp. 292–293.

43. Mann (1970).

44. For more on what it means to be an "expert," see Nichols (2017) and Collins and Evans (2007).

45. Drezner (2017), ch. 1.

46. Gellner (1983), ch. 7.

47. Economic historians are becoming an exception, e.g. Johnson and Koyama (2017).

48. Hattam (1993); Katznelson (1985).

49. Berman (1998).

50. McDaniel (1988).

51. For a discussion of American patriotism along these lines, see Duina (2017).

2 Phoenix from the Ashes

1. Held et al. (1999), p. 156.

2. Lieven (2000).

3. Chickering (1984), pp. 289–290.

4. Judson (2016), pp. 383–384.
5. Maddison (2019).
6. Digital History (2019).
7. Mazower (1998), p. 113.
8. Keynes (1920), p. 69.
9. Prasad (2014), pp. 16–17, 273–274.
10. Keynes (1920).
11. Ikenberry (2001), ch. 5.
12. Mann (2012), p. 215.
13. Bernanke (2015), pp. 33–36.
14. Mann (2012), p. 230.
15. Chase (2005), ch. 2.
16. Held et al. (1999), pp. 157–158.
17. Mann (2012), ch. 7.
18. Samuels (2003), pts. I and II.
19. Mazower (1998).
20. Maddison (2003), tables 16, 5b.
21. Bolt et al. (2018) and authors' calculations.
22. Ortiz-Ospina et al. (2018).
23. Maddison (2001), table 3–8.
24. Maddison (2001), table 3–8.
25. Pauly (1997).
26. Ikenberry (2001), p. 190.
27. Skidelsky (2000), p. 358.
28. Prasad (2014), pp. 16–17. Eventually, the vast majority of the world's international reserves were held in dollar-denominated assets, and the dollar provided a safe haven for investors in times of economic turmoil, which put a premium on the value of the dollar and afforded the United States tremendous political and economic advantages over other countries.
29. Bukovansky (2010), p. 80.
30. Eichengreen (2018), p. 90.

31. Mazower (1998), ch. 9; Milward (1992).
32. For especially detailed discussions about the United States, see Mizruchi (2013) and Ferguson and Rogers (1986).
33. Even in places where the Communist Party remained influential, such as France and Italy, it was incorporated into the liberal democratic system. Put differently, granting it a legitimate voice in political and economic affairs mollified its otherwise revolutionary ambitions.
34. Piketty (2014), pp. 291, 324.
35. Scheidel (2017), ch. 5. This is not to deny that considerable economic inequalities remained in several capitalist countries, particularly when it came to the gender and race pay gaps. The Golden Age was much less golden for some of these groups than others.
36. Campbell (2018), p. 22.
37. Salant (1989).
38. Gourevitch (1989); Lee (1989).
39. Salant (1989).
40. Maddison (2001), table 3–9.
41. Hall (1989); Weir and Skocpol (1985).
42. Katzenstein (1985); Shonfield (1965).
43. Duina (1999).
44. Medrano (2003).
45. Koh (1989).
46. Gao (1997); Samuels (1987, 2003).
47. Janelli (1993).
48. Finegold (2006); Keating (2018); Khoo (2017); Mediacorp (2017).
49. Weiss (1998), ch. 3.
50. Evans (1995); Weiss (1998), ch. 3.
51. Campbell and Hall (2009); Patsiurko et al. (2013).
52. Ruggie (1983).

53. Dixon (2020).
54. Kindleberger (2013); Webb and Krasner (1989).

3 Storm Clouds

1. Sergent et al. (2020).
2. Gilpin (2000), pp. 57–70.
3. Gill and Law (1988), pp. 172–174; Gilpin (2000), pp. 68–70.
4. Gill and Law (1988), p. 72; Gilpin (2000), pp. 61, 70.
5. Eichengreen (2007), pp. 242–245; Gilpin (2000), pp. 68–70; Judt (2005), pp. 453–455.
6. A trade deficit arises when a country's imports of goods and services exceeds its exports. A current account deficit arises when a country spends more on imports than on exports, including not only goods and services, but also investment, salaries, pensions, money sent abroad, and other things – i.e. when more money is leaving the country than is coming in. The problem posed by a current account deficit is that the longer it lasts, the more it lands future generations with the accumulated debt and resulting interest payments.
7. Kenworthy (1997), table 7.
8. Judt (2005), p. 456.
9. Vogel (2018), p. 51.
10. Among many other studies, Bowles et al. (1983) documented the flaws in neoliberalism early in its heyday, while Blyth (2013) did so again three decades later in the wake of the 2008 financial crisis.
11. Fligstein (2001), ch. 9.
12. Campbell (2003), pp. 239–240.
13. Guillén (2015), p. 60.
14. Guillén and García-Canal (2010); Jensen (2006).

15. Mudge (2011). See also Crouch (2011) and Harvey (2005).
16. Swank (2002).
17. Bunch (2009); Pierson (1994).
18. Vogel (1996).
19. Simmons (1999), p. 37.
20. Simmons (1999).
21. Simmons (1999), p. 43.
22. Eichengreen (2007), pp. 242–243. See also Simmons (1999), pp. 40–41, on the emergence of offshore accounts in the 1960s and 1970s.
23. Krippner (2011), ch. 2.
24. Vogel (2018), p. 59.
25. Babb (2001); Dezalay and Garth (2002); Fourcade-Gourinchas and Babb (2002); Yonay (1998).
26. MacLean (2018); Teles (2008).
27. Campbell and Pedersen (2014), ch. 2.
28. Babb (2001, 2009); Dezalay and Garth (2002); Harvey (2005); Prasad (2006), p. 179.
29. Amsden et al. (1994); Campbell (2003); Stark and Bruszt (1998); Stiglitz (2002), ch. 5.
30. Gereffi (2005).
31. Simply put, the VAX ratio is the difference between value added and gross export. A declining VAX ratio indicates a decline in the domestic content – i.e. the value added – to goods and services. It helps to illustrate the growing prominence of global supply chains.
32. Johnson and Noguera (2017).
33. Howard (2019).
34. Bronfenbrenner (2007); Fantasia and Voss (2004).
35. Palier and Thelen (2012); Thelen and Kume (1999).
36. Thelen (2014), pp. 14–18, 34, 36.

37. Freeman (1994); Freeman and Katz (1994); Goldfield (1987); Rosenfeld (2014); Western (1997).
38. Western (1997).
39. Vogel (2018), p. 46.
40. Hicks and Kenworthy (1998); Kenworthy (2020).
41. Kapstein (1994).
42. Alpert (2013), ch. 4, pp. 240–242.
43. Reinhart (2012).
44. Clark et al. (2004), p. 5.
45. Clark et al. (2004), table 3.5.
46. Clark et al. (2004); Jacks et al. (2011). Cross-national historical data from the Central Bank of England (2019) indicate that, since 1986, although the overall trend in commodity price volatility has been nearly unchanged, there have been some dramatic short-term periods of increased volatility – notably, in 1988, 1999, and much of the period from 2008 to 2019.
47. Reinhart (2012), chart 6; Reinhart and Rogoff (2009), figs. 12.3 and 13.1.
48. Guillén (2015), p. 2.
49. Babb (2001), chs. 5–7; Krugman (2009), ch. 2.
50. Babb (2001); Stiglitz (2002), pp. 7, 81.
51. Babb (2001), pp. 190–198.
52. Krugman (2009), ch. 2.
53. Babb (2001), p. 194.
54. Corsetti et al. (1999); Wade and Veneroso (1998a, 1998b).
55. Atinc and Walton (1998).
56. Stiglitz (2002), p. 89.
57. Stiglitz (2002), ch. 4; Wade and Veneroso (1998a, 1998b).
58. Stiglitz (2002), pp. 113–118.
59. Wade and Veneroso (1998a, 1998b).
60. Pinto and Ulatov (2010), tables 3 and 4.
61. Stiglitz (2002), ch. 5.

62. Dungery et al. (2002), pp. 6, 11.

63. Mortgage-backed securities are bonds created by mixing bits and pieces of mortgages with different levels of risk, including subprime mortgages – i.e. adjustable-rate mortgages often sold to naive first-time homebuyers at great risk of defaulting on their mortgages should their interest rate rise.

64. The average interest rate on a fixed-rate thirty-year mortgage declined from nearly 19 percent in 1981 to 3.4 percent in July 2016. It then rose to 4.75 percent by mid-September 2017 (U.S. Federal Reserve Bank 2019d).

65. Tooze (2018), ch. 3.

66. Tooze (2018), p. 159.

67. Campbell (2011).

68. Vogel (2018), pp. 74–75.

69. Nutting (2008).

70. Tooze (2018), ch. 8.

71. Kirshner (2014).

72. Keegan (2012).

73. Koranyi and Canepa (2017).

74. Verlaine (2017).

75. Tooze (2018), ch. 7.

76. Campbell and Hall (2017).

4 Nationalism and Social Cohesion

1. Judt (2010).

2. Troy (2017).

3. Judt (2005, 2010).

4. Scheidel (2017).

5. Scheidel (2017), p. 1.

6. Woods (2020).

7. Piketty (2014).
8. Scheidel (2017).
9. Allen (1988); Harrington (2016).
10. There has been debate recently about how much income and wealth inequality there really is and by how much it has been growing. Much of the debate boils down to differences in how to measure inequality. See, e.g., *The Economist* (2020b).
11. Scheidel (2017), table 15.1.
12. Kenworthy (2019b).
13. Scheidel (2017), table 15.1. See also Milanovic (2018), Ostry et al. (2014), Thévenot (2017), and Voitchovsky (2005).
14. Milanovic (2018).
15. Friedman (1970).
16. For a review of the literature, see Ostry et al. (2014).
17. Kenworthy (2019a), pp. 101–102.
18. Stiglitz (2012).
19. Voitchovsky (2005).
20. Ostry et al. (2014).
21. Kenworthy (2019b), ch. 4.
22. Stiglitz (2012).
23. Stiglitz (2012), p. 93.
24. Wilkinson and Pickett (2009), ch. 8.
25. According to the Social Progress Index, in 2019 the United States ranked first in the world in medical technology but 97th in access to quality health care – a remarkably low ranking comparable to countries such as Chile, Jordan, and Albania (Kristof 2020b).
26. Wilkinson and Pickett (2009), chs. 5–7.
27. Stiglitz (2012), chs. 2 and 4.
28. Pew Research Center (2013).
29. International Monetary Fund (2019b); Jensen (2006); Voitchovsky (2005).

30. So-called contact theory was first formulated by Gordon Allport, but it has since been studied and often confirmed in various settings by sociologists, psychologists, and political scientists many times (Pettigrew 1998).

31. Kenworthy (2019a), pp. 48, 103; Kenworthy (2019b), ch. 4.

32. Katzenstein (1985, 2000, 2006); Zak and Knack (2001).

33. The Hamilton Project (2013); Narayan et al. (2018), ch. 4. See also Kenworthy (2019b), ch. 4.

34. Narayan et al. (2018), fig. 0.2 and pp. 2, 6, 16, 139. See also Piketty (2015), p. 81.

35. Narayan et al. (2018), pp. 23–25. See also Stiglitz (2012), pp. 94–104.

36. Leicht and Fitzgerald (2014); Mishel et al. (2012), p. 179.

37. Mishel et al. (2012), p. 405. See also Leicht and Fitzgerald (2014), ch. 5.

38. Blyth (2013); Campbell and Hall (2017), ch. 3; Eichengreen (2018), pp. 134–135; U.S. Congress Joint Economic Committee (2010); Woll (2014).

39. BBC News (2010).

40. Statista (2019).

41. Duina (2017).

42. Sachs (2019).

43. Mudge (2011).

44. Gellner (1983).

45. Eichengreen (2018), p. 145.

46. Milanovic (2016), ch. 1.

47. Rodrik (2005, 2011); Rodrik (2018), p. 5.

48. Milanovic (2019), p. 18.

49. Pew Research Center (2019).

50. Pew Research Center (2018b).

51. Pew Research Center (2018b).

52. Wuthnow (2018). See also Hochschild (2016) and Vance (2016).

53. Case and Deaton (2020).
54. American Farm Bureau Federation (2019).
55. Duina (2018).
56. Pasieka (2020).
57. Mamonova (2019).
58. Milanovic (2005), pp. 154–157.
59. OECD (2014), p. 2. The term "foreign-born" refers to people born outside their country of residence, including both naturalized citizens and noncitizens.
60. Guillén (2015), p. 29.
61. Kenworthy (2019b).
62. OECD (2014).
63. Patsiurko et al. (2012).
64. Kenworthy (2020), ch. 12.
65. Judis (2016), p. 97.
66. Eichengreen (2018), pp. 137–139.
67. Campbell (2018), p. 72.
68. Campbell (2018), pp. 71–74; Eichengreen (2018), pp. 110–111, 156.
69. Problems of perception are linked to patterns of residential segregation. As noted earlier, the less contact different groups have with each other, the more likely they are to be prejudiced against and distrustful of each other. Immigrants in a new land tend to cluster in areas along with others from their home country at least at first. Less residential mixing means that people are living more in residentially segregated silos with relatively less interaction across groups (Iceland 2014). This exacerbates some of the prejudice that fuels nationalism in the first place.
70. Schmidt and Otterbeck (2014).
71. Walker (2019).
72. Guillén (2015), pp. 148, 156.
73. BBC News (2019).

74. Campbell (2018).
75. Judt (2005, 2010).
76. Ascherson (2016); Barnes (2017); Finlayson (2017).
77. Fligstein (2008).
78. O'Reilly (2016).
79. Boyer (2016), p. 837; Le Galès (2016).
80. Frerichs and Sankari (2016); Le Galès (2016); Warhurst (2016).
81. See the *Comparative Labor Law and Policy Journal* (2020) for several examples of such restrictive labor market policies.
82. Campbell (2018), p. 76.

5 State Failure

1. Meek (2019).
2. OECD (2020a); Campbell (2004), p. 140.
3. Araujo (2011).
4. OECD (1997), p. 5.
5. World Bank (2020a) and authors' calculations. The median for the full OECD population increased from 3.2 to 3.5.
6. Amsden et al. (1994); Bromley (1989); Evans (1995); Hall and Soskice (2001); Hodgson (1988); Katzenstein (1985); Roe (2003); Williamson (1985).
7. Katzenstein (1985).
8. Campbell and Hall (2017).
9. Mizruchi (2013). See also Ferguson and Rogers (1986), Mayer (2016), and Skocpol and Williamson (2012).
10. International Monetary Fund (2013).
11. Collins and Evans (2007); Hochschild and Einstein (2015); Nichols (2017).
12. Lewis (2018).
13. Lewis (2018), pt. II.

14. By 2019, dozens of top positions had been vacated, including several cabinet-level posts. The rate of turnover in the Trump administration far exceeded that of the Obama, George W. Bush, or Clinton administrations (Yu and Yourish 2019).

15. Plumer and Davenport (2019). See also Corrigan (2018) and Davenport and Friedman (2019).

16. Sanger and Barnes (2019).

17. Blom (2018); Tankersley (2018).

18. LeBlanc (2019).

19. Mattis (2018); Sanger and Barnes (2019); Straqualursi (2018).

20. Wolf (2019).

21. Philippon (2019).

22. Irfan (2019); Tully (2019).

23. Jacobson (2018).

24. Heeb (2019).

25. U.S. Bureau of Labor Statistics (2020a).

26. Nunn et al. (2019).

27. Richter (2019). Three caveats are necessary. First, rising wages were largely a result of states raising the minimum wage, which had nothing to do with Trump's economic policies. Second, borrowing was likely helped by low interest rates. Third, since the financial crisis, household debt as a percentage of net disposable personal income has dropped from a high of 143 percent in 2007 to a low of 105 percent in 2018, and debt service payments as a percentage of disposable household income have declined from 13 percent in 2007 to 9.6 percent in early 2020 (OECD 2020b; U.S. Federal Reserve Bank 2020). However, these data lump together borrowing by households spanning the income range. It is impossible to tell from these data how much better or worse different income groups fared in terms of their relative debt and debt service burdens.

28. Blom (2018); Tankersley (2018).

29. Committee for a Responsible Federal Budget (2019).
30. *Financial Times* (2020).
31. Sergent et al. (2020).
32. Koronowski et al. (2020) provide a detailed timeline of the Trump administration's moves to cut budgets for public health and emergency management agencies, ignore warnings, and delay responses as the crisis unfolded.
33. Reuters Fact Check (2020).
34. Glanz and Robertson (2020).
35. U.S. House Committee on Oversight and Reform (2020).
36. U.S. Bureau of Labor Statistics (2020b).
37. Guzman (2020); Sardana (2020).
38. OECD (2020c).
39. Smialek et al. (2020).
40. U.S. Federal Reserve Bank (2019c).
41. Cheng et al. (2020).
42. Cheng et al. (2020).
43. Sergent et al. (2020).
44. Brenner (2020).
45. HM Treasury (2016).
46. OECD (2016).
47. Grey (2016); Wood and Wright (2016).
48. Castle (2020).
49. Colson (2018).
50. The Conversation (2017). See also Whitman (2019).
51. OECD (2016).
52. McBride (2016).
53. Guillén (2015), p. 142.
54. Alpert (2013), pp. 93–97; Blyth (2013).
55. Ireland did better not because of austerity but in spite of it – because it had a well-educated, English speaking labor force, sound digital infrastructure, especially favorable tax rates for

FDI, and easy access to the European market, all of which were attractive to foreign and particularly American investment. While FDI remained flat in the other PIIGS from 2005 to 2017, hovering slightly below the OECD average, it soared in Ireland from 61 percent of GDP in 2008, already twice the OECD average, to 313 percent in 2015.

56. Alpert (2013), p. 6.
57. Blyth (2013), p. 87.
58. Eurostat (2020).
59. Ventura (2018); World Economic Forum (2019c).
60. Blyth (2013).
61. Kristof (2020a); Thompson (2020).
62. Helm et al. (2020).
63. OECD (2020c).
64. Ellyatt (2020); Johns Hopkins University and Medicine (2020).
65. Steinmo (2010), ch. 3. See also Dore (1987), Koh (1989), Samuels (1987), and Vogel (2018), ch. 4.
66. Steinmo (2010), ch. 3.
67. Vogel (2018), pp. 96–100.
68. Amyx (2004).
69. Krugman (2009), ch. 3.
70. Abe (2010).
71. Vogel (1996, 2018).
72. Vogel (2018), pp. 114–116.
73. Khanna (2019), chs. 4 and 6.
74. Finegold (2006); Khanna (2019), pp. 286–299.
75. Heijmans (2020); Helm et al. (2020); Pepinsky (2020).
76. Johns Hopkins University and Medicine (2020).
77. Focus Economics (2020); OECD (2020c).
78. Frankel (2020).
79. World Economic Forum (2019a).
80. Deloitte China (2018), p. 18.

81. Alpert (2013), pp. 12–15.
82. Prasad (2014), ch. 8; Scott (2019).
83. Khanna (2019), pp. 9, 20, 75–76.
84. Khanna (2019), pp. 309–310.
85. *The Economist* (2019d).
86. Rich (2006).
87. Crawford (2018), p. 3; Esterbrook (2002); Murphy (2011).
88. Pew Research Center (2018a).
89. Corrigan (2018).
90. Frankel (2020); Kirkpatrick et al. (2019); Smale and Erlanger (2017).
91. *The Economist* (2019a); Partington (2019); Rappeport (2019); Smialek and Ewing (2019); Smialek et al. (2020).
92. Sanger and Barnes (2019).
93. Guillén (2019).
94. Imbert (2019).
95. Goodman (2019).
96. The current account deficit represents the amount a country borrows from abroad to finance its consumption and investment. If it sells less to other countries than it buys from them, it needs to borrow the money from abroad to make up the difference. The current account balance reflects net capital flows through all channels – official and private (Prasad 2014, pp. 3, 35–36).
97. *The Economist* (2019c, 2019d); Guillén (2019); Smialek et al. (2019).
98. *The Economist* (2019b).
99. BBC News (2020).
100. *The Economist* (2020a, 2019c); Rappeport (2019).
101. Khanna (2019), p. 144; Prasad (2014), pp. 209–214, 239–247.
102. International Monetary Fund (2013); Kirshner (2014), ch. 6.
103. *The Economist* (2020a, 2019a).

104. Guillén (2015), p. 111.
105. *The Economist* (2020a).
106. Butler (2020); Oltermann (2020).
107. In fact, that is what we did in the first edition of our book *The World of States* (Campbell and Hall 2021).
108. Business Anti-Corruption Portal (2019a, 2019b); Xu (2014).

6 What Next?

1. Narayan et al. (2018), p. 23.
2. Kenworthy (2019a), ch. 2; Narayan et al. (2018), pp. 23–25.
3. Hirsch (1976).
4. Crouch (2013), p. 3.
5. Crouch (2011). See also Stiglitz (2019), ch. 8.
6. Collier (2018), p. 17.
7. Iversen and Soskice (2019).
8. Stiglitz (2019), ch. 8.
9. Block (2018), p. 2.
10. Gelles and Yaffe-Bellany (2019).
11. Streeck (2016), p. 13.
12. Streeck (2016), p. 14.
13. Kenworthy (2020, 2019a, 2014).
14. Apuzzo and Pronczuk (2020).
15. Pasieka (2020).
16. Varoufakis and McWilliams (2020).
17. Foroohar (2019); Stiglitz (2019), ch. 6.
18. Orlikowski and Scott (2014).
19. Bauman (2013); Lewis (2014).
20. Sanger (2018).
21. Sanger (2018), chs. 3 and 4.
22. D'Ancona (2017); Sunstein (2017).

23. U.S. National Oceanic and Atmospheric Administration (2019).
24. Intergovernmental Panel on Climate Change (2019a, 2019b).
25. World Bank (2019b).
26. World Bank (2019b).

REFERENCES

Abe, Naoki. 2010. "Japan's Shrinking Economy." *Brookings Institution*, February 12. www.brookings.edu/opinions/japans-shrinking-economy/

Allen, Michael Patrick. 1988. *The Founding Fortunes*. New York: Dutton.

Alpert, Daniel. 2013. *The Age of Oversupply*. New York: Penguin.

American Farm Bureau Federation. 2019. "Rural Opioid Epidemic." *AFBF News*, October 2. www.fb.org/issues/other/rural-opioid-epidemic/

Amsden, Alice, Jacek Kochanowicz, and Lance Taylor. 1994. *The Market Meets Its Match*. Cambridge, MA: Harvard University Press.

Amyx, Jennifer. 2004. *Japan's Financial Crisis: Institutional Rigidity and Reluctant Change*. Princeton, NJ: Princeton University Press.

Appuzzo, Matt, and Monika Pronczuk. 2020. "After 2 Years of Paralysis Belgium Forms a (Very Fragile) Government." *The New York Times*, October 2. www.nytimes.com/2020/10/01/world/europe/belgium-government-coalition.html

Araujo, Sonia. 2011. "Has Deregulation Increased Investment in Infrastructure? Firm-Level Evidence from OECD Countries." OECD Economics Department Working Papers No. 892. Paris: OECD.

Ascherson, Neal. 2016. "England Prepared to Leave the World." *London Review of Books* 38(22): 7–10.

Atinc, Tamar Manukelykan, and Michael Walton. 1998. "Responding to the Global Financial Crisis: Social Consequences of the East Asian Financial Crisis." World Bank Working Paper. https://pdfs.semanticscholar.org/fbca/156ef53c7be5abc036f f116eeb30f20200f6.pdf

Babb, Sarah. 2009. *Behind the Development Banks: Washington Politics, World Poverty and the Wealth of Nations.* Chicago, IL: University of Chicago Press.

Babb, Sarah. 2001. *Managing Mexico: Economists from Nationalism to Neoliberalism.* Princeton, NJ: Princeton University Press.

Barnes, Julian. 2017. "Diary: People Will Hate Us Again." *London Review of Books* 39(8): 41–43.

Bauman, Nick. 2013. "Too Fast to Fail: How High-Speed Trading Fuels Wall Street Disasters." *Mother Jones*, January/February. www .motherjones.com/politics/2013/02/high-frequency-trading-danger -risk-wall-street/

BBC News. 2020. "US–China Trade War Takes Toll on Their Global Competitiveness." June 17. www.bbc.com/news/business– 53060436

BBC News. 2019. "Europe and Nationalism: A Country-by-Country Guide." April 29. www.bbc.com/news/world-europe–36130006

BBC News. 2010. "European Cities Hit by Anti-Austerity Protests." September 29. www.bbc.com/news/world-europe–11432579

Berman, Sheri. 1998. *The Social Democratic Moment.* Cambridge, MA: Harvard University Press.

Bernanke, Ben. 2015. *The Courage to Act.* New York: Norton.

Block, Fred. 2018. *Capitalism: The Future of an Illusion.* Berkeley, CA: University of California Press.

Blom, Terry. 2018. "CBO's Projections of Deficits and Debt for the 2018–2028 Period." April 19. Washington, DC: Congressional Budget Office. www.cbo.gov/publication/53781

Blyth, Mark. 2013. *Austerity.* New York: Oxford University Press.

Bolt, Jutta, Robert Inklaar, Herman de Jong, and Jan Luiten van Zanden. 2018. "Rebasing 'Maddison': New Income Comparisons and the Shape of Long-Run Economic Development." *Maddison Project Data Base*, version 2018. www.rug.nl/ggdc/historicaldeve lopment/maddison/releases/maddison-project-database-2018

Bowles, Samuel, David Gordon, and Thomas Weisskopf. 1983. *Beyond the Waste Land*. New York: Anchor/Doubleday.

Boyer, Robert. 2016. "Brexit: The Day of Reckoning for the Neo-Functionalist Paradigm of European Union." *Socio-Economic Review* 14(4): 836–840.

Brenner, Robert. 2020. "Escalating Plunder." *New Left Review* 123: 5–22.

Bromley, Daniel. 1989. *Economic Interests and Institutions*. London: Blackwell.

Bronfenbrenner, Kate, ed. 2007. *Global Unions: Challenging Transnational Capital through Cross-Border Campaigns*. Ithaca, NY: Cornell University Press.

Bukovansky, Mlada. 2010. "Institutionalized Hypocrisy and the Politics of Agricultural Trade." In Rawi Abdelal, Mark Blyth, and Craig Parsons, eds. *Constructing the International Economy*. Ithaca, NY: Cornell University Press, 68–90.

Bunch, Will. 2009. *Tear Down This Myth*. New York: The Free Press.

Business Anti-Corruption Portal. 2019a. *Brazil Corruption Report*. www.ganintegrity.com/portal/country-profiles/brazil/

Business Anti-Corruption Portal. 2019b. *South Africa Corruption Report*. www.ganintegrity.com/portal/country-profiles/south-africa/

Butler, Katherine. 2020. "Europeans' Trust in U.S. as World Leader Collapses During Pandemic." *The Guardian*, June 29. www .theguardian.com/world/2020/jun/29/europeans-trust-in-us-as -world-leader-collapses-during-pandemic

Campbell, John L. 2018. *American Discontent: The Rise of Donald Trump and Decline of the Golden Age*. New York: Oxford University Press.

Campbell, John L. 2011. "The U.S. Financial Crisis: Lessons for Theories of Institutional Complementarity." *Socio-Economic Review* 9: 211–234.

Campbell, John L. 2004. *Institutional Change and Globalization*. Princeton, NJ: Princeton University Press.

Campbell, John L. 2003. "States, Politics and Globalization: Why Institutions Still Matter." In T.V. Paul, G. John Ikenberry, and John A. Hall, eds. *The Nation State in Question*. Princeton, NJ: Princeton University Press, 234–259.

Campbell, John L., and John A. Hall. 2021. *The World of States*, 2nd ed. New York: Cambridge University Press.

Campbell, John L., and John A. Hall. 2017. *The Paradox of Vulnerability: States, Nationalism and the Financial Crisis*. Princeton, NJ: Princeton University Press.

Campbell, John L., and John A. Hall. 2009. "National Identity and the Political Economy of Small States." *Review of International Political Economy* 16(4): 1–26.

Campbell, John L., and Ove K. Pedersen. 2014. *The National Origin of Policy Ideas*. Princeton, NJ: Princeton University Press.

Case, Anne, and Angus Deaton. 2020. *Death of Despair*. Princeton, NJ: Princeton University Press.

Castle, Stephen. 2020. "Brexit Border Bureaucracy Looms for Truckers, Pet Owners and Travelers." *The New York Times*, July 13. www.nytimes.com/2020/07/13/world/europe/brexit-border-bureaucracy.html

Central Bank of England. 2019. VIX Index Historical Data. www.cboe.com/products/vix-index-volatility/vix-options-and-futures/vix-index/vix-historical-data

Chase, Kerry. 2005. *Trading Blocs: States, Firms and Regions in the World Economy*. Ann Arbor, MI: University of Michigan Press.

Cheng, Jeffrey, Dave Skidmore, and David Wessel. 2020. "What's the Fed Doing in Response to the COVID-19 Crisis? What More

Could It Do?" Washington, DC: Brookings Institution. www
.brookings.edu/research/fed-response-to-covid19/

Chickering, Roger. 1984. *We Men Who Feel Most German: A Cultural Study of the Pan-German League, 1886–1914.* London: George Allen and Unwin.

Clark, Peter, Natalia Tamirisa, Shang-Jin Wei, Azim Sadikov, and Li Zeng. 2004. "Exchange Rate Volatility and Trade Flows: Some New Evidence." Washington, DC: International Monetary Fund. www.imf.org/external/np/res/exrate/2004/eng/051904.pdf

Collier, Paul. 2018. *The Future of Capitalism.* New York: HarperCollins.

Collins, Harry, and Robert Evans. 2007. *Rethinking Expertise.* Chicago, IL: University of Chicago Press.

Colson, Thomas. 2018. "Chronic Mismanagement at Liam Fox's Trade Department Could Derail May's Brexit Plans." *Business Insider*, June 5. www.businessinsider.com/brexit-chronic-lack-of-expertise-could-derail-foxs-trade-plans–2018–6

Committee for a Responsible Federal Budget. 2019. "CBO's Analysis of the President's FY 2020 Budget." May 9. www.crfb.org/papers/cbos-analysis-presidents-fy-2020-budget

Comparative Labor Law and Policy Journal. 2020. Special Issue on Labor Law and Policy under New Nationalism. Fall.

The Conversation. 2017. "EU Agencies: A Brexit Loss Nobody's Talking About." April 13. http://theconversation.com/eu-agencies-a-brexit-loss-nobodys-talking-about–76222

Corrigan, Jack. 2018. "The Hollowing-Out of the State Department Continues." *The Atlantic*, February 11. www.theatlantic.com/international/archive/2018/02/tillerson-trump-state-foreign-service/553034/

Corsetti, Giancarlo, Paolo Pesenti, and Nouriel Roubini. 1999. "What Caused the Asian Currency and Financial Crisis?" *Japan and the World Economy* 11(3): 305–373.

Crawford, Neta C. 2018. "United States Budgetary Costs of the Post-9/11 Wars through FY2019: $5.9 Trillion Spent and Obligated." Watson Institute of International and Public Affairs, Brown University. https://watson.brown.edu/costsofwar/files/cow/imc e/papers/2018/Crawford_Costs%20of%20War%20Estimates%20 Through%20FY2019.pdf

Crouch, Colin. 2013. *Making Capitalism Fit for Society*. London: Polity Press.

Crouch, Colin. 2011. *The Strange Non-Death of Neoliberalism*. London: Polity Press.

D'Andona, Matthew. 2017. *Post-Truth: The New War on Truth and How to Fight Back*. London: Ebury Press.

Davenport, Coral, and Lisa Friedman. 2019. "Science Panel Staffed with Trump Appointees Says E.P.A. Rollbacks Lack Scientific Rigor." *The New York Times*, December 31. www.nytimes.com/2 019/12/31/climate/epa-science-panel-trump.html

Deloitte China. 2018. *A New Era of Education: China Education Development Report*. www2.deloitte.com/content/dam/Deloitt e/cn/Documents/technology-media-telecommunications/deloi tte-cn-tmt-china-education-development-en-report-2018.pdf

Dezalay, Yves, and Bryant Garth. 2002. *The Internationalization of Palace Wars*. Chicago, IL: University of Chicago Press.

Digital History. 2019. *Overview of World War I*. Digital History ID 2919. www.digitalhistory.uh.edu/era.cfm?eraid=12&smtid=1

Dixon, Marc. 2020. *Heartland Blues: Labor Rights in the Industrial Midwest*. New York: Oxford University Press.

Dore, Ronald. 1987. *Taking Japan Seriously*. Stanford, CA: Stanford University Press.

Drezner, Daniel. 2017. *The Ideas Industry*. New York: Oxford University Press.

Duina, Francesco. 2018. *Broke and Patriotic: Why Poor Americans Love Their Country*. Stanford, CA: Stanford University Press.

Duina, Francesco. 1999. *Harmonizing Europe*. Albany, NY: State University of New York Press.

Dungery, Mardi, Renee Fry, Brenda Gonzalez-Hermosillo, and Vance Martin. 2002. "International Contagion Effects from the Russian Crisis and the LTCM Near-Collapse." www.bis.org/cgfs/Gonzalez-Hermosillo-et-al.pdf

Economic Policy Uncertainty. 2019a. *Financial Stress Indicator*. Fourth quarter data. www.policyuncertainty.com/financial_stress.html

Economic Policy Uncertainty. 2019b. *World Uncertainty Index*. First quarter data. www.policyuncertainty.com/wui_quarterly.html

The Economist. 2020a. "Dethroning the Dollar." January 18, 62–64.

The Economist. 2020b. "Measuring the 1%." November 30, 21–24.

The Economist. 2019a. "Weapons of Mass Disruption." June 8, 13.

The Economist. 2019b. "America First Trade Policy." June 8, 65–66.

The Economist. 2019c. "Global Technology: Pinch Points." June 8, 58–59.

The Economist. 2019d. "A New Kind of Cold War: A Special Report." May 18, pp. 3–16.

Eichengreen, Barry. 2018. *The Populist Temptation: Economic Grievance and Political Reaction in the Modern Era*. New York: Oxford University Press.

Eichengreen, Barry. 2007. *The European Economy since 1945*. Princeton, NJ: Princeton University Press.

Ellyatt, Holly. 2020. "UK Jobless Claims Jumped 70% in April as the Coronavirus Hit Employment." *CNBC*, May 19. www.cnbc.com/2020/05/19/uk-jobless-claims-rise-by-70percent-in-april-to-2point1-million.html

Esterbrook, John. 2002. "Rumsfeld: It Would Be a Short War." *CBS News*, November 15. www.cbsnews.com/news/rumsfeld-it-would-be-a-short-war/

Eurostat. 2020. Unemployment Statistics. https://ec.europa.eu/euro stat/statistics-explained/index.php/Unemployment_statistics

Evans, Peter. 1995. *Embedded Autonomy: States and Industrial Transformations.* Princeton, NJ: Princeton University Press.

Fantasia, Rick, and Kim Voss. 2004. *Hard Work: Remaking the American Labor Movement.* Berkeley, CA: University of California Press.

Ferguson, Thomas, and Joel Rogers. 1986. *Right Turn.* New York: Hill and Wang.

Financial Times. 2020. "Can Government Afford the Debts They Are Piling up to Stabilize Economies?" May 3. www.ft.com/con tent/53cb3f6a-895d-11ea-a109-483c62d17528

Finegold, David. 2006. "The Role of Education and Training Systems in Innovation." In Jerald Hage and Marius Meeus, eds. *Innovation, Science and Institutional Change.* New York: Oxford University Press, 391–413.

Finlayson, Alan. 2017. "Brexitism." *London Review of Books* 39(10): 22–23.

Fligstein, Neil. 2008. *Euro-Clash.* New York: Oxford University Press.

Fligstein, Neil. 2001. *The Architecture of Markets.* Princeton, NJ: Princeton University Press.

Focus Economics. 2020. "Singapore Economic Outlook." May 26. www.focus-economics.com/countries/singapore

Foroohar, Rana. 2019. "Lina Khan: 'This Isn't Just about Antitrust. It's About Values'." *Financial Times,* March 29. www.ft.com/con tent/7945c568-4fe7-11e9-9c76-bf4a0ce37d49

Fourcade, Marion. 2010. *Economists and Societies.* Princeton, NJ: Princeton University Press.

Fourcade-Gourinchas, Marion, and Sarah Babb. 2002. "Rebirth of the Liberal Creed: Paths to Neoliberalism in Four Countries." *American Journal of Sociology* 108: 533–579.

Frankel, Jeffrey. 2020. "Is China Overtaking the U.S. as a Financial and Economic Power?" *The Guardian*, May 29. www.theguardian.com /business/2020/may/29/is-china-overtaking-the-us-as-a-finan cial-and-economic-power

Freeman, Richard. 1994. "How Labor Fares in Advanced Economies." In Richard Freeman, ed. *Working under Different Rules*. New York: Russell Sage Foundation, 1–28.

Freeman, Richard, and Lawrence Katz. 1994. "Rising Wage Inequality: The United States vs. Other Advanced Countries." In Richard Freeman, ed. *Working under Different Rules*. New York: Russell Sage Foundation, 29–62.

Frerichs, Sabine, and Suvi Sankari. 2016. "Workers No Longer Welcome? Europeanization of Solidarity in the Wake of Brexit." *Socio-Economic Review* 14(4): 840–844.

Friedman, Milton. 1978. "The Role of Government in a Free Society." Lecture delivered at the Hoover Institution, Stanford University, February 9. In *Milton Friedman Speaks* (videotape publication). New York: Harcourt Brace Jovanovich.

Friedman, Milton. 1970. "The Social Responsibility of Business is to Increase Profits." *New York Times Magazine*, September 13, 32–33, 122, 124, 126.

Friedman, Milton. 1962. *Capitalism and Freedom*. Chicago, IL: University of Chicago Press.

Gao, Bai. 1997. *Economic Ideology and Japanese Industrial Policy*. New York: Cambridge University Press.

Gelles, David, and David Yaffe-Bellany. 2019. "Shareholder Value is No Longer Everything, Top C.E.O.s Say." *The New York Times*, August 19. www.nytimes.com/2019/08/19/business/business-roundtable-ceos-corporations.html

Gellner, Ernest. 1983. *Nations and Nationalism*. Oxford: Blackwell.

Gereffi, Gary. 2005. "The Global Economy: Organization, Governance and Development." In Neil Smelser and Richard Swedberg, eds. *The*

Handbook of Economic Sociology, second ed. Princeton, NJ: Princeton University Press, 160–182.

Gill, Stephen, and David Law. 1988. *The Global Political Economy*. Baltimore, MD: Johns Hopkins University Press.

Gilpin, Robert. 2000. *The Challenge of Global Capitalism*. Princeton, NJ: Princeton University Press.

Glanz, James, and Campbell Robertson. 2020. "Lockdown Delays Cost at Least 36,000 Lives, Data Show." *The New York Times*, May 22. www.nytimes.com/2020/05/20/us/coronavirus-distancing -deaths.html?auth=linked-google

Goldfield, Michael. 1987. *The Decline of Organized Labor in the United States*. Chicago, IL: University of Chicago Press.

Goodman, Peter. 2019. "Globalization is Moving Past the U.S. and Its Vision of World Order." *The New York Times*, June 19. www.nytimes.com/2019/06/19/business/globalization-us-world-order.html

Gourevitch, Peter. 1989. "Keynesian Politics: The Political Sources of Economic Policy Choices." In Peter Hall, ed. *The Political Power of Economic Ideas*. Princeton, NJ: Princeton University Press, 87–106.

Grey, Christopher. 2016. "The New Politics of Cosmopolitans and Locals." *Socio-Economic Review* 14(4): 829–832.

Guillén, Mauro. 2019. "Bullying China Now Will Just Leave Us with Welts Later." *The Hill*, May 16. https://thehill.com/opinion/fina nce/443895-bullying-china-now-will-leave-us-with-welts-later

Guillén, Mauro. 2015. *The Architecture of Collapse: The Global System in the 21st Century*. New York: Oxford University Press.

Guillén, Mauro, and Estaban García-Canal. 2010. *The New Multinationals: Spanish Firms in Global Context*. New York: Cambridge University Press.

Guzman, Joseph. 2020. "More than 100,000 Small Businesses Have Permanently Closed Due to Coronavirus, Study Estimates."

Changing America, May 13. https://thehill.com/changing-america /well-being/longevity/497519-more-than-100000-small-businesses -have-permanently

Hall, Peter, ed. 1989. *The Political Power of Economic Ideas: Keynesianism across Nations.* Princeton, NJ: Princeton University Press.

Hall, Peter, and David Soskice, eds. 2001. *Varieties of Capitalism.* New York: Oxford University Press.

The Hamilton Project. 2013. Countries with High Income Inequality Have Low Social Mobility. www.hamiltonproject.org/charts/ the_relationship_between_income_inequality_and_social_mobility

Harrington, Brooke. 2016. *Capital without Borders: Wealth Managers and the One Percent.* Cambridge, MA: Harvard University Press.

Harvey, David. 2005. *A Brief History of Neoliberalism.* New York: Oxford University Press.

Hattam, Victoria. 1993. *Labor Visions and State Power: The Origins of Business Unionism in the United States.* Princeton, NJ: Princeton University Press.

Heeb, Gina. 2019. "U.S. Income Inequality Jumps to Highest Level Ever Recorded." *Markets Insider*, September 27. https://markets .businessinsider.com/news/stocks/income-inequality-reached-highest-level-ever-recorded-in-2018-2019-9-1028559996

Heijmans, Philip. 2020. "Singapore Contained Coronavirus: Could Other Countries Learn from its Approach?" *World Economic Forum*, March 5. www.weforum.org/agenda/2020/03/singapore-response-contained-coronavirus-covid19-outbreak/

Held, David, Anthony McGrew, David Goldblatt, and Jonathan Peraton. 1999. *Global Transformations.* Stanford, CA: Stanford University Press.

Helm, Toby, Emma Graham-Harrison, and Robin McKie. 2020. "How Did Britain Get Its Coronavirus Response So Wrong?"

The Guardian, April 18. www.theguardian.com/world/2020/apr/18/how-did-britain-get-its-response-to-coronavirus-so-wrong

Hicks, Alexander, and Lane Kenworthy. 1998. "Cooperation and Political Economic Performance in Affluent Democratic Capitalism." *American Journal of Sociology* 103: 1631–72.

Hirsch, Fred. 1976. *Social Limits to Growth.* Cambridge, MA: Harvard University Press.

Hirschman, Albert O. 1992. *Rival Views of Market Society.* Cambridge, MA: Harvard University Press.

Hirschman, Albert O. 1970. *Exit, Voice and Loyalty.* Cambridge, MA: Harvard University Press.

HM Treasury. 2016. *HM Treasury Analysis: The Long-Term Economic Impact of EU Membership and the Alternatives.* London: HMSO, April. https://assets.publishing.service.gov.uk/government/upload s/system/uploads/attachment_data/file/517415/treasury_analysis_e conomic_impact_of_eu_membership_web.pdf

Hochschild, Arlie. 2016. *Strangers in Their Own Land.* New York: New Press.

Hochschild, Jennifer, and Kathrine Levine Einstein. 2015. *Do Facts Matter? Information and Misinformation in American Politics.* Norman, OK: University of Oklahoma Press.

Hodgson, Geoffrey. 1988. *Economics and Institutions.* Philadelphia, PA: University of Pennsylvania Press.

Howard, Phoebe Wall. 2019. "Mexican Strike Leads to Steering Wheel Shortages on Mustang, Explorer." *Detroit Free Press*, February 25. www.freep.com/story/money/cars/2019/02/25/ford-mustang-explorer-no-steering-wheels-mexico-strike/2984225002/

Iceland, John. 2014. *Residential Segregation: A Transatlantic Analysis.* Washington, DC: Migration Policy Institute. www.migrationpolicy.org/sites/default/files/publications/TCM_Citie s_Residential-SegregationFINALWEB.pdf

Ikenberry, G. John. 2001. *After Victory: Institutions, Strategic Restraint, and the Rebuilding of Order after Major Wars*. Princeton, NJ: Princeton University Press.

Imbert, Fred. 2019. "Fed Chief Powell Says Trade Policy Is Weighing on Investment Decisions." *CNBC*, September 6. www.cnbc.com/2019/0 9/06/fed-chief-powell-says-trade-policy-is-weighing-on-investment -decisions.html

Intergovernmental Panel on Climate Change. 2019a. "Summary for Policymakers." In *IPCC Special Report on the Ocean and Cryosphere in a Changing Climate*. Geneva: IPCC.

Intergovernmental Panel on Climate Change. 2019b. "Summary for Policymakers." In *IPCC Special Report on Climate Change, Desertification, Land Degradation, Sustainable Land Management, Food Security, and Greenhouse Gas Fluxes in Terrestrial Ecosystems*. Geneva: IPCC.

International Monetary Fund. 2019a. IMF DataMapper. www .imf.org/external/datamapper/DEBT1@DEBT/OEMDC/ADVE C/WEOWORLD/FAD_G20Emg/FAD_G20Adv

International Monetary Fund. 2019b. IMF's Work on Income Inequality. www.imf.org/external/np/fad/inequality/

International Monetary Fund. 2013. "IMF Releases Data on the Currency Composition of Foreign Exchange Reserves with Additional Data on Australian and Canadian Dollar Reserves." Press release, June 28. www.imf.org/external/np/sec/pr/2013/p r13236.htm

Irfan, Umair. 2019. "2019 Was a Brutal Year for American Farmers." *Vox*, December 27. www.vox.com/2019/12/27/21038054/american-farmer-2019-climate-change-agriculture-flood-trade-war-corn-soy

Iversen, Torben, and David Soskice. 2019. *Democracy and Prosperity: Reinventing Capitalism through a Turbulent Century*. Princeton, NJ: Princeton University Press.

Jacks, David, Kevin O'Rourke, and Jeffrey Williamson. 2011. "Commodity Price Volatility and World Market Integration since 1700." *The Review of Economics and Statistics* 93(3): 800–813.

Jacobson, Louis. 2018. "What Percentage of Americans Own Stocks?" *Politifact*, September 18. www.politifact.com/factchecks/2018/sep/18/ro-khanna/what-percentage-americans-own-stocks/

Janelli, Robert. 1993. *Making Capitalism: The Social and Cultural Construction of a South Korean Conglomerate*. Stanford, CA: Stanford University Press.

Jensen, Nathan. 2006. *Nation-States and the Multinational Corporation: A Political Economy of Foreign Direct Investment*. Princeton, NJ: Princeton University Press.

Johns Hopkins University and Medicine. 2020. Coronavirus Resource Center, July 29. https://coronavirus.jhu.edu/data/mortality

Johnson, Noel, and Mark Koyama. 2017. "States and Economic Growth: Capacity and Constraints." *Explorations in Economic History* 64: 1–20.

Johnson, Robert C., and Guillermo Noguera. 2017. "A Portrait of Trade in Value-Added over Four Decades." *The Review of Economics and Statistics* 99(5): 896–911.

Johnson, Robert C., and Guillermo Noguera. 2012. "Fragmentation and Trade in Value-Added over Four Decades." National Bureau of Economic Research Working Paper 18186. www.nber.org/papers/w18186

Jones, Laura, Daniele Palumbo, and David Brown. 2020. "Coronavirus: A Visual Guide to the Economic Impact." *BBC News*, April 27. www.bbc.com/news/business-51706225

Judis, John. 2016. *The Populist Explosion: How the Great Recession Transformed American and European Politics*. New York: Columbia Global Reports.

Judson, Pietor. 2016. *The Habsburg Empire: A New History*. Cambridge, MA: Harvard University/Belknap Press.

Judt, Tony. 2010. *Ill Fares the Land*. New York: Penguin.

Judt, Tony. 2005. *Postwar: A History of Europe since 1945*. New York: Penguin.

Kapstein, Ethan. 1994. *Governing the Global Economy*. Cambridge, MA: Harvard University Press.

Katzenstein, Peter. 2006. "Denmark and Small States." In John L. Campbell, John A. Hall, and Ove K. Pedersen, eds. *National Identity and the Varieties of Capitalism: The Danish Experience*. Montreal: McGill-Queens University Press, 431–440.

Katzenstein, Peter. 2000. "Confidence, Trust, International Relations, and Lessons from Smaller Democracies." In Susan Pharr and Robert Putnam, eds. *Disaffected Democracies: What's Troubling the Trilateral Countries?* Princeton, NJ: Princeton University Press, 121–148.

Katzenstein, Peter. 1985. *Small States in World Markets*. Ithaca, NY: Cornell University Press.

Katznelson, Ira. 1985. "Working-Class Formation and the State: Nineteenth-Century England in American Perspective." In Peter Evans, Dietrich Rueschemeyer, and Theda Skocpol, eds. *Bringing the State Back In*. New York: Cambridge University Press, 257–286.

Keating, Sarah. 2018. "Can Singapore's Social Housing Keep up with Changing Times?" *BBC News*, December 14. www.bbc.com/cap ital/story/20181210-can-singapores-social-housing-keep-up-with -changing-times

Keegan, William. 2012. "Bank Deregulation Leads to Disaster: Shout It from the Rooftops." *The Guardian*, May 5. www.theguardian.com /business/2012/may/06/shout-rooftops-bank-deregulation-leads-to-disaster

Kenworthy, Lane. 2020. "Would Socialism Be Better?" Unpublished manuscript, Department of Sociology, University of California-San Diego.

Kenworthy, Lane. 2019a. *Social Democratic Capitalism*. New York: Oxford University Press.

Kenworthy, Lane. 2019b. *The Good Society*. Department of Sociology, University of California-San Diego. https://laneken worthy.net/

Kenworthy, Lane. 2014. *Social Democratic America*. New York: Oxford University Press.

Kenworthy, Lane. 1997. "Globalization and Economic Convergence." *Competition and Change* 2: 1–64.

Keynes, John Maynard. 1964 [1936]. *The General Theory of Employment, Interest, and Money*. New York: Harcourt.

Keynes, John Maynard. 1926. *The End of Laissez-Faire*. London: Hogarth Press.

Keynes, John Maynard. 1920. *The Economic Consequences of the Peace*. New York: Harcourt, Brace and Howe.

Khanna, Parag. 2019. *The Future is Asian*. New York: Simon & Schuster.

Khoo, Louisa-May. 2017. "Living with Diversity the Singapore Way." *Urban Solutions* 10: 38–45. www.clc.gov.sg/docs/default-source/urba n-solutions/urb-sol-iss-10-pdfs/essay-inclusion_through_interven tion.pdf

Kindleberger, Charles. 2013. *The World in Depression: 1929–1939*. Berkeley, CA: University of California Press.

Kirkpatrick, David D., Ben Hubbard, and David Halbfinger. 2019. "Trump's Abrupt Shifts in Middle East Unnerve U.S. Allies." *The New York Times*, October 13, 1.

Kirshner, Jonathan. 2014. *American Power after the Financial Crisis*. Ithaca, NY: Cornell University Press.

Koh, B.C. 1989. *Japan's Administrative Elite*. Berkeley, CA: University of California Press.

Koranyi, Balazs, and Francesco Canepa. 2017. "ECB Sees Seeds of Next Crisis in Trump Deregulation Plan." *Reuters*, February 6.

www.reuters.com/article/us-ecb-policy/ecb-sees-seeds-of-next-crisis-in-trump-deregulation-plan-idUSKBN15L1LH

Koronowski, Ryan, Jeremy Venook, and Will Ragland. 2020. " 'Blinking Red': A Running Timeline of How the Trump Administration Ignored Warnings, Misled the Public and Made the Coronavirus Crisis Worse." *Center for American Progress*, April 27. www.americanprogress.org/issues/democracy/news/2020/04/27/483986/blinking-red-trump-administration-ignored-warnings-misled-public-made-coronavirus-crisis-worse/

Krippner, Greta. 2011. *Capitalizing on Crisis: The Political Origins of the Rise of Finance*. Cambridge, MA: Harvard University Press.

Kristof, Nicholas. 2020a. "McDonald's Workers in Denmark Pity Their U.S. Colleagues." *The New York Times*, International Edition, May 13, 10–11.

Kristof, Nicholas. 2020b. "We're No. 28! And Dropping." *The New York Times*, October 10. www.nytimes.com/2020/09/09/opinion/united-states-social-progress.html

Krugman, Paul. 2009. *The Return of Depression Economics and the Crisis of 2008*. New York: Norton.

Lakner, Christoph, and Branko Milanovic. 2013. World Panel Income Distribution (LM-WPID) data, 1988–2008. www.worldbank.org/en/research/brief/World-Panel-Income-Distribution

LeBlanc, Paul. 2019. "Ex-WH Economic Advisor Says He's Concerned No One is Left in White House to Challenge Trump." *CNN Politics*, December 3. www.cnn.com/2019/12/03/politics/gary-cohn-trump-white-house/index.html

Le Galès, Patrick. 2016. "Brexit: UK as an Exception or the Banal Avant Garde of the Disintegration of the EU?" *Socio-Economic Review* 14(4): 848–854.

Lee, Bradford. 1989. "The Miscarriage of Necessity and Invention: Proto-Keynesianism and Democratic States in the 1930s." In

Peter Hall, ed. *The Political Power of Economic Ideas*. Princeton, NJ: Princeton University Press, 129–170.

Leicht, Kevin, and Scott Fitzgerald. 2014. *Middle Class Meltdown in America*. New York: Routledge.

Lewis, Michael. 2018. *The Fifth Risk*. New York: W.W. Norton.

Lewis, Michael. 2014. *Flash Boys: A Wall Street Revolt*. New York: W.W. Norton.

Lieven, Dominic. 2002. *Empire: The Russian Empire and Its Rivals*. London: John Murray.

List, Friedrich. 2005a [1841]. *National System of Political Economy, Vol. 1: The History*. New York: Cosimo Classics.

List, Friedrich. 2005b [1841]. *National System of Political Economy, Vol. 2: The Theory*. New York: Cosimo Classics.

Luxembourg Income Study. 2019. "Inequality and Poverty Key Figures." *LIS Cross-National Data Center*. www.lisdatacenter.org/lis-ikf-webapp/app/search-ikf-figures

MacLean, Nancy. 2018. *Democracy in Chains: The Deep History of the Radical Right's Stealth Plan for America*. New York: Penguin.

Maddison, Angus. 2019. Historical Statistics of the World Economy: 1–2006 AD. www.ggdc.net/maddison/historical_statistics/horizontal-file_03–2009.xls

Maddison, Angus. 2003. *The World Economy: Historical Statistics: 1–2001 AD*. Paris: OECD.

Maddison, Angus. 2001. *The World Economy: A Millennial Perspective*. Paris: OECD.

Mamonova, Natalia. 2019. "Right-Wing Populism and Counter-Movements in Rural Europe." *Emancipatory Rural Politics Initiative*, February 27. www.arc2020.eu/right-wing-populism-emancipatory-rural-politics-initiative-europe/

Mann, Michael. 2012. *The Sources of Social Power, Vol. 3*. New York: Cambridge University Press.

Mann, Michael. 1970. "The Social Cohesion of Liberal Democracies." *American Sociological Review* 35(3): 423–439.

Mattis, James. 2018. "Letter of Resignation." December 20. Washington, DC: U.S. Department of Defense. https://media.defense.gov/2018/D ec/20/2002075156/-1/-1/1/LETTER-FROM-SECRETARY-JAMES-N-MATTIS.PDF

Mayer, Jane. 2016. *Dark Money*. New York: Doubleday.

Mazower, Mark. 1998. *Dark Continent: Europe's Twentieth Century*. New York: Vintage.

McBride, James. 2016. "Weighing the Consequences of 'Brexit'." *Council on Foreign Relations*, June 10. www.cfr.org/expert-roundup/weighing-consequences-brexit

McDaniel, Tim. 1988. *Autocracy, Capitalism and Revolution in Russia*. Berkeley, CA: University of California Press.

Mediacorp. 2017. "Building a Nation: Lee Kuan Yew (1923–2015)." *YouTube*, December 21. www.youtube.com/watch?v=JAvNqAv G7bk&t

Medrano, Juan Diez. 2010. *Framing Europe: Attitudes to European Integration in Germany, Spain and the United Kingdom*. Princeton, NJ: Princeton University Press.

Meek, James. 2019. "The Two Jacobs." *London Review of Books*, August 1. www.lrb.co.uk/the-paper/v41/n15/james-meek/the-two -jacobs

Milanovic, Branko. 2019. *Capitalism Alone*. Cambridge, MA: Belknap/Harvard University Press.

Milanovic, Branko. 2018. "Inequality Is Bad for Growth of the Poor (but Not for That of the Rich)." *The World Bank Economic Review* 32(3): 507–530.

Milanovic, Branko. 2016. *Global Inequality*. Cambridge, MA: Belknap/Harvard University Press.

Milanovic, Branko. 2005. *Worlds Apart: Measuring International and Global Inequality*. Princeton, NJ: Princeton University Press.

Milward, Alan. 1992. *The European Rescue of the Nation State*. Berkeley, CA: University of California Press.

Mishel, Lawrence, Josh Bivens, Elise Gould, and Heidi Shierholz. 2012. *The State of Working America*, 12th ed. Ithaca, NY: Cornell University Press.

Mizruchi, Mark. 2013. *The Fracturing of the American Corporate Elite*. Cambridge, MA: Harvard University Press.

Mudge, Stephanie. 2011. "What's Left of Leftism? Neoliberal Politics in Western Party Systems, 1945–2008." *Social Science History* 35(3): 337–338.

Murphy, Dan. 2011. "Would the War Be Cheap and Would Iraq Pay for It?" *The Christian Science Monitor*, December 22. www.csmonitor/World/Backchannels/2011/1222/Iraq-war-Predictions-made-and-results

Narayan, Ambar, Roy Van der Weide, Alexandru Cojocaru, Christoph Lakner, Silvia Redaelli, Daniel Gerszon Mahler, Rakesh Gupta N. Ramasubbaiah, and Stefan Thewissen. 2018. *Fair Progress? Economic Mobility across Generations around the World*. Washington, DC: World Bank. www.worldbank.org/en/events/2018/05/22/intergenerational-mobility-around-the-world

Nichols, Tom. 2017. *The Death of Expertise: The Campaign against Established Knowledge and Why It Matters*. New York: Oxford University Press.

Nunn, Ryan, Jana Parsons, and Jay Shambaugh. 2019. "Race and Underemployment in the U.S. Labor Market." *Brookings Institution Up Front* [blog], August 1. www.brookings.edu/blog/up-front/2019/08/01/race-and-underemployment-in-the-u-s-labor-market/

Nutting, Rex. 2008. "Paulson Admits Deregulation Has Failed Us All." *Market Watch*, March 13. www.marketwatch.com/story/paulsons-lament-deregulation-has-been-a-failure

OECD. 2020a. OECD Data, Social Spending. https://data.oecd.org/socialexp/social-spending.htm

OECD. 2020b. OECD Data, Household Debt. https://data.oecd.org /hha/household-debt.htm

OECD. 2020c. Real GDP Forecast. https://data.oecd.org/gdp/real-gdp-forecast.htm

OECD. 2019a. OECD Data. https://data.oecd.org/

OECD. 2019b. OECD Data, Permanent Immigrant Inflows. https:// data.oecd.org/migration/permanent-immigrant-inflows.htm#indicator-chart

OECD. 2019c. OECD Data, Harmonized Unemployment Rate. https:// data.oecd.org/unemp/harmonised-unemployment-rate-hur.htm

OECD. 2019d. OECD Data, Real GDP Forecast. https://data .oecd.org/gdp/real-gdp-forecast.htm#indicator-chart

OECD. 2019e. OECD Data, General Government Debt. https://data .oecd.org/gga/general-government-debt.htm

OECD. 2016. "The Economic Consequences of Brexit: A Taxing Decision." OECD Economic Policy Paper No. 16, April. Paris: OECD.

OECD. 2014. "Is Migration Really Increasing?" *Migration Policy Debates*, May. www.oecd.org/berlin/Is-migration-really-increasing.pdf

OECD. 1997. *The OECD Report on Regulatory Reform: Synthesis.* Paris: OECD.

Oltermann, Philip. 2020. "Do Not Assume U.S. Still Aspires to Be a World Leader, Merkel Warns." *The Guardian*, June 26. www .theguardian.com/world/2020/jun/26/do-not-assume-us-still-aspires-to-be-world-leader-merkel-warns

O'Reilly, Jacqueline. 2016. "The Fault Lines Unveiled by Brexit." *Socio-Economic Review* 14(4): 808–814.

Orlikowski, Wanda, and Susan Scott. 2014. "What Happens When Evaluation Goes Online? Exploring Apparatuses of Valuation in the Travel Sector." *Organization Science* 25(3): 868–891.

Ortiz-Ospina, Esteban, Diana Beltekian, and Max Roser. 2018. Trade and Globalization. https://ourworldindata.org/trade-and-globalization

Ostry, Jonathan, Andrew Berg, and Charalambos Tsangarides. 2014. "Redistribution, Inequality and Growth." IMF Research Department Discussion Paper SDN/14/02. New York: International Monetary Fund.

Palier, Bruno, and Kathleen Thelen. 2012. "Dualization and Institutional Competitiveness: Industrial Relations, Labor Market and Welfare State Changes in France and Germany." In Patrick Emmeneger, Silja Häusermann, Bruno Palier, and Martin Seeleib-Kaiser, eds. *The Age of Dualization: Structures, Policies, Politics and Divided Outcomes.* New York: Oxford University Press, 201–225.

Partington, Richard. 2019. "Donald Trump Attacks ECB for 'Currency Manipulation'." *The Guardian*, June 18. www.theguardian.com/business/2019/jun/18/donald-trump-attacks-ecb-for-currency-manipulation?CMP=share_btn_link

Pasieka, Agnieszka. 2020. "In Search of a Cure? Far-Right Youth Activism and the Making of a New Europe." Paper presented at the workshop on Europe: A World of Yesterday? McGill University, Montreal.

Patsiurko, Natalka, John L. Campbell, and John A. Hall. 2013. "Nation-State Size, Ethnic Diversity and Economic Performance in the Advanced Capitalist Countries." *New Political Economy* 18(6): 827–844.

Patsiurko, Natalka, John L. Campbell, and John A. Hall. 2012. "Measuring Cultural Diversity: Ethnic, Linguistic and Religious Fractionalization in the OECD." *Ethnic and Racial Studies* 35(2): 195–217.

Pauly, Louis. 1997. *Who Elected the Bankers? Surveillance and Control in the World Economy.* Ithaca, NY: Cornell University Press.

Pepinsky, Thomas. 2020. "The Political and Economic Impact of COVID-19 in Southeast Asia." National Bureau of Asian Research, June 11. www.worldometers.info/coronavirus/?utm_campaign=ho meAdvegas1?%22

Pettigrew, Thomas. 1998. "Intergroup Contact Theory." *Annual Review of Psychology* 49: 65–85.

Pew Research Center. 2019. "Many across the Globe are Dissatisfied with How Democracy is Working." April 29. www.pewglobal.org /2019/04/29/many-across-the-globe-are-dissatisfied-with-how-democracy-is-working/

Pew Research Center. 2018a. "Trump's International Ratings Remain Low, Especially among Key Allies." October 1. www .pewglobal.org/2018/10/01/trumps-international-ratings-remain-low-especially-among-key-allies/

Pew Research Center. 2018b. "In Western Europe, Populist Parties Tap Anti-Establishment Frustration but Have Little Appeal across Ideological Divide." July 12. www.pewglobal.org/2018/07/12/in-western-europe-populist-parties-tap-anti-establishment-frustration -but-have-little-appeal-across-ideological-divide/

Pew Research Center. 2013. "Economies of Emerging Markets Better Rated during Difficult Times." May 23. www.pewresearch.org/glo bal/2013/05/23/economies-of-emerging-markets-better-rated-during -difficult-times/

Philippon, Thomas. 2019. *The Great Reversal.* Cambridge, MA: Belknap/Harvard University Press.

Pierson, Paul. 1994. *Dismantling the Welfare State? Reagan, Thatcher, and the Politics of Retrenchment.* New York: Cambridge University Press.

Piketty, Thomas. 2015. *The Economics of Inequality.* Cambridge, MA: Belknap/Harvard University Press.

Piketty, Thomas. 2014. *Capital in the Twenty-First Century.* Cambridge, MA: Belknap/Harvard University Press.

Pinto, Brian, and Sergei Ulatov. 2010. "Financial Globalization and the Russian Crisis of 1998." World Bank Policy Research Working Paper 5312. https://openknowledge.worldbank.org/bitstream/handle/10986/3797/WPS5312.pdf

Plumer, Brad, and Coral Davenport. 2019. "Science under Attack: How Trump Is Sidelining Research and Their Work." *The New York Times*, December 28. www.nytimes.com/2019/12/28/climate/trump-administration-war-on-science.html

Polanyi, Karl. 1944. *The Great Transformation*. Boston, MA: Beacon Press.

Prasad, Eswar. 2014. *The Dollar Trap: How the U.S. Dollar Tightened Its Grip on Global Finance*. Princeton, NJ: Princeton University Press.

Prasad, Monica. 2006. *The Politics of Free Markets*. Chicago, IL: University of Chicago Press.

Rappeport, Alan. 2019. "At G-20 Meeting, U.S.–China Trade Dispute Sours Global Economic Outlook." *The New York Times*, June 10, A9.

Reinhart, Carmen. 2012. "The Return of Financial Repression." *Financial Stability Review* No. 16. Paris: Banque de France.

Reinhart, Carmen, and Kenneth Rogoff. 2009. "This Time is Different: Eight Centuries of Financial Folly." Online datasets. www.carmenreinhart.com/this-time-is-different/

Reuters Fact Check. 2020. "Partly False Claim: Trump Fired Entire Pandemic Response Team in 2018." *Reuters*, March 25. www.reuters.com/article/uk-factcheck-trump-fired-pandemic-team/partly-false-claim-trump-fired-pandemic-response-team-in-2018-idUSKBN21C32M

Rich, Frank. 2006. *The Greatest Story Ever Sold: The Decline and Fall of Truth from 9/11 to Katrina*. New York: Penguin.

Richter, Felix. 2019. "This is What Nearly $14 Trillion of Household Debt Looks Like." *World Economic Forum*, November 25. www

.weforum.org/agenda/2019/11/u-s-household-debt-climbs-to-13–95-trillion/

Rodrik, Dani. 2018. *Straight Talk on Trade*. Princeton, NJ: Princeton University Press.

Rodrik, Dani. 2011. *The Globalization Paradox*. New York: Oxford University Press.

Rodrik, Dani. 2005. *Has Globalization Gone Too Far?* Washington, DC: Institute for International Economics.

Roe, Mark. 2003. *Political Determinants of Corporate Governance*. New York: Oxford University Press.

Rogan, Tim. 2017. *The Moral Economists*. Princeton, NJ: Princeton University Press.

Rosenfeld, Jake. 2014. *What Unions No Longer Do*. Cambridge, MA: Harvard University Press.

Ruggie, John. 1983. "International Regimes, Transactions and Change: Embedded Liberalism in the Postwar Economic Order." In Stephen Krasner, ed. *International Regimes*. Ithaca, NY: Cornell University Press, 195–232.

Sachs, Jeffrey. 2019. "America's Illusions of Growth." *Project Syndicate*, May 14. www.project-syndicate.org/commentary/america-growth-illusions-declining-wellbeing-by-jeffrey-d-sachs–2019–05

Salant, Walter. 1989. "The Spread of Keynesian Doctrines and Practices in the United States." In Peter Hall, ed. *The Political Power of Economic Ideas*. Princeton, NJ: Princeton University Press, 25–51.

Samuels, Richard. 2003. *Machiavelli's Children: Leaders and Their Legacies in Italy and Japan*. Ithaca, NY: Cornell University Press.

Samuels, Richard. 1987. *The Business of the Japanese State*. Ithaca, NY: Cornell University Press.

Sanger, David. 2018. *The Perfect Weapon: War, Sabotage, and Fear in the Cyber Age*. New York: Crown.

273

Sanger, David, and Julian Barnes. 2019. "On North Korea and Iran, Intelligence Chiefs Contradict Trump." *The New York Times*, January 29. www.nytimes.com/2019/01/29/us/politics/kim-jong-trump.html

Sardana, Saloni. 2020. "Yelp Says 60% of U.S. Businesses that Closed Due to COVID-19 Won't Reopen." *Markets Insider*, September 17. https://markets.businessinsider.com/news/stocks/yelp-business-closures-permanent-covid-report-2020-9-1029598577

Scheidel, Walter. 2017. *The Great Leveler*. Princeton, NJ: Princeton University Press.

Schmidt, Garbi, and Jonas Otterbeck. 2014. "Scandinavian Countries." In Jocelyne Cesari, ed. *The Oxford Handbook of European Islam*. New York: Oxford University Press, 391–427.

Schumpeter, Joseph. 1942. *Capitalism, Socialism and Democracy*. New York: Harper Torchbooks.

Scott, Robert. 2019. "A Radical Plan to Fix the Dollar." *The New York Times*, June 16. www.nytimes.com/2019/06/16/opinion/elizabeth-warren-dollar.html

Sergent, Jim, Ledyard King, and Michael Collins. 2020. "4 Coronavirus Stimulus Packages. $2.4 Trillion in Funding. See What That Means to the National Debt." *USA Today*, May 8. www.usatoday.com/in-depth/news/2020/05/08/national-debt-how-much-could-coronavirus-cost-america/3051559001/

Shonfield, Andrew. 1965. *Modern Capitalism*. New York: Oxford University Press.

Simmons, Beth. 1999. "The Internationalization of Capital." In Herbert Kitschelt, Peter Lange, Gary Marks, and John Stephens, eds. *Continuity and Change in Contemporary Capitalism*. New York: Cambridge University Press, 36–69.

Skidelsky, Robert. 2009. *Keynes: The Return of the Master*. New York: Public Affairs.

Skidelsky, Robert. 2000. *John Maynard Keynes: Fighting for Freedom, 1937–1946*. New York: Penguin.

Skocpol, Theda, and Vanessa Williamson. 2012. *The Tea Party and the Remaking of Republican Conservatism*. New York: Oxford University Press.

Smale, Alison, and Steven Erlanger. 2017. "Merkel, After Discordant G-7 Meeting, Is Looking Past Trump." *The New York Times*, May 28. www.nytimes.com/2017/05/28/world/europe/angel-merkel-trump-alliances-g7-leaders.html?_r=0

Smialek, Jeanna, and Jack Ewing. 2019. "Trump Accuses Europe of Bolstering Its Economy at America's Expense." *The New York Times*, June 18. www.nytimes.com/2019/06/18/business/ecb-mario-draghi-stimulus.html

Smialek, Jeanna, Jim Tankersley, and Ben Casselman. 2020. "Low Interest Rates Worry the Fed: Ben Bernanke Has Some Ideas." *The New York Times*, January 5. www.nytimes.com/2020/01/04/business/economy/low-interest-rates-ben-bernanke.html

Smialek, Jeanna, Jim Tankersley, and Mark Landler. 2019. "Trump's Trade War Escalation Will Exact Economic Pain, Adviser Says." *The New York Times*, May 12. www.nytimes.com/2019/05/12/us/politics/trump-us-china-economy.html

Smith, Adam. 2016 [1759]. *The Theory of Moral Sentiments*. Los Angeles, CA: Enhanced Media.

Smith, Adam. 2012 [1776]. *The Wealth of Nations*. San Bernardino, CA: Simon and Brown.

Stark, David, and László Bruszt. 1998. *Postsocialist Pathways*. New York: Cambridge University Press.

Statista. 2019. Major Foreign Holders of U.S. Treasury Securities, as of October 2018. www.statista.com/statistics/246420/major-foreign-holders-of-us-treasury-debt/

Steinmo, Sven. 2010. *The Evolution of Modern States*. New York: Cambridge University Press.

Stiglitz, Joseph. 2019. *People, Power and Profits: Progressive Capitalism for an Age of Discontent*. New York: Norton.

Stiglitz, Joseph. 2012. *The Price of Inequality: How Today's Divided Society Endangers Our Future*. New York: Norton.

Stiglitz, Joseph. 2010. *Freefall*. New York: Norton.

Stiglitz, Joseph. 2002. *Globalization and Its Discontents*. New York: Norton.

Straqualursi, Veronica. 2018. "Rex Tillerson Said Trump Got 'Frustrated' When Told He Couldn't Do Something That 'Violates the Law'." *CNN*, December 7. www.cnn.com/2018/12/0 7/politics/rex-tillerson-donald-trump/index.html

Streeck, Wolfgang. 2016. *How Will Capitalism End?* London: Verso.

Sunstein, Cass. 2017. *#republic: Divided Democracy in the Age of Social Media*. Princeton, NJ: Princeton University Press.

Swank, Duane. 2002. *Global Capital, Political Institutions and Policy Change in Developed Welfare States*. New York: Cambridge University Press.

Swedberg, Richard, ed. 1991. *Joseph A. Schumpeter: The Economics and Sociology of Capitalism*. Princeton, NJ: Princeton University Press.

Tankersley, Jim. 2018. "How the Trump Tax Cut Is Helping Push the Federal Deficit to $1 Trillion." *The New York Times*, September 25. www.nytimes.com/2018/07/25/business/trump-corporate-tax-cut -deficit.html

Teles, Steven. 2008. *The Rise of the Conservative Legal Movement: The Battle for Control of the Law*. Princeton, NJ: Princeton University Press.

Thelen, Kathleen. 2014. *Varieties of Liberalization and the New Politics of Social Solidarity*. New York: Cambridge University Press.

Thelen, Kathleen, and Ikuo Kume. 1999. "The Effects of 'Globalization' on Labor Revisited: Lessons from Germany and Japan." *Politics and Society* 27(4): 476–504.

Thévenot, Celine. 2017. "Inequality in OECD Countries." *Scandinavian Journal of Public Health* 45(supplement 18): 9–16.

Thompson, Derek. 2020. "Denmark's Idea Could Help the World Avoid a Great Depression." *The Atlantic*, March 21. www.theatlantic.com/ideas/archive/2020/03/denmark-freezing -its-economy-should-us/608533/

Tooze, Adam. 2018. *Crashed: How a Decade of Financial Crises Changed the World*. New York: Viking.

Troy, Tevi. 2017. "Can Conservatives Find Their Way?" *The New York Times*, Sunday Review section, July 8. www.nytimes.com/2017/07/ 08/opinion/sunday/can-conservatives-find-their-way.html? mcubz=0

Tully, Shawn. 2019. "Trump's Tariffs Were Supposed to Ding China, But the U.S. Economy is Getting Hit 2.5× Harder." *Fortune*, October 8. https://fortune.com/2019/10/08/trump-china-tariffs- trade-war-us-economy-impact/

U.S. Bureau of Labor Statistics. 2020a. Graphics for Economic News Releases: Employment–Population Ratio. www.bls.gov/charts/e mployment-situation/employment-population-ratio.htm

U.S. Bureau of Labor Statistics. 2020b. Economy at a Glance. www .bls.gov/eag/eag.us.htm

U.S. Congress Joint Economic Committee. 2010. Income Inequality and the Great Recession. www.jec.senate.gov/public/_cache/files/91 975589-257c-403b-8093-8f3b584a088c/income-inequality-brief-fall-2 010-cmb-and-ces.pdf

U.S. Federal Reserve Bank. 2020. Household Debt Service Payments as a Percentage of Disposable Personal Income. https://fred .stlouisfed.org/series/TDSP

U.S. Federal Reserve Bank. 2019a. Federal Debt Held by Foreign and International Investors as a Percentage of Gross Domestic Product. https://fred.stlouisfed.org/series/HBFIGDQ188S#0

U.S. Federal Reserve Bank. 2019b. Federal Debt: Total Public Debt as Percent of Gross Domestic Product. https://fred.stlouisfed.org/s eries/GFDEGDQ188S#0

U.S. Federal Reserve Bank. 2019c. Recent Balance Sheet Trends. www.federalreserve.gov/monetarypolicy/bst_recenttrends.htm

U.S. Federal Reserve Bank. 2019d. 30-Year Fixed Rate Mortgage Average. https://fred.stlouisfed.org/graph/?g=NUh

U.S. House Committee on Oversight and Reform. 2020. "New Document Shows Inadequate Distribution of Personal Protective Equipment and Critical Medical Supplies to States." Press release, April 8. https://oversight.house.gov/news/press-releases/new-document-shows-inadequate-distribution-of-personal-protective-equipment-and

U.S. National Oceanic and Atmospheric Administration. 2019. Climate Change: Global Sea Level. August 2019. www.climate.gov/print/8438

Vance, J.D. 2016. *Hillbilly Elegy: A Memoir of a Family and Culture in Crisis*. New York: HarperCollins.

Varoufakis, Yanis, and David McWilliams. 2020. "There Is a Glimmer of Hope: Economists on Coronavirus and Capitalism." *The Guardian*, May 6. www.theguardian.com/world/2020/may/06/there-is-a-glimmer-of-hope-economists-on-coronavirus-and-capitalism

Ventura, Luca. 2018. "Percentage of Public Debt to GDP around the World 2018." *Global Finance*, January 18. www.gfmag.com/glo bal-data/economic-data/public-debt-percentage-gdp

Verlaine, Julia-Ambra. 2017. "Europe Vows to Maintain Postcrisis Financial Rules, Despite Trump Deregulation." *The Wall Street Journal*, February 10. www.wsj.com/articles/e urope-vows-to-maintain-postcrisis-financial-rules-despite-trump-deregulation–1486735932

Visser, Jelle. 2009. Database on Institutional Characteristics of Trade Unions, Wage Setting, State Intervention and Social Pacts in 34 Countries between 1960 and 2007, version 2. Amsterdam: Amsterdam Institute for Advanced Labour Studies AIAS, University of Amsterdam.

Vogel, Steven. 2018. *Marketcraft*. New York: Oxford University Press.

Vogel, Steven. 1996. *Freer Markets, More Rules*. Ithaca, NY: Cornell University Press.

Voitchovsky, Sarah. 2005. "Does the Profile of Income Inequality Matter for Economic Growth?" *Journal of Economic Growth* 10: 273–296.

Wade, Robert, and Frank Veneroso. 1998a. "The Asian Crisis: The High Debt Model versus the Wall Street–Treasury–IMF Complex." *New Left Review* 228: 3–24.

Wade, Robert, and Frank Veneroso. 1998b. "The Gathering World Slump and the Battle over Capital Controls." *New Left Review* 231: 13–42.

Walker, Shaun. 2019. "Viktor Orbán Trumpets Hungary's 'Procreation, not Immigration' Policy." *The Guardian*, September 6. www.theguardian.com/world/2019/sep/06/viktor-orban-trumpets-far-right-procreation-anti-immigration-policy

Warhurst, Chris. 2016. "Accidental Tourists: Brexit and Its Toxic Employment Underpinnings." *Socio-Economic Review* 14(4): 819–825.

Webb, Michael, and Stephen Krasner. 1989. "Hegemonic Stability Theory: An Empirical Assessment." *Review of International Studies* 15: 183–198.

Weir, Margaret, and Theda Skocpol. 1985. "State Structures and the Possibilities for 'Keynesian' Responses to the Great Depression in Sweden, Britain and the United States." In Peter Evans, Dietrich Rueschemeyer, and Theda Skocpol, eds. *Bringing the State Back In*. New York: Cambridge University Press, 107–167.

Weiss, Linda. 1998. *The Myth of the Powerless State*. Ithaca, NY: Cornell University Press.

Western, Bruce. 1997. *Between Class and Market: Postwar Unionization in the Capitalist Democracies*. Princeton, NJ: Princeton University Press.

Whitman, Richard. 2019. "Britain Is Failing to Plan for a Post-Brexit Europe." *Chatham House*, May 21. www.chathamhouse.org/expe rt/comment/britain-failing-plan-post-brexit-europe

Wilkinson, Richard, and Kate Pickett. 2009. *The Spirit Level*. New York: Bloomsbury Press.

Williamson, Oliver. 1985. *The Economic Institutions of Capitalism*. New York: Free Press.

Wolf, Zachary. 2019. "Trump Wants Radically Less Government. Here's What That Looks Like." *CNN Politics*, April 12. www .cnn.com/2019/04/12/politics/trump-deregulation/index.html

Woll, Cornelia. 2014. *The Power of Inaction: Bank Bailouts in Comparison*. Ithaca, NY: Cornell University Press.

Wood, Geoffrey, and Mike Wright. 2016. "What Brexit Tells Us about Institutions and Social Action." *Socio-Economic Review* 14(4): 832–836.

Woods, Hiatt. 2020. "How Billionaires Got $637 Billion Richer during the Coronavirus Pandemic." *Business Insider*, August 3. www .businessinsider.com/billionaires-net-worth-increases-coronavirus- pandemic–2020–7

World Bank. 2020a. Burden of Government Regulation. TCdata360. https://tcdata360.worldbank.org/indicators/govt.regu?country= COL&indicator=689&countries=PRT&viz=line_chart&year s=2007,2017

World Bank. 2020b. World Development Indicators. https://data .worldbank.org/indicator/NY.GDP.MKTP.KD.ZG

World Bank. 2019a. World Bank Data. https://data.worldbank.org/ indicator/NE.TRD.GNFS.ZS

World Bank. 2019b. Climate Change Overview. www.worldbank.org /en/topic/climatechange/overview

World Economic Forum. 2019a. Global Competitive Index Historical Dataset, 2007–2017, version 20180712. Davos: World Economic Forum.

World Economic Forum. 2019b. *Global Competitiveness Report, 2018.* Davos: World Economic Forum.

World Economic Forum. 2019c. "These EU Countries Have the Most Government Debt." May 8. www.weforum.org/agenda/201 9/05/european-countries-with-most-government-debt-chart/

Wuthnow, Robert. 2018. *The Left Behind.* Princeton, NJ: Princeton University Press.

Xu, Beina. 2014. "Governance in India: Corruption." *Council on Foreign Relations,* September 4. www.cfr.org/backgrounder/gov ernance-india-corruption

Yonay, Yuval. 1998. *The Struggle over the Soul of Economics.* Princeton, NJ: Princeton University Press.

Yu, Denise, and Karen Yourish. 2019. "The Turnover at the Top of the Trump Administration Is Unprecedented." *The New York Times,* January 14. www.nytimes.com/interactive/2018/03/16/us/politics/all-the-major-firings-and-resignations-in-trump-administration.html

Zak, Paul, and Steven Knack. 2001. "Trust and Growth." *The Economic Journal* 111: 295–321.

Introductory Note

References such as '178–79' indicate (not necessarily continuous) discussion of a topic across a range of pages. Wherever possible in the case of topics with many references, these have either been divided into sub-topics or only the most significant discussions of the topic are listed. Because the entire work is about 'capitalism', the use of this term (and certain others which occur constantly throughout the book) as an entry point has been minimised. Information will be found under the corresponding detailed topics.

.